"FOR FORTY YEARS MY ACT CONSISTED OF ONE JOKE. AND THEN SHE DIED."

She was from California. He was from New York. She was Catholic. He was Jewish. She produced laughs. He puffed on his cigar. They couldn't have children, so they adopted them, and raised two great kids. What they created together in show biz was magic. What they created together in life was love. Now both that magic and tha love come alive again in the most wonderful book George Burns has ever written and the most wonderful book you have ever read.

"This lovingly written book, with an abundance of photos, has got to be the sweetest biography of the year . . . it will siphon off a gallon or two of years of joy and laughter. All husbands and wives—and lovers—should read it. It is a lesson in devotion."
—*Chattanooga Times*

"You can hear George Burns's voice in these pages, loving but unsentimental. . . . His book is a very dear tribute to a very talented woman. Goodnight, Gracie. Good job, George."
—*Cosmopolitan*

(for more hoorays for *Gracie*, please turn page . . .)

GRACIE

A Love Story

GEORGE BURNS

A SIGNET BOOK

SIGNET
Published by the Penguin Group
Penguin Books USA Inc., 375 Hudson Street,
New York, New York 10014, U.S.A.
Penguin Books Ltd, 27 Wrights Lane,
London W8 5TZ, England
Penguin Books Australia Ltd, Ringwood,
Victoria, Australia
Penguin Books Canada Ltd, 2801 John Street,
Markham, Ontario, Canada L3R 1B4
Penguin Books (N.Z.) Ltd, 182–190 Wairau Road,
Auckland 10, New Zealand

Penguin Books Ltd, Registered Offices:
Harmondsworth, Middlesex, England

Published by Signet, an imprint of New American Library, a division of Penguin Books USA Inc. This is an authorized reprint of a hardcover edition published by G. P. Putnam's Sons.

First Signet Printing, February, 1991
10 9 8 7 6 5 4 3 2 1

Special thanks to Ned Comstock of the Archives of Performing Arts, University of Southern California, for his assistance with a portion of the interior photographs.

Ⓢ REGISTERED TRADEMARK—MARCA REGISTRADA

Printed in the United States of America

Acknowledgments

Now that *Gracie: A Love Story* is done, it hardly seems possible that I needed so much urging to begin it. How could I have put off what turned out to be such a rewarding and somehow comforting experience for me? And if the pages that follow bring you half the pleasure I got from reliving all those wonderful times with Gracie, you can join me in thanking Putnam's Phyllis Grann for being so insistent that I get on with it.

There are many, many others I am indebted to. If I were to thank them all individually you'd never get to the book. But let me specifically express my appreciation and gratitude to David Fisher. David is a fine writer and I could not have done this book without him. But then he couldn't have done it without me.

And of course, neither of us could have done it without Gracie.

—GEORGE BURNS

To all the fans
who love Gracie

"Gracie, why should I give your mother a bushel of nuts? What'd she ever give me?"

"Why, George, she gave you me. And I'm as good as nuts."

1

For forty years my act consisted of one joke. And then she died.

Her real name was Grace Ethel Cecile Rosalie Allen. Gracie Allen. But for those forty years audiences in small-time and big-time vaudeville houses and movie theaters and at home listening to their radios or watching television knew her, and loved her, simply as Gracie. Just Gracie. She was on a first-name basis with America. Lovable, confused Gracie, whose Uncle Barnum Allen had the water drained from his swimming pool before diving one hundred feet into it because he knew how to dive but didn't know how to swim, and who once claimed to have grown grapefruits that were so big it took only eight of them to make a dozen, Gracie, who confessed to cheating on her driver's test by copying from the car in front of her, who decided that horses must be deaf because she saw so few of them at concerts, who admitted making ice cubes with hot water so she would be prepared in case the water heater broke, and who realized it was much better for a quiz show contestant to know the questions beforehand rather than the answers because, ''The people who know the answers come and go, but the man who asks the questions comes back every week.'' Just Gracie, who stated with absolute certainty, ''I've got so many brains I haven't used some of them yet.''

There was only one Gracie, and that was half of her. That Gracie was a real character. But there was a lot more to Gracie than that funny little girl whose mind was made up—mostly by me and our writers. Gracie was a beautiful, elegant lady with real style and class. You never saw Gracie looking anything but perfect. And she was charming. And she was very smart, smart enough to become the dumbest woman in show-business history.

Gracie was a great actress. I don't think she ever received enough credit for that. When she wasn't performing, she was nothing like the dizzy character she played. Nothing at all. Well, except maybe for the time she backed up into a parked car and managed to convince the driver of that car that he'd hit her. Or the time she inaugurated the Chicago Exposition by swinging a bottle of champagne at the cornerstone of the building and instead threw it through a plate-glass door. Gracie never quite understood gambling either—when she gambled she'd always keep her winnings in a separate pile from her stake, so she would spend $50 to win $20 and when I asked her how she was doing she'd tell me, ''Great. I'm winning twenty dollars.''

I never thought about it, but maybe the character was the real Gracie and she was just playing the role of that elegant lady. Like I said, she was a great actress.

I would have known. We were together day and night for forty years and she never stopped amazing me. She was just a tiny little thing, barely five feet tall and never more than one hundred pounds, but she was capable of so much. Gracie was just as comfortable discussing fancy dresses with the top designers in the world, dining with Al Capone at his place in Chicago, and playing jacks on the kitchen table with the kids as she was serving as the first Mistress of Ceremonies at the Palace Theatre on Broadway—during which she asked the audience, "If I say the right thing, please forgive me," launching National Donut Week by pushing a button to start donut-making machines across the country, dancing on screen with Fred Astaire or running for President of the United States on the Surprise Party ticket.

Gracie was my partner in our act, my best friend, my wife and my lover, and the mother of our two children. We were a team, both on and off the stage. Our relationship was simple; I fed her the straight lines and she fed me. She made me famous as the only man in America who could get a laugh by complaining, "My wife understands me."

We had a good marriage. We knew it was a good marriage because we never read anything bad about it in the papers. They only wrote about us once in the big gossip magazine, *Confidential*. They wrote a story that said we'd had a big fight and I'd moved into the west wing of our house. I knew that couldn't be true—our house didn't have a west wing.

This book is about Gracie and our life together. It's the story of a marriage without scandals, separations, bitter accusations, or Hollywood gossip. But I'm going to write about it anyway. Those of you who have seen me perform know I smoke a cigar and use it as a prop. When I tell a joke, I pause and puff on my cigar. That way, when I take a puff on my cigar, the audience knows I've told a joke. It works very well. But since you can't see me smoking a cigar while reading this book, you'll just have to believe me when I tell you something is funny.

This book is funny.

The other thing it's important you know about me is that I lie a lot. That's the truth. But usually, when I tell a lie, I admit it. I'm a very honest liar. But when I talk about Gracie I don't lie. I don't have to. The truth is unbelievable enough.

I'm not puffing on my cigar.

I never knew how old Gracie was. I never asked. The newspapers reported that she had been born in 1906, and that she was only fifty-eight years old when she died in 1964. Maybe she was. When I met her in 1923 she could sing and she could dance and she was willing to work cheap. Who cared how old she was? I know she was born in San Francisco just after the turn of the century. She often said that her birth certificate had been destroyed in the great earthquake of 1906. Gracie always thought that was very funny: all the glamour girls in Hollywood lied about their age, and claimed that their birth certificates had been destroyed. She was a great comedienne, and hers actually had been destroyed.

I once asked her about those newspaper stories that said she was born after the quake. "If that's true," I said, "how could your birth certificate have been destroyed."

"Well, you know," she explained, "that was a terribly powerful earthquake."

Or, maybe she didn't say that. I told you, I lie a lot. Gracie never claimed responsibility for the quake. In fact, some people wondered if just the opposite was true. The only thing Gracie ever said about her birth was that "I was so surprised at being born that I didn't speak for a year and a half." Her father, George Allen, was a well-known song and dance man, an Irish clog and minstrel dancer who worked up and down the West Coast. But after having five kids he did a disappearing act.

Now I'm puffing on my cigar. See how it works?

Gracie's father went on tour, permanently, when she was about five years old. She didn't hear a word from him for years. But one night, when we were headlining the bill at the Palace, he showed up to see her. Gracie and I often used separate dressing rooms, so I didn't even know he'd been there until after the show. "He wanted to talk," she told me, "so I let him."

"What'd you say?" I asked.

"Nothing," she said. "He had nothing to say to me when I was growing up, so now I had nothing to say to him." Gracie could be very cool when she felt someone had done something wrong to her, but I never saw her as cold as this. I'm not a psychologist, I'm barely a comedian, but even I could tell she was hurting inside. I just put my arm around her shoulders and took her home.

Everybody called Gracie's mother "Pidgie," because after divorcing George Allen she'd married a San Francisco police department captain named Edward Pidgeon. Pidgie loved show business. She lived next door to a famous opera singer named Alice Nielsen, and when she was pregnant with Gracie, she'd go over there every day to hear Alice Nielsen sing, hoping her child would be a born singer. Pidgie used to say that the first time Gracie opened her mouth, and she heard *that* voice, she went out and bought her a pair of dancing shoes.

Much later in life, though, Gracie made a major contribution to the opera world. She stayed out of it.

Gracie took after her mother. On our radio show she used to joke that the bill collectors took after her father. Pidgie was no more than five feet tall, and she had absolutely perfect manners and a wonderful sense of humor. But she was Irish and could be very tough when she needed to be. That was Gracie. Gracie always demanded I treat her like the lady that she was. Once, I remember, we were walking into the Brown Derby restaurant and I forgot to hold the door open for her. So she got behind me and kicked me as hard as she could. "What'd you do that for?" I asked, rubbing my shoulder. I couldn't rub the place she'd kicked me.

"Next time you'll remember to hold the door for me," she said, then marched past me. That was Gracie too—if you didn't treat her like a lady, she'd pull up her skirt and kick you.

Pidgie had all kinds of rules of proper etiquette. "When you leave the house," she used to tell her four daughters, "you always take your kid gloves and your hat. Because that's the way a lady goes out of the house." So that was the way Gracie went out of the house. Gracie made some of her own rules, too. The last thing she would do before leaving the house, every time, was look at herself in the mirror and take one thing off. It could have been anything. A necklace, a bracelet, a scarf, it didn't matter, she had to take one thing off. That way, she believed, she'd never be overdressed. I was probably the only husband in the country who could ask his wife if she was ready to go and have her say, "One minute— just let me take something off."

The Allen family lived in a three-story white

stucco house at 668 Fourth Avenue in San Francisco. It was a great old house. It had a long, open basement with a polished redwood floor, which was used as a dancing school, a large aviary in the garden filled with canaries, a gymnasium out back and the very first marble bathroom in the city. Pidgie was really proud of that bathroom. The first thing she would do every morning was wipe off her marble. A marble bathroom, can you believe that? When Gracie was born I was ten years old and living on the Lower East Side of New York City. Her bathroom may have been marble, but ours, which was out in back of the building, was air conditioned—at least it was whenever there was a breeze blowing.

In one of our vaudeville routines, I asked Gracie, "Did the maid ever drop you on your head when you were a baby?"

"Don't be silly, George," she'd answer in an astonished voice, with a little wave of her gloved hand. "We couldn't afford a maid. My mother had to do it."

Maybe she never did get dropped on her head, but Gracie did have a lot of serious accidents during her childhood. Few people ever knew this, but when Gracie was about a year and a half she reached up to the stove and pulled down a large pot of boiling tea. Her left arm and shoulder were scalded badly, and for a while it looked like they might have to amputate the arm. They finally saved it, but it was terribly scarred and she could never completely straighten it out. She was always embarrassed about that scar and kept it hidden from just about everybody except me and our kids. She never wore anything but long-sleeved dresses and blouses or full-length gloves. In fact, after she became famous in vaudeville, all the other women doing a "Dumb Dora" act, as that type of character was known, began wearing gloves or long sleeves. What they should have realized was that the long sleeves were a cover—the real secret to our success was my cigar.

Gracie's relatives told me that long before I met her, she used to try to strengthen that arm by hitting a punching bag. Imagine that, Gracie hitting a punching bag. I'll bet the bag won.

That arm bothered her her entire life, but she never complained about it. It wasn't a physical problem, but the way it looked. Gracie always took such pride in her appearance; her seams were always straight, her hair was always in place, her makeup was always just right, and I think she believed her arm made her less than perfect. Once, after she'd retired and was sick, we were sitting alone in our den having dinner, and I asked her if there was anything she wanted to do that we hadn't had the time or opportunity to do before. This was long after she'd earned a fortune, performed for royalty, even worked with Clark Gable. She thought about it for a minute, then said, yes, there was one thing—she had always wanted to spend one evening wearing a strapless, sleeveless evening gown.

There wasn't anything I could do about that. This was long before I became God.

I'll tell you how much that scalded arm bothered her. After we'd been married for maybe twenty-five years we were in bed one night, reading scripts, and she suddenly put hers down and said, "You know, Nattie"—she always called me Nattie—"the nicest thing you've ever done for me is that you never said anything about my bad arm."

"Oh, really," I said, continuing to read my script, "which arm is the bad one?"

Gracie also had two different color eyes. One eye was green, the other was blue. Of course it didn't matter—on radio they were the same color and on black and white television they were both gray. But she did have an eye problem. Not too long after she'd scalded her arm, she knocked over a glass storm lamp and several tiny shards of glass flew into her eye. Doctors got all of them, or most of them out, but she lost some sight and had limited vision for the rest of her life. Gracie also suffered from terrible migraine headaches. No one knew anything about migraines in those days, except that they were terrible, and I always wondered if that eye injury might have had something to do with causing the headaches.

When Gracie had a migraine, she would tie a damp bandana as tightly as possible around her forehead and lie down in a dark, absolutely quiet room. But if she had a show to do, she worked. No matter what happened, she worked. Once, in vaudeville, for example, we were playing in Oakland and after our last show we were in a cab going back across the bridge to San Francisco. Gracie was asleep, her head resting against my shoulder. Suddenly the cab stopped short and she went flying forward, smashing her face again the partition and breaking her nose. We rushed to St. Mary's Hospital where they stopped the bleeding and bandaged her nose. In those days the best painkiller was ice; it wasn't addictive and it was particularly effective if you poured some whiskey over it. Gracie didn't miss a single performance. She was in pain and could barely speak, but she did three shows the next day. In fact, the cab company refused to pay any damages, claiming we didn't lose anything because Gracie had worked the next day.

In all the years we performed together she missed only one performance. That was a radio show, and her headache was so bad she couldn't get out of bed. Our friend Janie Wyman, who'd just won the Academy Award as Best Actress, played Gracie's part. That was about right.

There was only one other thing that bothered Gracie—her feet. Gracie had nice feet—they came as a matched set—but for some reason I never knew, she always kept her feet covered. There was nothing wrong with them, she certainly didn't have the same problem as that character on our show, whom she felt so sorry for when she heard he'd grown another foot, but she just didn't consider it proper to expose her feet.

So Gracie had a badly scarred left arm, two different color eyes, she suffered from migraines, and she didn't like her feet. And all those years people thought Gracie's only problem was her mind.

Gracie grew up in a big, loving Irish family. They were so Irish that her sister Hazel spoke Gaelic—and they don't even speak Gaelic in Ireland. I loved her family too. The only mother-in-law problem I ever had was that I didn't see my mother-in-law enough. At one point during her childhood, though, Gracie went to live with her aunt, Clara Burke. Clara was a beautiful girl who'd married an older man everybody called Papa Burke. Papa Burke was a very wealthy chief of police. If I had ever asked Gracie if that was redundant, she would have told me, No, silly, that was his job. Papa Burke gave his young bride everything, including a large estate with several barns. So Gracie grew up among horses and cows.

On our television show, whenever Gracie was supposed to be working in the house she would wear a pretty apron. Now, Gracie could do a lot of things, but cooking was not one of them. Truthfully, the only thing Gracie knew about the kitchen was that it wasn't the room with the marble counters. She admitted it, she claimed she didn't need a fancy kitchen just to burn food, she could do that anywhere. But her Aunt Clara was a great cook, and Aunt Clara always wore lovely aprons. And so on our show, Gracie always wore a lovely apron.

Let me tell you a little story about Aunt Clara. She wasn't really rich, but Papa Burke left her a little money. When Gracie and I were starting out in vaudeville we weren't doing very well, so every week Aunt Clara would send us a check for $25. Every week. Even after we'd become big stars, earning thousands of dollars a show, we still received that $25 check every week from Aunt Clara. Well, Aunt Clara never knew it, but she lost almost everything she had in the stock-market crash. But she never knew about it, because Gracie found out and arranged to have enough money deposited in Clara's account each month to cover all her expenses. This went on for years. It's a good thing Gracie did that, too, otherwise we would have stopped getting those $25 checks.

Gracie made her first appearance onstage when she was three years old, performing an "Interpretative Irish Dance" at a church social. At least it was *her* interpretation of an Irish dance. For the occasion her father dressed her up in the coat of a man's full-dress suit, a top hat, and a set of bright-red "sluggers," false whiskers that ran from ear to ear under her chin and fastened around her head with a tie. Every Irish comedian wore them. But even with the whiskers, Gracie knew no one was going to mistake her for an Irishman. Besides, they made her itch. So as she walked onstage she pulled them off and carried them over her arm as she did her routine. That was Gracie too—if she didn't want to do something onstage, she simply didn't do it.

Obviously, her performance wasn't a disaster. The church is still in business.

She even got a nice little review in the paper. *"La petite Gracie,"* they called her. No wonder Gracie was always confused by show business. She dressed up like a man to do an Irish dance and they gave her a French nickname.

That night was probably the first time she heard the warm sound of a laughing audience, and she fell in love with it. One thing about Gracie, she never performed for an audience, she just shared some of her funny thoughts with some nice people.

There was never any doubt in Gracie's mind that she was going to be in show business, whatever else is said about Gracie's mind. Pidgie encouraged her— she'd often stay up late at night sewing dresses for Gracie and her sisters Bessie, Pearl, and Hazel to wear to dancing school. Gracie's brother George probably got the whiskers. The one thing Gracie's father gave her before he left was some smart advice. Looking at her wearing one of the beautiful dresses her mother had made, he said, "You'll never make a nickel all dolled up in a spangled skirt. If you're going to get anywhere in show business, you have to be a character."

Maybe I'm wrong, maybe Gracie did get the whiskers.

All of the Allen sisters were talented Irish and Scottish dancers. At the holiday picnics they used to win all the prizes. Bessie, in fact, was so good that Sid Grauman used to tell people, "If you want to learn tap, you have to go to Bessie Allen." And Hazel could dance *and* play the piano at the same time. Gracie never believed she was as good a dancer as her sisters, but she was good enough to hold her own in a specialty number opposite Fred Astaire in *Damsel in Distress*. I could dance. I was a real smoothie on the ballroom floor. Probably the only thing I ever had in common with Gracie's family was that we all taught dancing. They taught private students in the basement of their house, I taught new immigrants at B.B.'s College of Dancing on Avenue B and 2nd Street in Manhattan and on Pitkin Avenue in Brownsville, Brooklyn. I always had a lot of students—I'd meet the ferries coming over from Ellis Island and tell everybody who got off that ballroom dancing was a requirement for citizenship. A few years later I was doing a song and dance act in vaudeville. And I was certainly one of the greatest dancers on radio.

But I could never match Gracie when she did those Irish clog dances. Usually, when Gracie and I visited someone's house, she would sit quietly on the couch and I would sing until the room cleared out. It rarely took longer than two verses of "I Am Tying the Leaves So They Won't Fall Down, So Daddy Won't Go Away." But whenever we went to Jimmy Cagney's house, I would sit, and Cagney and his wife, Bill, and Gracie would literally roll up the carpet and spend the entire night doing Irish dances.

Gracie was the only one of her sisters who didn't love dancing, but she learned because she thought it would help her get into show business. She was determined to get into show business. Practically every day after coming home from the Star of the Sea School, the Catholic school all the girls attended, she would go downtown and stroll from theater to theater, just looking at the pictures in the lobby. In fact, when Pidgie wanted Gracie to run an errand, she'd use the theaters to give directions. "Make a right at the Alhambra," she'd say, "and go all the way up to the Rialto. Turn left at the Rialto until you get to the Orpheum . . ." In vaudeville, every performer was required to give the theater manager a black and white glossy photograph when he or she arrived for a booking. The manager would post the picture out front. Normally, at the end of the booking, they would give you back your pictures. But if the act turned out to be terrible, the manager would take down the picture right away and give it back to the performer. Nobody in vaudeville "got fired," instead they got their pictures back. Gracie would stand in front of the theaters, looking at those pictures, dreaming of the day her picture would be there.

When there was no school, or on Saturdays, Gracie spent her allowance on a ticket to a matinee; ten cents downstairs or twenty-five cents upstairs at famous San Francisco theaters like the Orpheum and Alcazar.

She loved the vaudeville, but her idol was a film star, Charlie Chaplin. He was the first man she ever wanted to marry. "I had decided that I was going to marry the richest man in the world," she told me once. "Charlie Chaplin was far from that then, but

I watched his salary grow with great excitement, and although I eventually realized I was going to have to compromise, I finally decided he was the only man for me.''

In 1912 Chaplin was making a movie in San Francisco, and Captain Pidgeon met him. So, a few days before Gracie's birthday, he gave her a choice: she could take a flight in an airplane or meet Charlie Chaplin. Gracie picked Chaplin. On the morning of her birthday, her stepfather took Gracie to Golden Gate Park, where the film was being made. Chaplin was great, he kissed her on the cheek, then he had a cameraman take moving pictures of the two of them waving to the camera. So Gracie made her film debut co-starring with Charlie Chaplin.

Gracie claimed she didn't wash the spot where he had kissed her for a week. That was another difference between my childhood and Gracie's—I didn't have to be kissed not to wash my face.

Gracie never really got over her crush on Chaplin. For the rest of her life, whenever I asked her to say something funny, she would reply, ''Charlie Chaplin.''

Gracie began her professional career as a singer. She had an unusual voice for a little girl. Actually, it was an unusual voice for a living person. During vacations she was able to get bookings in local movie houses singing songs from colored magic-lantern slides projected on the screen. So it would be accurate to say that Gracie sang in the movies long before she met me.

Starring with Chaplin, singing in the movies . . . sounds to me like I ruined the kid's career.

Bessie was the first of the girls to work in vaudeville. She was a singer and dancer and magician's

assistant on the Sullivan and Considine time, a West
Coast theater chain. When Gracie was six years old
she went to see Bessie perform, and Bessie brought
her out onstage. One surprising thing about Gracie,
she was always nervous before a show. Always. She
used to say, "If my hands aren't damp before I go
on, it's not going to be a good show." So Bessie
brought her out onstage, Gracie looked at the audience, started crying, and ran off the stage. For a
dramatic actress that would have been a fine debut,
but there wasn't too much demand on the circuit for
crying dancers.

Bessie dragged her back onstage, still crying, and
the two of them did an Irish jig and a sailor's horn-
pipe. Twenty years later Shirley Temple stole Gracie's act.

It was right about this time that I started my career
in vaudeville. The difference between me and Gracie
is that when I went out onstage it was the audience
that started crying.

When Gracie graduated from the convent school
she joined her sisters in a harmony singing and dancing act called The Four Colleens. The act was based
on an illusion—the girls would appear out of a mist
and do a Highland reel, then disappear again.

Supposedly, during their first show at the San
Francisco Hippodrome, the girls were doing great
until Gracie started slipping on some talcum powder
that had been left on the stage by an acrobatic act.
She fell several times dragging her sisters down with
her. The audience thought it was part of the act and
kept laughing. But for the next show The Four Colleens were perfect. After that show the manager gave
the girls their pictures back for cutting out the laughs.

I read that story, Gracie never told it to me. Maybe

it happened, maybe it didn't. One of the things I've found to be true about show business is that the more successful a comedian becomes, the funnier he or she used to be. Imagine what a great comedienne Gracie must have been—she was so funny she was getting laughs in an Irish dance act.

Gracie was still a teenager when The Four Colleens broke up, and by that time she had become a really beautiful girl. A lot of guys wanted to marry her. She used to tell me about a wealthy Guatemalan named Frank, who evidently had problems with the English language. He used to say things like, ''Gracie, did you saw me yesterday?'' And when she laughed, he'd complain to Hazel, ''Gracie laughs for me.'' Frank wanted her to marry him and go live in South America, or South Jersey, she was never quite sure.

Gracie didn't want to marry anybody, she wanted to be on the stage. She went into a dramatic act owned by a dashing fellow named Larry Reilly. It was an Irish act in which Reilly played the hero, Gracie and another girl were the heroines, and another man played the Priest. An Irish act without a priest was like a Jewish act without heartache. Gracie was paid $22 a week for her first speaking part. The funny thing was, Gracie naturally spoke with a thick Irish brogue, but Larry Reilly wanted her to learn stage Irish, which was very different. ''But that's not the way real people speak,'' Gracie insisted.

''We're not real people,'' Larry Reilly reminded her. ''We're actors.''

Gracie learned the fake Irish accent, which audiences believed was a real accent, and Reilly raised her pay. The act was pretty successful on the coast circuits. They worked. In vaudeville that was the definition of success. Eventually, Reilly made some changes in the act: he hired Bessie and Hazel, then took Larry Reilly and Company out on tour.

Their first major booking was at the Hippodrome in Chicago. After viewing the act, a local newspaper critic wrote, "Larry, look out, the girls are stealing the show." In show business there are good reviews, bad reviews, good bad reviews, and bad good reviews. For example, a good bad review would be, "This is the worst picture ever made. Don't miss it." The Larry Reilly review was a bad good review. There was a reason the act was named Larry Reilly and Company, not Company and Larry Reilly. Larry Reilly was the reason. By the time the act reached the East Coast, Bessie had returned to San Francisco to get married and Hazel had gone back to help Pearl with the dancing school. Hazel eventually got married and became Samuel Gompers' secretary when he was president of the AF of L. That left Gracie as the "and Company."

If Larry Reilly had been a little smarter, the act would have been called Reilly and Allen and I would have spent my show-business career working with a trained seal. But he wasn't. That's a good thing, because I never could get used to eating fish seven nights a week. They were opening in Hoboken, and when Gracie got to the theater, she went into the lobby to check the pictures and discovered the name of the act had been changed to "Larry Reilly." She was infuriated. "I didn't get any billing before," she told me, "but no billing I couldn't stand." She quit the act in New Jersey.

So there she was, this little girl, maybe eighteen

years old, alone, living in New York City without a job. She started making the rounds, trying to find a partner for a dance act. Hazel sent her a little money, but asked her not to tell Pidgie or the other girls. Bessie sent her a little money, but asked her not to tell anyone. Pearl sent her a little bit, but asked her not to tell anyone. As long as Gracie could keep a secret, she was doing pretty good.

After going six months without finding a partner, Gracie enrolled in stenography school. If she had to, she had decided, she'd work as a secretary until she found the right partner. Just imagine Gracie working as a secretary. She could have put the Pentagon out of business. Actually, she played my secretary in one of our movies. In the first scene she was reading a newspaper when I arrived at the office. I walked in and asked her what the date was, and she told me she didn't know.

"Look at the newspaper," I said.

"Oh, that won't do any good," she explained. "It's yesterday's paper."

It was about this time that Gracie met a well-known songwriter and actor named Benny Ryan. Benny Ryan wrote some great songs. A lot of people don't know this, but he wrote "When Frances Dances With Me." In case you've forgotten the lyrics, Maestro, music please:

She does a new step that goes one, two, three, kick.
And she can't count so good, that's the worst of the trick.
My shin bones look like they've been hit with a brick.
When Frances dances with me.

* * *

Pretty good, huh? That's why it became the classic it is today. As we used to say in my old neighborhood, from this he made a living. Well, Benny Ryan wrote an act for his new girlfriend, Grace Allen. The problem with the act was that it required $300 worth of scenery and a male partner. Male partners were easy to find; Gracie didn't have the $300. Meanwhile she continued trying to figure out why it took so long to learn shorthand.

After Bessie and Hazel had returned to San Francisco, Gracie had moved into a small rooming house with two other girls in show business, Mary Kelly and Rena Arnold. Rena Arnold did a hokey act, a low-comedy act in which she banged her partners around, and in 1923 she was headlining the bill at a small-time theater in Union City, New Jersey. Also appearing on that bill was the wonderful variety act Burns and Lorraine.

I had already become a big star in vaudeville. How big a star was I? Well, even stars like Eddie Cantor, Al Jolson, and Blossom Seeley had only one act and one name. I was too big for one name. I was so good that I probably worked in fifty different acts using a dozen different names. I was Glide of Goldie, Fields, and Glide; I was Jed Jackson of Jackson and Malone; I was Maurice Valente of Maurice Valente and His Wonder Dog; Harris of Harris and Dunlop; Jose of Jose and Dolores; at various times I was both Brown and Williams of Brown and Williams. I was Jack Garfield, but I became Eddie Delight when the real Eddie Delight got out of show business and gave me all his leftover business cards. The only qualification for a name was that I had to be able to spell it.

I never cared what name I was working under, as long as I was working. And usually it was easier to change the name of the act than the act. And why should I have felt bad about changing my name? Even my real name wasn't my real name.

My real name was Nathan Birnbaum. I was born in 1896, one of twelve kids. I began calling myself George because I had an older brother named Isadore. Everybody called him Izzy, which he hated, so he named himself George. I loved Izzy, and if George was good enough for him, it was good enough for me. The Burns came from the name of the coal company, Burns Brothers, that I used to steal coal from. I took it because if I ever forgot how to spell it, all I had to do was look at the side of one of their trucks.

I'll tell you how poor we were. My sister Sarah had only one ambition—she wanted to be able to wash floors wearing a silk dress. She wanted to have so many silk dresses that she would be able to wear a different one every time she got down on her hands and knees to scrub the floor. It never even occurred to her that someday she might not have to wash floors. I was going to be in show business. That's all I ever wanted to do. I found out very early that I loved making people laugh; of course, I was too young at the time to know that they weren't supposed to laugh at singers. Show business had a lot of appeal to me: you got to wear nice clothes, you got to travel, sometimes you got paid, and it didn't require heavy lifting.

I started entertaining when I was seven years old. I'd dance on street corners and people would throw pennies and nickels into a hat. After a while I started to sing, then they'd take their pennies and nickels out of the hat. I stayed in school all the way through the fourth grade. I went to a very difficult school—

my teacher couldn't get out of the fourth grade either. But I really didn't care about school—nobody came to the theater to watch you spell.

Show business in those days was vaudeville. You needed three things to work in small-time vaudeville; glossy pictures, business cards, and an act. You didn't really need much talent to get started in vaudeville, and if there was one thing I had, it wasn't much talent. The pictures were probably most important—you couldn't fake pictures. Sometimes you didn't even need an act. Hammerstein's, for example, the best-known house before the Palace opened, used to book celebrities out of the newspaper. Jack Johnson, the heavyweight champion of the world, appeared there. A woman who killed her husband in a crime of passion, then was acquitted by a jury, was a big success at Hammerstein's. But I was too small to be a heavyweight, and I hadn't killed anybody. I had to have an act.

Fortunately it didn't have to be a good act. To be successful in vaudeville, you had to be either the best in the world or the worst. In fact, if you were the best at being the worst, you were the best. Eva Tanguay, for example, used to come onstage and say, "I can't sing, I can't dance, but I don't care. I've got no talent, but I don't care." Her talent was she didn't care. I didn't have that particular talent— I cared.

The Cherry Sisters were the worst act in the world. That was their act, the worst act in the world. They were bad singers. Before they came out onstage a net would be lowered to protect them. Then they would come out and stand behind the net and start singing, and the audience would throw fruit at them. They were considered one of the toughest acts to follow—you had to be careful about slipping on the fruit.

I remember a comedian named Roy Cunningham who used to dive headfirst into the orchestra pit. Lucan and Lillian were acrobatic contortionists. Eddie Leonard would come out and tell the audience that this was his final performance. How could an audience boo a man doing his last show? He did that act for twenty years.

I wasn't good, and I wasn't bad enough to be good. I was just bad. I tried every different type of act. I did a dancing act in which my partner and I dressed in Spanish costumes and did a Russian mazurka. I did a straight dancing act with the Rosebud Sisters. I did a singing and talking act with Sid Gary and another singing act with The Wonder Dog. I did a double buck dance on roller skates. (I'll tell you a secret: in roller-skating dance acts the back wheels of the skates don't move. They're frozen. Makes it easy to dance on them.) I did a patriotic skit with eight other teenagers called The Fourth of July Kids. Nobody dared boo The Fourth of July Kids. I did several song and dance acts, singing songs like "If You're Crazy About the Woman, You're Not Crazy at All" and "Augustus J. McCann was a Henpecked Married Man."

When animal acts were popular I did animal acts. Once, my partner Sid Gary and I heard there was an opening for a dog act. We were a song and dance team, but we went out and found two stray dogs and became a dog act. That's a description of the act, not a critique. We brought the dogs onstage with us, let them do whatever they wanted to do, and we did our song and dance act.

I did a single, a double, I was the entire company

of Mac Fry and Company. I had only one rule: I worked only with people who would work with me. I even worked with Captain Bett's seal for a few months. I was the straight man for the seal.

I'd toss a beach ball to the seal and he would juggle it on his nose. Then I'd point to the seal and the audience would applaud and I would take a bow. Then I'd set up a ladder and the seal would climb the ladder. I'd point to the seal and the audience would applaud and I'd take a bow. Sometimes I'd toss a large ring to the seal and he'd stick his head through it. There wasn't too much else the seal could do. A seal can't get down on one flipper and do Jolson.

The only thing all of my acts had in common was that they weren't very good. In those days an act was usually booked for a week, two to five shows a day, depending on the theater. Most acts were booked on the circuits out of New York, so very often the first time a theater manager saw an act was at the opening show Monday morning. If he didn't like the act, after that show he would hand them their pictures. Backstage in almost every theater there was a large sign listing the Don'ts: DON'T SAY HELL. DON'T SAY DAMN. DON'T SAY RISQUÉ THINGS. DON'T SEND YOUR LAUNDRY OUT UNTIL THE SECOND SHOW.

I got canceled a lot. Goldie, Fields, and Glide got canceled after the first show at Miner's Bowery. Another act I did made history—we got canceled *before* the first show. On Monday morning all the acts would rehearse their music with the orchestra. The manager of the Follies in Brooklyn came in early and heard me rehearsing and canceled me. I didn't care, there was always another theater, or a new act, or a new name. About five months after being canceled in Scranton, Pennsylvania, for example, I returned to the same theater. The theater manager looked at me and asked suspiciously, "Aren't you Burns?"

"Nah," I told him, "and besides, I got a new act."

It was tough, but I loved every minute of it. I was in show business and that was all I cared about. There's a great story about Wilton Lackaye, a very famous actor who did dramatic readings in vaudeville. He was doing six weeks at the Keats in Cincinnati when he received a telegram informing him that his mother had died suddenly. There was nothing he could do, he had to stay in Cincinnati and do his show, so he went into the hotel bar to have a drink. Appearing on the bill with him was a dancing act named Bowen and Keating. After finishing their Monday-morning rehearsal, Bowen and Keating walked into the same bar. When they saw the famous Wilton Lackaye drinking by himself, they went over to him and introduced themselves. "We're honored to be on the same bill with you," Keating said.

Bowen added, "We'd be pleased if you'd let us buy you a drink."

"Thank you boys," Lackaye said sadly, "but I just got this wire saying I lost my mother. If you don't mind, I'd rather drink alone."

"Of course," Bowen said sympathetically. "We know just how you feel. Our trunk is missing."

I'm puffing on my cigar because that's a funny story. It's also a true story, whether it actually happened or not. Working in vaudeville, whether it was the big-time circuit or the small-time, was the most important thing in the world. Everybody felt that way. Believe me, there was nothing in the world that could match the feeling of standing in front of an

audience and singing a beautiful love ballad and
hearing their laughter.

So it was tough, and sometimes it got frustrating,
but we kept going. Every vaudevillian in the small-
time believed that our next act or our next partner or
our next name or our next booking was going to be
the break that led directly to the Palace. When we
played the back end of a horse, we always knew that
if we worked hard and did a good job, someday we
could become the front end.

I wasn't making a lot of money, but in my mind
I was a star. I was a mental hit. I had never been a
hit, so I didn't know what I was missing. I was
working; three days in Scranton, three days in Al-
toona, a week in Boonton, but I was working. I had
pictures, I had cards, I had music, as far as I was
concerned, I was a hit.

Let me tell you something—every song and dance
man who ever lived believed he was the greatest song
and dance man in the business. I believed that, what
did I know? When I wasn't working, I put the blame
directly where it belonged—I blamed my agent.
When I didn't have an agent, I spent time looking
for a new agent so I would have somebody to blame.

I was doing an act with Billy Lorraine called Burns
and Lorraine—Two Broadway Thieves, when I met
Grace Allen. In the act Billy and I impersonated famous Broadway stars like Jolson, Cantor, George
White and George M. Cohan. Actually, neither Billy
nor I had ever seen any of these people perform in
person, but in the theaters we played neither had
anyone in the audience. So our act wasn't difficult
to do. You wore a little blackface, got down on one
knee, and sang "Mammy," you were Jolson. Of

course, Powers' Elephants was a little tougher to fake.

Onstage, Billy Lorraine was a fine performer, but offstage he had a stammering problem. Whenever he was upset, or nervous, he would stutter. But when he sang, he was fine. We were in Toledo once, and I was sitting in a restaurant, and Billy came rushing in. "W-w-w-we-we-we-b-b-b-be-be . . ."

"Slow Billy," I said, "say it slow."

"W—w—w—w—we—we—we—b—b . . ."

"Sing it," I suggested.

He nodded, took a deep breath, spread his arms wide, and sang beautifully: "We've been robbed!"

After working together for almost a year, Billy and I had decided to split up. About the only kind of act I'd never done was a talking double, so I had decided to try a boy-girl comedy act, a flirtation act. I figured I'd been getting laughs for years as a singer and dancer, I might as well try to do it intentionally. I wrote the entire act myself. I read dozens of issues of *College Humor* and *Whiz Bang* magazines and whenever I found a joke I liked I wrote it down. It was a pretty clever act. For example, I'd say to my straight man, the "feeder," "Ask me why I brush my teeth with gunpowder."

The straight man's job was to repeat the question. It was not a hard job. If Captain Bett's seal had had a little better diction, the seal could have been a good straight man. "Okay," the straight man would ask. "Why do you brush your teeth with gunpowder?"

"Because I like to shoot my mouth off." Listen, if the magazines had been funnier, I could have written a much better act.

I'd decided to work with a woman because most of the jokes I wrote were about dating. Dating was popular them. I didn't expect to have much problem finding a woman to be my straight man. In those days men were men and women were also men; there was no such thing as a mailperson. Acts were always splitting up, and when someone was looking for a new partner he just spread the word or posted notices at places like the National Variety Artists Club or at the White Rats Union hall, a vaudeville union.

When Rena Arnold heard that Billy Lorraine and I were breaking up, she told her roommate, Grace Allen, and suggested she catch our show in Union City and see if she wanted to work with either one of us. Actually, Rena was partial to Billy because I told risqué jokes to all the girls in the show. Maybe Billy told dirty jokes too, but nobody had the time to find out.

The bill consisted of four acts and a movie. After our last show Rena brought Gracie into the dressing room to meet us. Gracie was so pretty. She had long black hair, with curls that spun down over her shoulders. Her skin was that Irish peach-bloom and she was wearing just a touch of makeup. She wasn't wearing any lipstick, it was well know that the only people who wore lipstick were prostitutes and actors. "Nattie," Rena said—offstage everybody called me Nat or Nattie—"This is Grace Allen."

"How do?" I said smartly. Gracie was so small and delicate I was almost afraid to shake her hand.

"I liked your act," she said. The moment I heard her voice I figured she had to be a dancer. She sounded like the bird who had been thrown out of the nest for singing offkey. In fact, it turned out to be a perfect voice. It had no lows, so it projected beautifully in a theater. Gracie never had to yell to be heard, her voice just cut through everything else.

And years later, when she started singing on the radio, it turned out she had a lovely singing voice. Like Gracie herself, her voice was unforgettable.

I remember looking down at her, looking right into her green eye and her blue eye, and thinking, what a pretty little girl she is. I was hoping she'd work with me.

The next day Rena told me Gracie wanted to form an act with me. As I later found out, the reason she picked me rather than Billy was because I didn't stammer. That was my big talent—I didn't stammer.

Gracie and I met at Wiennig and Sberber's restaurant on 45th Street, an old show-business hangout, to work out the details. After comparing our two acts we decided to do mine, mainly because we couldn't afford to buy scenery for the act Benny Ryan had written for Gracie. We agreed to bill ourselves as Burns and Allen because it was my act and I was going to be the comedian. Gracie didn't mind, it was better to be billed second than to be "Larry Reilly" without company. I suggested I get 60 percent of our salary and she get 40 percent because I owned the act and I was the star. Gracie later claimed that she had called for a showdown over that split and had demanded that she get 40 percent while I get 60 percent. After it became obvious that Gracie was the whole act, we agreed to a 50–50 split. I thought that was fair. She did 95 percent of the work and I got 50 percent of the money.

We couldn't afford to hire a rehearsal hall, so we met at a different music publisher's office every day and worked in their rehearsal rooms. We told each publisher we were going to use their songs in our act, so they gave us the space. I was always good in rehearsal; I showed up on time and I knew my lines.

In fact, Gracie's other roommate, Mary Kelly, or Pretty Mary Kelly as she was known, told Gracie after our first rehearsal, "You know, you ought to marry that guy. Any hoofer who shows up on time for a rehearsal is a pearl beyond price."

At that point I wasn't interested in marrying Gracie, I just wanted a feeder. We rehearsed for three weeks, adding jokes or cutting them from the act as we worked. It was a simple flirtation act. For example, Gracie would ask me, "Why don't you ever buy me something? Why don't you buy me a necklace or a diamond ring or a diamond bracelet?"

I'd respond, "You have all those things."

"I had them," she corrected, "but where are they now?"

"I'm holding them for you. And why? Because every day you read in the papers, 'Girl gets hit on the head and they take away her jewelry.' But I'm considerate, I don't want that to happen to you. So I'm holding them, and that way you can go home by yourself every night and if they hit you on the head you won't be out anything."

Even puffing on my cigar wouldn't help that joke. But in the 1920s, that was funny.

Gracie wasn't very good in rehearsal, as I was to learn Gracie was never very good in rehearsal. She knew her lines, but I was concerned that her Irish brogue would make it difficult for the audience to understand her.

Finally, we were ready to break in the act. We named it 60–40, after our agreement. If it had been Gracie's act we probably would have called it 40-60. We were booked into the Hill Street Theatre, in Newark, at five dollars a day. It wasn't very much, but they did guarantee us three days.

The Hill Street was one of those decaying theaters that had never seen better days. If the dressing room had had ceilings, the plaster would have been falling from them. In Gracie's dressing room a large, unframed mirror was balanced on the dressing table. As Gracie sat down she shook the table, the mirror fell, and was smashed into countless pieces. When I heard the crash I went running in to see if she was okay. She was practically in tears. Being Irish, she was very superstitious. As far as she was concerned, that broken mirror meant that Burns and Allen were finished even before we did our first show.

I calmed her down, then explained that there was an old Jewish superstition that said breaking a mirror is actually good luck, that's why they break a wineglass at the end of a wedding ceremony. She believed me. Actually, that's a lie, the only people who believe breaking a mirror is good luck are the people in the mirror replacement business. But there is an old show-business superstition that says if you don't work you aren't going to eat.

Just to make sure the audience knew I was the funny one in the act, I dressed like a comedian. Actually, I often dressed like a comedian, but this time I did it intentionally. I'd seen a newspaper photograph of Joe E. Brown, so I knew how a big-time comedian dressed onstage. I wore wide pants and a short coat, a hat with the brim turned up in front, and a trick bow tie on a swivel. That jazzbo tie was very important; this was long before I smoked a cigar onstage; I let the audience know I'd told a joke by whirling my bow tie.

Being the straight man, Gracie wore a lovely dress.

There were maybe fifteen people in the audience

when Grace Allen and I walked out onstage together
for the first time. I was nervous, I admit it. The kid
was cute, but who knew how she was going to do
onstage? If she froze up, she could ruin my act.

The reality was, that act was so bad, the Ice Age
couldn't have ruined it.

Then she gave me the opening line. She said it
very differently than she'd done it in rehearsal, with
a totally new inflection. The line that had been basically a throwaway suddenly had some life. I realized instantly that this was a different person than
the little girl I'd been rehearsing with. Something
had happened to her. Some kind of magical transformation had taken place. As the act progressed I
realized that the audience felt it too. They loved her,
I could feel it. It was the most amazing thing, and
it happened just like that.

The act did not go the way it was supposed to.
Gracie fed me a straight line and the audience chuck-
led. I answered with my topper. Nothing. She gave
me another line, this time a few people laughed. I
answered. Again, nothing. I spun my bow tie. Still
nothing. When the audience doesn't laugh at a spinning bow tie, you're in trouble. I had gotten more
laughs with Jose and Dolores than I was getting with
Burns and Allen. By the time we finished our first
show Gracie was getting good laughs with funny
lines like, "Oh, how stingy is her father?"

I didn't have to be a genius to understand that
there was something wrong with a comedy act when
the straight lines got more laughs than the punch
lines. So between the first and second show I decided to give Gracie a few of my toppers, just to see
how the audience reacted. During the second show

I asked Gracie, "Who was that guy I saw you kissing backstage?"

"Oh, I don't know," she said.

"You mean, you kiss a guy and you don't know who he is?"

"Well," she said quickly—she always spoke quickly—"I was standing in the wings and he said, 'How about you and me having a bite tonight?' And I said, 'No, I'm busy tonight, but if you'd like I'll bite you now.' "

The audience roared. Either I was the greatest straight man who ever lived or Gracie was something special. By the time we finished those three days in Newark, Gracie had three-quarters of the punch lines. I didn't mind, I still had 60 percent of our salary.

The audience had created Gracie's character. I listened to the jokes they laughed at and gave Gracie more of that type. Gracie certainly wasn't the first comedienne in vaudeville. There had been a long line of "Dumb Doras," as "silly" women were called. Harriet Lee had worked with Benny Ryan. Gracie Deagon. The "Martin Family" had a "dumb" mother. What made Gracie different was her sincerity. She didn't try to be funny. Gracie never told a joke in her life, she simply answered the questions I asked her as best she could, and seemed genuinely surprised when the audience found her answers funny. Onstage, Gracie was totally honest, and honesty is the most important thing a performer can have. And if a performer can fake that, he can do anything.

After our first show we'd taken some of Gracie's friends out to dinner to celebrate, among them Pretty Mary Kelly and her boyfriend, a kind of good-looking, violin-playing vaudevillian named Jack Benny. I liked Benny right away, he had something I enjoyed very much—a worse singing voice than mine. Gracie told me that Benny was in love with Mary, but that she wouldn't give him a tumble. At that moment I was falling in love too. Everytime I looked at Gracie I realized I'd finally found the thing I'd been searching for my whole life—a good act.

2

We were hot. Our agent got us a week in Boonton, New Jersey, at double the money. So if we didn't eat for that week, we'd end up just about even. Actually, I never had a problem getting booked with a new act. It was only after people saw the act that I had a problem. But new acts filled a bill—the audience hadn't seen them before, so they didn't know what they were missing. And they worked for practically nothing.

Our bus was a little late getting into Boonton, and when we got to the theater the manager and his son were busy setting up the folding chairs for the audience. "Glad you made it," the manager said. "So tell me, what kind of act you got?"

"Dialogue," I told him.

"Oh, that's good," he said. "Just make sure you cut out all the talk."

"If there's one thing people around here hate," the manager's son added, "it's all that talk."

But Gracie proved to be as successful in Boonton as she'd been in Newark. We were conquering New Jersey, one theater at a time.

By the end of the month Gracie was the whole

act. My part had been reduced to little more than walking onstage with her and asking, "So how's your brother?" Or, "Your brother thinks he's a ghost?" Or, "Nudist camp? Aren't the police looking for him?" Playing the stooge for Gracie's toppers did bother me a little, but at least I got to wear my own clothes onstage and I didn't have to carry fish in my pockets for the seal. And the act was good, really good. People were laughing when they were supposed to laugh. I wasn't used to that. It threw off my timing. But gradually I made the adjustment. The response of the audience made me realize I had a very special talent—Gracie Allen.

Each show we did I learned a little more about Gracie's character, and Gracie. The audience loved both of them. The character was simply the dizziest dame in the world, but what made her different from all the other "Dumb Doras" was that Gracie played her as if she were totally sane, as if her answers actually made sense. We called it illogical-logic.

For example, she would ask me, "Where do you keep your money?"

"In a bank," I'd respond.

"What interest do you get?"

"Four percent."

"Ha. I get eight."

"You get eight?"

"Yep—I keep it in two banks."

Several things about Gracie's character immediately became apparent. Gracie couldn't be sarcastic or nasty. Some acts could fight onstage; Barry and Woolridge, for example, used to scream at each other. That was their act, screaming at each other. We couldn't do anything like that. The audience was very protective of Gracie. I couldn't argue with her.

And I couldn't touch her. If I had to touch her, I had to do so very delicately. When I began smoking my cigar onstage—mainly so I'd have something to do while Gracie did the act—I'd go onstage before the show began to find out which way the air was blowing, just to make sure my cigar smoke didn't blow in her face. Sometimes I worked on her right, sometimes I worked on her left; Gracie didn't care. I don't know if she even realized I was doing it differently.

Believe me, the audience was so protective of Gracie that if my cigar smoke had blown in her face they might have stood for it, but after standing, they would have come right up on the stage after me.

I remember once we were playing the Victoria Palace in London. At the end of our act we did a brief encore. We left the stage, then returned, and I told the audience, "Gracie and I thank you very much. We'd love to do a little encore, but we're not prepared. So we just—"

"I'm prepared," Gracie interrupted.

I ignored her. "As I was saying, we just want to—"

"I'm very prepared," she insisted.

Our encore consisted of my explaining that we didn't do an encore, while Gracie insisted that she was prepared. We went on like that for several minutes until finally a very distinguished looking, formally dressed gentleman sitting in the front row stood up and pointed his walking stick at me. "See here," he demanded loudly. "Let the little lady carry on!"

So the audience found my character too. Next to Gracie, I was wonderful. All I had to do was stand next to her and imagine some of their applause was for me. Believe me, next to Gracie, even the seal could have been wonderful.

Acts had to be between fourteen and seventeen minutes long. We were constantly making changes, trying new bits, dropping jokes that didn't work. At first we had some difficulty finding the right finish. The most important parts of any act were the beginning and the finish. Powers' Elephants, for example, did the Charleston as they left the stage. That's a big finish. I had this wonderful idea. We would do the act, then dance for several seconds, then interrupt the music for a short joke, dance a bit more, stop and tell another joke, then dance off the stage. Nobody had ever done that before. We tried it several times. Maestro, music please: dum-de-dum-de-dum, dum-de-dum-de-dum, "Tell me, Gracie, did you ever dream you went out with me?"

"Oh no, George, I never have nightmares."

Dum-de-dum-de-dum, dum-de-dum-de-dum, "Gracie, I heard you were mad at your mother."

"I'm very mad at her, George. It was thundering and she didn't wake me. And she knows I can't sleep when it's thundering."

Dum-de-dum-de-dum, dum-de . . . Well, that finish didn't work. So we took advantage of our respective talents. When we finished the act the orchestra would start playing, Gracie would do an Irish jig and I would point to her feet. I was a lot younger then, I could point for a long time.

The act kept changing and it kept getting better. The better it got, the less I did. The less I did, the better it got. People think I'm kidding when I say all I did in the act was ask Gracie, "How's your brother?" I'm not. After a while we dropped the jig from the act, so I didn't even have to point. The only reason we kept the name Burns and Allen was so people would think I did something.

I'll tell you how little I actually did. We would come onstage and I'd ask Gracie, "How's your brother?" She would begin talking and I would leave the stage and return with a carpet. I'd spread the carpet on the stage and lie down until she finished telling me about her brother.

And would you believe it, when we were working in England another performer on the bill stole *my* act. He came out and did his act lying down. He wasn't nearly as good as I was, though, he wasn't lying next to Gracie.

The thing that continued to amaze me about Gracie was how easy she was to work with. She was the most natural performer I'd ever seen. She simply came onstage and said her lines the way she felt that night. She never tried to act, that was probably the main reason she could make the audience believe that she really believed that by shortening the vacuum cleaner cord she could save on electricity. And because she said her lines differently every performance, those lines always sounded fresh. It was only when she started thinking about how to say a line that she had trouble. When we first started in vaudeville, for example, we did a bit that began with Gracie demanding, "Take me home, George."

I said, "I'll take you home if you'll give me a kiss."

"All right," she agreed, "if you take me home, I'll give you a kiss."

We started walking across the stage, and I suddenly stopped. "Wait a second," I asked suspiciously. "Is your mother home?"

"Sure she is, but my father won't let you kiss my mother."

Jack Benny thought that was one of the funniest bits he'd ever seen. After watching us do it at the Keith's in Newark, he came backstage and told Gracie, "I just love the way you read that last line." Now, that was a mistake. Because from that moment on, Gracie became conscious of the way she said that line, and tried to do it just the way Jack liked it every show. It no longer sounded natural. It was no longer funny. Eventually we had to take it out of the act.

Believe me, if Jack Benny had liked our act any more, we would have been out of the business.

I think that if it hadn't been for the presence of the audience, Gracie would have loved performing. She loved people, the difficulty she had with audiences was that they insisted on watching her. Gracie could appear to be so natural only because she was able to block out the audience. Onstage, Gracie talked to me. She would deliver a line, I'd look at the audience, smoke my cigar, and when they stopped laughing I'd look back and Gracie would still be looking at me.

After Gracie retired I worked with Carol Channing. Carol was also a natural actress, but because she was used to working on the Broadway stage, she worked directly to the audience. It took me awhile to get used to that. I'd ask her, "How do you feel, Carol?" She'd look at the audience and say, "I feel fine." So after a few days of that I looked at the audience and said, "I wonder how Carol feels?" That way we could both work to the audience.

Gracie never worked to the audience or, later, to the camera. In radio, for example, most performers kept the house lights on during their shows so they could watch the reaction of the audience. Our first few years we didn't even let anyone in the studio, and when our sponsor finally demanded that we did, we kept the house dark when we were on the air. After we'd been doing our television program for two seasons, Gracie happened to notice that a red light on one of the cameras kept blinking on and off. I explained to her that the red light meant the camera was "live," the picture it was shooting was what was being broadcast to the audience at home. I should have known better. But you always hope. In the middle of a scene the next day, she stopped. "Something wrong, Gracie?" the director asked.

"The red light is on again," she said, pointing to the camera.

The director started to tell her that the red light didn't mean stop, but I interrupted him. Maybe it didn't mean stop to him, but he hadn't been working with Gracie for thirty-five years. Believe me, that red light meant stop. For the next seven years we covered the red lights on every camera.

Because Gracie worked so naturally, "she had no hands." That's an old theatrical expression meaning a performer never thinks about his hands. I had hands, I was always aware of the fact that they were right there at the end of my arms. I used my cigar as a prop. It gave me something to do with my hands. I always held the cigar in my left hand so I could use my right hand to adjust the microphone. I probably could have just as easily held the cigar in my right hand, but I would have looked pretty silly trying to smoke the microphone.

Jack Benny had terrible hands; he was never comfortable with his hands. That's why he was always folding his arms or touching his cheek. He just needed someplace to keep his hands. Onstage, Jack was so conscious of his hands that he couldn't dial a telephone and speak at the same time; he dialed, then he read his lines. Gracie could do many things at the same time without knowing she was doing any of them.

She never relied on props either. If I had been forced to work without my cigar, I probably would have forgotten my lines. But Gracie always did the same things differently. Sometimes she'd walk onstage carrying a purse, sometimes she'd be without a purse; sometimes she wore a dress with pockets and kept her hands in the pockets, sometimes the dress didn't have pockets; sometimes she'd wear gloves, sometimes she'd wear a hat—with Gracie I never knew what to expect. That was just her way of keeping the act fresh. She planned it all. I asked her after a performance once, "Why'd you carry that pocketbook with you today?"

She looked at me as if I were the dizzy one in the act. "A lady always carries a purse," she explained.

All of these things came naturally to Gracie. She didn't need to go to acting school to learn that the essence of acting is to act like you're not acting. Gracie never acted, that's why she was such a great actress.

After the first month we started working pretty regularly. In 1924 we were what was known as a disappointment act. That was a type of act, not a description. A "dissy" was an act that filled in on short notice for scheduled acts that got sick or couldn't perform for some reason. Every Monday and Thursday—the days that theaters changed their bills—we'd sit by the phone, with our bags packed, until two o'clock, when the call usually came telling us where to go. A good disappointment act could get sixty to seventy-five bookings a year. The definition of a "good" disappointment act was an act that showed up. So for two years, wherever there was a flu epidemic, Burns and Allen wouldn't be far behind. Let me put it this way: penicillin would have ended our act.

It seemed like we were always on a bus or truck or short-hop freight. Gracie once said that we did so much traveling that for years afterward she couldn't get used to sleeping in a bedroom that didn't have a number on the door.

As long as we stayed healthy, we worked. We worked bad theaters and worse theaters. We dressed in boiler rooms, bathrooms, and closets. One week in St. Louis we appeared right after a troupe of Hungarian midget acrobats. In Syracuse we followed the Hilton Sisters, the very pretty Siamese twins. That was memorable—we came onstage and everybody in the theater was crying. It made me feel like I was working with Billy Lorraine again.

But we kept getting better and Gracie's character kept evolving. When we were booked for ten weeks by Faly Markus, I changed the name of the act. I named it after Gracie. "Dizzy," as it was known, opened with Gracie and I walking out holding hands. She pulled her hand away from mine and waved toward the wings. A strange man came out, put his arms around her, and they kissed. Then he left the stage, and she waved goodbye. Finally she turned to me and asked, "Who's that?"

"Who's that? You mean to say you kiss people you don't know?"

"Sure."

"Well, if you kiss people you don't know, what do you do to people you do know?"

"People I know I don't kiss."

"Well, suppose that fellow wouldn't kiss *you?*"

"Oh, George, he'd have to. It's a certain little trick I have."

"Certain little trick, huh? Suppose your mother saw you do that?"

"My mother showed me the trick."

"Well, what's the idea of kissing people?"

"I'm practicing. I'm going into pictures. I made up my mind I'm going to be a picture star."

"You made up your mind?"

"Yes, and my father is going to be President of the United States."

"Your father . . ."

"That's right, he told me so this morning. He said, 'When you're a picture star, I'll be President of the United States.' "

Later in the act I shook my head in disbelief at something Gracie said, then told her, "You're dizzy."

"Well, I'm glad I'm dizzy," she replied, "because boys like dizzy girls and I like boys."

"Well, I'm glad you're glad you're dizzy."

"And I'm glad that you're glad that I'm glad I'm dizzy."

"And I'm glad that you're glad that I'm glad that you're glad I'm dizzy."

"And I'm glad . . ."

"Dizzy" was the act that gained us recognition. Audiences left the theater repeating our line, and repeating our line, and repeating our line . . .

In addition to becoming successful, something else was happening between me and Gracie. Well, at least between me. I was falling in love with her. That was hard for me to believe. Gracie was precisely the type of woman I'd never been attracted to—a nice girl.

When Gracie and I teamed up I was a gay blade, a real ladies' man. I wore checkered four-button suits and spats, and I was usually attracted to blondes who called me things like "babe" and "slick." Before meeting Gracie I'd lived with one girl and married another. Actually, I got married because I had to— we were booked.

Back then the only men who lived with women were husbands, fathers, and brothers, and even brothers were suspect. But when Billy Lorraine and I were on the Pantages circuit I met a singer named Harriet Gibson. She was an awful cute little number, and she was making $350 a week. That was another cute number. Billy and I were only making $250 a week as a team, or $125 each, less 10 percent agent's commission. By the time we got through paying transportation, hotel, and food bills, we cleared about two dollars a week.

I was a spiffy-looking fellow, and Harriet and I hit it off. We moved in together, pooled our salaries, and split them down the middle. So now I was making $237.50 without changing my act. The only problem was that Harriet was also going around with a gangster who lived in Chicago. Unlike movie gangsters, a lot of real gangsters weren't too smart. One day Harriet got a letter from this gangster warning, "I understand you're going around with some Jewish kid. You break it off or I'll come back there and shoot him in the ass. To prove I'm serious, I'm going to shoot myself in the leg." And he did.

His plan worked. He shot himself in the leg, and a thousand miles away I got scared. I figured any man who would shoot himself in the leg to prove he was serious was serious. Or stupid. Or worse, both. Either way, when Harriet and I were going together I refused to play the Midwest.

A couple of years later I married Hermosa Jose, my partner in a dance act. Her name was actually Hannah Siegel, but I named her after my cigar. The marriage lasted twenty-six weeks; it would have lasted longer if we had had a better act. She came from a very religious family, and when we were offered a twenty-six-week tour, her parents wouldn't let her go with me unless we were married. So on Friday we went to City Hall and got married for better, for worse, and for twenty-six weeks. I said, "I do," and then I said, "I'll see you at the train Monday morning." The whole marriage we never slept together—I wasn't the type of man who slept with married women. When we came home we got divorced. She was a lovely girl, but I wouldn't have married her for a sixteen-week booking. She eventually married one of the Klein brothers and they played happily ever after on the Shubert circuit.

I wasn't in love with her, but I was in love with Gracie. There wasn't one moment when I looked at Gracie and suddenly realized I was in love. It just happened. Love is a lot like a backache, it doesn't show up on X rays, but you know it's there. And falling in love doesn't leave bruises unless the person you've fallen in love with isn't in love with you. Gracie wasn't in love with me, she was in love with Benny Ryan. At one point, in fact, Benny Ryan sent her a wire advising her to "Stay away from hoofers, particularly that Burns." When Gracie showed it to me I was very pleased. Benny Ryan was a big star— I didn't even think he knew who I was.

I fell in love with Gracie because she was pretty, smart, nice, and talented. But I'll tell you the truth. I also fell in love with Gracie because I fell in love with making a good living. If she had married Benny Ryan, what was I going to do for an act? I had no real affection for the seal. The Siamese twins already had partners. Where was I going to find another Gracie? Remember, she was born Gracie, she wasn't manufactured. Gracie didn't come by the dozen.

I fell in love with her just like our audiences did. Before meeting her, I was splitting $250 a week with Billy Lorraine when we worked a full week. Gracie and I were working regularly, splitting much more than that, and audiences really liked our act. At that time I wasn't sure if I was falling in love with Gracie or falling in love with the better dinners. Until I had become a success, I didn't know that I'd been a failure. Once I'd found out, I realized that success was much better.

I loved Gracie, for whatever reasons. That I was sure of. I hadn't fallen in love with Gracie's face, or her legs, or her bust, or her voice, or her timing. I fell in love with the whole package. But she did have great timing. And years later, when we were rich, I still loved her. And I still love her today. So whatever my reasons at first, it worked. It worked for a long, long time.

It took me almost a year to tell Gracie how I felt about her. I knew she was planning to marry Benny Ryan and I was afraid if I told her I loved her she'd get upset and quit the act. Before this, whenever I'd told a girl I loved her, the only people who had been upset were her parents. So I touched Gracie only when I was supposed to in the act, and I only kissed her softly on the cheek, and most importantly, I kept my mouth shut.

That wasn't easy because we spent so much time together. When we were on the road we'd be at the theater for three or four shows a day, and after the last show we'd go to a local hotel for dinner and rooftop dancing. I knew Gracie wasn't going to fall in love with me, but I was hoping I might dazzle her with my dancing. People danced differently then; when a man and a woman got up from the table they both went in the same direction. And a couple was always a man and a woman. We waltzed, we did the two-step and the foxtrot and the Peabody, and when we danced, we held each other.

That was the only time I got to hold her. We slept in separate hotel rooms, and when we traveled by train we never took a compartment—they were expensive, they had doors!—instead we took bunks. As the gentleman, I always slept in the upper. I guarantee you, there is no way to look sophisticated when climbing into an upper.

I tried subtle ways to make Gracie realize she was in love with me. I'd give her flowers, I'd tell her about all the other girls who were chasing me, sometimes I'd even put a dab of lipstick on my shirt collar to try to make her jealous. Gracie and I became very close friends, so close she would often tell me how much she loved Benny Ryan.

Finally I told her I loved her. And she laughed. Maybe audiences didn't think I was funny; Gracie thought I was hysterical. She didn't believe me at all. "Oh, Nattie," she used to say. "Don't be such a kidder." The more I insisted, the more she thought I was doing a routine. I used to tell her, "Please,

Gracie, marry me. Benny Ryan won't mind." And she'd laugh some more.

Once, because I was competing with Benny Ryan, I wrote a song for her. Mr. Maestro, if you please:

I love you, love you, love you, I do,
You're the only girl I adore.
I love you, love you, love you, I do,
And every day I love you more.
Someday I may build a little home,
For two or three or more,
We'll settle down for life, if you'll be my wife,
Oh, I love you, love you, I do.

Sweet, isn't it? Gracie laughed and told me, "If you write another song like that, I *will* marry Benny Ryan."

I don't remember the first time I kissed Gracie for real. It happened gradually. Instead of kissing her on the cheek, I kissed her lightly on the lips. The next time I pressed a little harder, and maybe the time after that I put my arms around her. Finally, I was kissing her for real. I did notice that when I put my arms around her and kissed her, she knew what was going on. Only once, I remember, did she pull away. "It's not right, Nat," she told me. "What about Benny?"

"I'll kiss him later," I said.

She almost married Benny Ryan in 1925. He returned from a long tour, planning to marry her. I was saved when we got a last-minute booking, sixteen-weeks-guaranteed, on the Orpheum circuit at $400 a week. We were just beginning to break into the big time. Critics would see our act. Gracie couldn't decide whether to stay in New York and

marry Benny Ryan or go with me. Mary Kelly and
Jack Benny urged her to go. I think Jack said something like, ''Oh, Nattie isn't as bad as all that, and
you can always get married when you come back.''
Mary pointed out that the tour included San Francisco, which would allow Gracie to fulfill at least
one of her ambitions—she could see her picture dis-
played in the lobby of the San Francisco Orpheum
Theatre. Gracie finally agreed to go, but only on the
condition that our salary be raised to $450 a week.

It was obvious the kid was crazy about me.

Mary was also going out with an Orpheum booker,
the man she eventually married, and convinced him
that Burns and Allen were worth another $50 a week.

Upon hearing that, Gracie decided she couldn't go
because she didn't have a large trunk.

It was amazing how much she loved me. The only
thing standing between us was a large trunk. So,
during a raging snowstorm, Jack Benny and I went
downtown and bought a steamer for Gracie, then
dragged it back uptown on our backs. Don't ask me
why we didn't take the subway. It was hard to be a
hero in vaudeville. Besides, when they make the
movie about Gracie, I want to see the actor playing
me carrying a trunk on his back in a snowstorm.

Finally, because of her deep love for me, and the
fact that she had run out of excuses, Gracie agreed
to go on the tour. She even made the train with at
least thirty or forty seconds to spare.

It was during that trip that I seriously asked her to
marry me. I'll never forget her response: if I could
have gotten that kind of laughter from an audience,
I would have been successful years earlier. I even
bought a ring. It sold for $35 but I managed to get
it for $20. It was a very special ring—the metal band

actually changed colors as it aged in my pocket. I didn't get down on one knee when I asked her to marry me, though. If I'd have done that, she would have thought I was doing Jolson.

Gracie said she really cared for me, but turned me down. I think what she really wanted from a man, more than anything else, was a sense of security. Gracie never forgave her father for leaving, and I think she wanted someone she could rely on to always be there for her. I was a song and dance man, and hoofers did not have a reputation for being reliable. If a hoofer even did the same step two performances in a row, people began wondering what was wrong with him. Benny Ryan was Irish, successful, talented, handsome, and he loved her. All I had going for me were my intelligence, cleverness, and the fact that I loved her. I knew I was in serious trouble.

Fortunately for me, Benny Ryan was Irish, successful, talented, handsome, and always late. If he told Gracie he'd pick her up at seven, he got there at nine. If he said nine, he would always send flowers the next day to apologize for not showing up. I was always right on time. In vaudeville, when you had my kind of talent, you were on time or you were off the bill. Being on time was another one of my talents.

The one issue that never came up between Gracie and me was religion. Gracie was a practicing Irish Catholic. She tried to go to Mass every Sunday. I was Jewish, but I was out of practice. My religion was always treat other people nicely and be ready when they play your music. Mary Kelly, who was also Irish Catholic, wouldn't marry Jack Benny because she didn't want to marry out of her faith, but

Gracie didn't seem to care. In fact, I was a lot more concerned about what my mother thought than I was about Gracie.

Immigrant parents put a lot of pressure on their children to marry someone of the same religious and ethnic background. My parents were Orthodox Jews. My mother came from Poland, my father came from Austria, and their parents had arranged their marriage. My mother had even cut off all her hair when she was fourteen—that was the custom—and wore a wig. It was a hand-me-down wig that was much too big for her, so every time she'd turn her head the wig would stay straight ahead. Even my mother got more laughs than I did.

My father had died long before I started working with Gracie. My mother was a wonderful woman whom I loved very deeply, and I was very nervous the first time she met Gracie. We were filling in for an equilibrist, a high-wire walker, for four days at the Myrtle Theatre, and she came to see us perform. Afterward we took her out for dinner.

"What did you think of your son?" Gracie asked.

"I think you're very talented, Gracie," my mother said.

"But what about Nattie? Wasn't he terrific?"

My mother raised her eyebrows and shrugged. "To tell you the truth, I think sometimes he acts like a relative got him the job."

After that I knew I wasn't going to have any problems with my mother about marrying an Irish Catholic girl—as long as it was this particular Irish Catholic girl.

And after Gracie's mother met me she felt the same way—she didn't care if I married an Irish Catholic girl. At one point though, she wrote me a long letter, threatening, "You be good to Gracie or she's coming right home!"

So my mother approved of my marrying Gracie, and Gracie's mother approved of my marrying Gracie; the only one who objected was Gracie.

The sixteen-week Orpheum tour opened at the Palace Theatre in Chicago. We were a big hit. Then we went to Winnipeg for a week, then did a split week in Vancouver and Seattle. Then Portland and Oakland. It was a great feeling for me to go into a town knowing that after I'd done my act I would still be welcomed back. Audiences loved us.

Oakland was our last date before San Francisco, and while we were there Gracie told me she wasn't feeling very well. At first I thought she was getting nervous about going home, but her condition continued to get worse. By this time I knew all about Gracie's migraines, and I'd seen her work when other people wouldn't have gotten out of bed, so when she said she was sick, I believed her. When we arrived in San Francisco I took her right to the hospital.

It was an appendicitis attack. Maybe appendicitis isn't dramatic enough for any movie producers reading this, and for the right offer I'd be willing to change it to some sort of more fashionable attack, but it was appendicitis, and in the 1920s it was extremely serious. I lived at Gracie's house while she was in the hospital, but I spent most of my time with her, proving she could depend on me.

Ironically, we'd finally made the big time—and a disappointment act had to fill in for us.

I'd changed a lot because of Gracie. It wasn't just that I'd become a straight man—anyone who'd seen me do comedy knew I'd been born to be a straight man—but that I was finally a success, I was trying to act responsibly, and I'd fallen head over heels for a nice girl.

I was still a pretty clever fellow, though. I knew how much Gracie loved flowers, so I borrowed $200 from her and filled her hospital room with beautiful arrangements. There was one thing I didn't do. She'd asked me to send a wire to Benny Ryan in New York telling him what had happened. Unfortunately I'd spent all of Gracie's money on the flowers, so I couldn't send the wire. Since I knew Gracie would worry about me if I told her I was broke, I lied and told her I'd sent it. I just didn't want her worrying about me. That's the kind of guy I am, always thinking about someone else's peace of mind. I could tell Gracie was very disappointed when she didn't hear from Ryan. I could tell that because I made sure to ask her several times a day if she'd heard from him.

After Gracie recovered we resumed the tour in Denver, eventually finishing at Chicago's State-Lake Theatre in September. We were a success everywhere we played, and the more successful we were, the more depressed I became. The situation was tough for me to accept: I'd been so happy as a failure before I met Gracie, now I was a success, I was in love, and I was miserable. I knew that even though Benny Ryan had let Gracie down, she still intended to marry him. That not only meant the end of our relationship, it meant the end of the act.

Fortunately, Benny Ryan was out on tour when we got back to New York. I pressed Gracie to marry me before he came home, but even that $20 ring wasn't enough to convince her to change her mind. Faly Markus had booked us into Cleveland in January, and I'd decided to use that tour to break in a new routine we were calling Lamb Chops that I'd written with a bright young comedy writer named Al Boasberg.

Lamb Chops was perfect for Burns and Allen. The only problem was that I didn't think there'd be a Burns and Allen in January. I just couldn't take it anymore. A week before Christmas I finally lost my temper and gave Gracie an ultimatum—agree to marry me within ten days or we were splitting up. I think until that moment she didn't believe I was serious about marrying her. I think she believed it was just another one of my jokes. Like the ring.

On Christmas Eve Mary Kelly threw a small party and asked me to play Santa Claus. Gracie was late getting to the party because she'd been waiting for a phone call from Benny Ryan. I was dressed in a bright-red costume, but I was probably the meanest Santa Claus in Christmas history. "Here," I'd snarl as I handed a gift to Mary or Rena or Jack Benny. "Take this!" I'd bought a silver bracelet with a small diamond in it for Gracie; she'd gotten a lounging robe for me. On the card she'd written, "To Nattie, with all my love." I read that card and laughed out loud. "All your love? Ha, ha, ha. You don't even know what love means."

Gracie began to cry and went into the bedroom and closed the door. I took off my beard and went home.

Gracie was supposed to call Benny Ryan at midnight to wish him a Merry Christmas, but she didn't do it. Instead, she sat talking with Mary Kelly, trying to decide between the two of us. Finally Benny Ryan called and complained, "You didn't call me at midnight like you were supposed to."

"I know," she said softly.

"How come?" She didn't answer. "Don't you love me anymore?" he asked.

"No," she said softly. "I don't."

"What'd you say?"

"I said, I don't think I love you anymore, Benny."

After a long silence Benny Ryan said, "Then please hang up the phone."

I was home in bed, but I wasn't asleep. The only telephone in the place I was living in was downstairs, and I don't remember if I heard it ringing. Maybe I thought it was the bells on Santa's sleigh. But at three o'clock someone knocked on my door to tell me that I wasn't supposed to be getting phone calls at three o'clock. I ran downstairs and grabbed the phone. "Yeah?"

"You can buy the wedding ring if you want to."

I didn't have to ask who it was. "You'll never be sorry," I promised. I was so happy I didn't even mention that I'd already spent $20 on a perfectly fine wedding ring.

That phone call was the second-best Christmas present I'd ever received. The next day I asked her why she'd changed her mind. "Well," she explained, "you're the only boy who ever made me cry. And I decided that if you could make me cry, I must really love you."

That was Gracie. I made her so unhappy she knew it had to be love. If I'd known before that that was all I had to do, I would have made her miserable and she probably would have married me much sooner.

Christmas night we slept together for the first time. Now *that* was the best Christmas present I've ever received. Actually, calling what we did "sleeping" is like expecting a lawyer's brief to be short. We made love. We had sex. This is about as risqué as this story is going to get, so I'd better repeat it. We made love. We had sex.

Sex is certainly a very important part of any marriage. Gracie and I had a wonderful life together, and a wonderful marriage, and sex was part of it, but not the major part. Probably the most important thing about sex is that it helps sell a lot of books. I have to be honest. I was a lousy lover. Fortunately Gracie married me for laughs, not for sex. Of course she got both of them—when we had sex, she laughed.

Gracie and I always had a nice time together, but after we'd made love she never gave me a standing ovation. In our marriage—I suspect in every marriage—the really important things became, "How do you feel?" "Is the soup hot?" "Want to see a movie tonight?" Those are the things that keep a marriage together.

We decided to get married in Cleveland at the end of January. But first we were going to break in Lamb Chops. We were both very nervous; getting married was one thing, but breaking in a new act was serious business. A divorce was a lot easier to get than a good act. We played the sticks in Ohio for three weeks, testing our relationship and the new material. Both of them were pretty funny.

After finishing a date in Canton, we caught a late-night milk train, arriving in Cleveland at about five A.M. When we reached the Statler Hotel we were told that if we checked in before seven o'clock we'd have to pay for an extra day. We knew the act was good, but we weren't sure it was that good, so we sat in the lobby for two hours trying to look like we belonged there. Believe me, nobody belongs in a hotel lobby at six o'clock in the morning.

We had asked Jack Benny to give the bride away, but Jack said he never gave anything away. Besides, he was playing a date in California. Instead, my brother Izzy, the original George, and his wife came in from Akron, where he was a department store executive, and Mary Kelly came in from Chicago, where her act, Swift and Kelly, was performing.

Gracie had gotten a new pair of white kid gloves, new shoes, and a new nightgown for the wedding. Actually, the nightgown was for later. I had my snazzy four-button suit pressed.

As soon as Izzy and Mary arrived, we hopped into a cab and drove to the justice of the peace. The justice of the peace was ready to leave on a fishing trip when we got there, and he wasn't interested in spending time marrying folks. Remember Al Kelly, who did a great double-talking act? I think Al Kelly got his act from the justice. He spoke so fast I didn't know if Gracie and I had gotten married or had bought land in Florida. All I remember is he asked, "Do you?" I said, "I do." He said, "Good—I'm going fishing."

Our cab was waiting for us. The entire ceremony had cost twenty cents on the meter.

❧

Years later, Gracie and I were remembering our wedding on the radio. "It seems like only yesterday," Gracie told our listeners, "that my mother tripped him as we walked down the aisle."

"I guess your family didn't approve," I suggested.

"Oh, sure they did," she explained. "In fact, they applauded her when she did it."

But at the end of the show Gracie got a little emotional, which was very unusual for her to do on the air. "I just want everyone to know one thing," she said. "I'm a very lucky woman. I was courted by the youngest, handsomest, most charming, most sought-after star in show business—"

"Thank you very much," I said.

"—but I still married George because I loved him."

At two-thirty in the morning on our wedding night the phone in our hotel room rang. When I answered, I heard a gruff voice say, "Hello, George?"

Jack Benny trying to disguise his voice sounded exactly like Jack Benny trying to disguise his voice. "Listen," I said, "send up two orders of ham and eggs." Then I hung up.

About a half hour later he called again. "George, I just—"

"The eggs were cold," I interrupted, "now send up some hot coffee." And I hung up again. Actually, I hung up on Jack only to make him happy. Even then he loved it when I played practical jokes on him. After hanging up for the second time I imagined him sitting in his hotel room in California laughing hysterically. I figured he'd probably keep laughing until he realized he had to pay for two long-distance telephone calls.

So there I was, married to a woman who knew she loved me because I made her cry, and best friends with a hack violin player who thought it was hysterical when I hung up the phone on him. And they were the comedians while I was the straight man.

Now that Gracie and I were married, we could

concentrate on the really important matter between two people very much in love with each other: the act. Breaking in a new act in vaudeville was very risky. If the audience didn't like it, an entire tour might be canceled.

Lamb Chops was a great act. It began with my asking Gracie, "Do you like to love?"

"No," she said.

"Well, then, do you like to kiss?"

"No," she said firmly.

"Well, what do you like?"

"Lamb chops."

I considered that for a moment. Considering was another one of my talents. Then I asked, "How many lamb chops can you eat?"

"Four."

"You mean, a little girl like you can eat four lamb chops alone?"

"No, silly, not alone. But with potatoes I could."

Gracie's relatives began showing up in our act for the first time: "My brother was held up by two men last night," she told me.

I was particularly sharp in this bit. "Your brother?"

"Yes."

"Was held up last night?"

"Yes."

"By two men?" It hadn't taken me long to learn my lines.

"Yes, my poor dear brother was held up last night by two men."

"Where?"

"All the way home."

I don't know if it had anything to do with the fact that Gracie had married me, but suddenly everybody decided she was crazy, and we were in demand. They loved us in Cleveland. In Detroit, they kept us onstage for thirty-four minutes, a house record, doing both Lamb Chops and Dizzy. After we wowed them in Syracuse, the B.F. Keith Agency offered us a week at the big-time Jefferson Theatre in New York City. The Jefferson was considered the toughest house in New York; it was where bookers from every agency came to look at acts trying to break into the big time. A failure there often meant a career in the sticks.

They loved us at the Jefferson even more than they had in Detroit. Married life was working out very well; six weeks after Gracie and I were married we signed a five-year contract to play the Keith-Orpheum circuit for a salary ranging from $450 to $600 a week.

It was a big-time tour, nothing but two-a-days. In small-time vaudeville, performers usually worked three or four shows a day for very little money. Sometimes, at the five o'clock show, there would be fifteen people sitting in a 1200-seat house. Big-time was two shows a day, a matinee and an evening show. Ironically, in vaudeville, the better known you were, the less you worked and the more they paid you. That sounds like a system in which Gracie could become a star.

Gracie was about twenty years old and she was a star. I was thirty and living with a star. Audiences and critics just fell in love with this charming little girl with a birdlike voice and a birdlike brain. In Boston, a critic wrote, "Burns and Allen are making a hit at the Rialto the first half of this week, chiefly due to the ingratiating ways of the pretty little Miss

Allen, who skips across the boards of the stage directly into the hearts of the audience.''

These were the best notices I'd ever received. "Lamb Chops is a snappy and bright little offering," a *Philadelphia Inquirer* critic wrote. "It is really the clever work of Miss Allen as a comedienne of rare ability that makes the act stand out. . . . Here is a young lady that will bear watching as her work is original and refreshing.''

They couldn't have been kinder to me in Chicago. "It is a happy situation for the patrons of the Imperial this week that Burns and Allen are here. . . . Miss Allen, who is just about the best characterization of the 'Dumb Dora' seen on the vaudeville boards on many a day, is thoroughly at home in her role. She has many rollicking bits of repartee and the unique manner in which she puts her stuff across makes her the main spot of a pleasing bill of entertainment. Mr. Burns is a good feeder for Miss Allen and that's all for him. He tries at times to steal the spot, but he simply can't do it, for Miss Allen is wholly master of the situation and the audience shows its approval.''

They loved me in Louisville. "One who has heard Miss Allen . . . could never forget her. She is delightfully vivacious as either a quipster or a dancer. Burns makes a good foil for the little lady.''

And finally, they adored me in Pittsburgh. "Burns has original ideas," a reviewer noted. "He cracks jokes while lying on his back.''

In 1928 we went to England with Lamb Chops for the first time. Initially, the booking agent didn't quite understand what kind of act we did.

"I play a dizzy girl," Gracie explained.

"You mean you're daft?''

"No, I'm dumb," Gracie emphasized.

"Oh, I see," he said quite properly. "You're a pantomime artist."

I could have interrupted and straightened out the whole thing, but if they had kept going long enough Gracie and I might have had a whole new routine. In fact, we had some trouble in England at first because they didn't understand what Gracie was talking about. That was not unusual. If people had understood what Gracie was talking about, we wouldn't have had an act. But the problem was that they didn't understand the meaning of certain words. Gracie once said, when she was asked how to speak French, "You speak it the same way you speak English, you just use different words." That was true in England, too. They don't eat lamb chops, for example, they eat lamb cutlets. So we had to change the name of the act. But once we made the necessary changes, we were a smash.

This trip was Gracie's first trip abroad. Not mine. Wherever I've gone I've had a broad.

Now I'm puffing on Groucho's cigar.

Actually, as far as Gracie was concerned, the best thing about England was the food. Somehow that figures. But during the entire time we were there she didn't have a single migraine headache, and she guessed it might have had something to do with the lack of spices in the food. That could be a great advertisement for British cooking: Eat our food, it doesn't cause headaches. They could use a good ad campaign, too. You don't hear too many Californians suggesting, "Let's go out and eat British food tonight."

They liked us though. We played twenty-one weeks all over the country. Our act became so well known that the audience used to shout out the punch lines with us. The critics loved me just as much in England as they had in the States: "Burns and Allen have a string of the niftiest gags heard here for a long time, and she can put them over with full effect. The lady partner I particularly liked; she has personality, she can talk, she can ogle and she can dance. The act should stay here for a long time."

I thought that notice was actually a bit unfair to me. I happen to be a fine ogler. Ogling is another one of my real talents. But that review was nothing compared to the raves I got in the *Observer:* "Miss Allen is a golden-faced brunette, with blue eyes, blue-black hair, crimson lips, a sylph-like form, and a baby voice all innocent guile and coquetry. She oozes personality from every pore and broadcasts wholesale sex appeal from the batteries of her pert good looks.

"Burns is all right too."

See that: *"Burns is all right too."*

I never minded Gracie getting better notices than I did, she was the whole act, but it did bother me when Gracie's dresses got better reviews than I did. From the very beginning Gracie had insisted on dressing like a lady onstage, often wearing a different gown for every show we did in a town. That was revolutionary in vaudeville because female performers, particularly comediennes, always wore the same costume every show, day after day. Comediennes always appeared in a little middy blouse and pleated skirt. Gracie dressed like she was going to a party. "Crowned in at least $500 worth of satin and lace," a reviewer wrote after we'd hit the big time, "Gracie Allen was both a beauty and a comedienne at the same time, and that should make any actress happy."

And: "Miss Allen wears another stunning creation, white this time." And: "Burns and Allen will always be more than welcome . . . if only to see more of Miss Allen's new frocks, of which she wears another this week." And: "George Burns and Gracie Allen, the latter wearing yet another stunning creation, cornered laughs galore." Of course, if I had worn a stunning creation we probably would have cornered even more laughs, but that was Milton Berle's act.

Of all the notices we received, the one that meant the most to me and Gracie was a two-line mention in Sidney Skolsky's New York newspaper column. At that time Alfred Lunt and Lynn Fontanne were considered the finest actors in America. Like many people in show business, we idolized them. They came to see us work at Loew's State, and after the show Lunt told Skolsky, "I predict that Burns and Allen are going to be very big stars." Four years earlier Gracie hadn't been good enough to be billed as "company" and I'd been tossing beach balls to an extremely self-centered seal, and now we were being praised by one of the country's finest actors. That felt great. All the seal was getting was fish.

The worst review I received, once I'd started working with Gracie, appeared in an Oklahoma paper. "Miss Allen can extract oodles of mirth from the most commonplace remark," the critic wrote, "and there's no telling how far she could go if she worked alone." I think there were a lot of people who felt that way, but I never let it bother me. Did Mrs. Einstein care? Once, on a movie set, the head of Paramount's publicity department called me "Mr. Allen." He started apologizing and I stopped him. "As long as they get Burns and Allen on the check,"

I said, "I don't care whether Gracie's Mrs. Allen or Mr. Burns, or I'm Miss Burns or Miss Allen."

Gracie was bothered by it a lot more than I was. She was always worried about my feelings. I'll tell you how we dealt with it. Before I'd met Gracie I'd done a lot of running around. One day my mother and I were eating breakfast and she started to lecture me. "Nattie," she said, "you have seven sisters, and every one of them was a virgin when she was married."

"You're right, Ma," I agreed, "but that's because they're all homely."

My mother glared at me for a moment, considering that—I got my talent for consideration from my mother—then said, "Pass the salt."

Gracie loved that story, and during our whole life together, whenever there was something either of us didn't want to talk about, we'd simply say, "Pass the salt." That meant, drop it. The subject, not the salt. So when this review was printed in the Oklahoma paper, I asked her, "Did you read this notice?"

"Pass the salt," she said.

There was never any professional jealousy between me and Gracie. Acts would run into trouble when they began competing for laughs. We never did; Gracie got the laughs, and at the end of the night, I got to bring Gracie home. It was so obvious that she was the whole act that we made it part of the act. That's why people thought it was funny when I laid down on a rug while she performed. On one of our radio shows, our accountant was doing our tax return and he said to me, "By the way, George, I see you're getting money from a new source this year."

"No," I told him. "I'm still married to Gracie." My real contribution to the act took place offstage. I made sure nothing happened to Gracie.

A magazine writer once asked Gracie and me how we dealt with the fact that she got all the laughs. "It doesn't matter," I explained. "We both know which side our bread is buttered on."

I often wrote material for Gracie to use in interviews, but I hadn't written her next line: "I don't see what difference it makes what side it's buttered on," she said. "I always eat both sides."

We were a team, Burns and Allen. The laughs we got were community property. In fact, I don't think Gracie ever fully understood how popular she was. I remember an evening in 1958—I know it was then because it was just after she'd retired—and we were sitting by ourselves in our den watching television, and she asked me, "Nattie, are we stars?"

" 'Course we are," I told her. "You're known all over the world. You can't even go shopping without someone asking you for an autograph. Why'd you ask?"

"Oh, I don't know," she said, sounding a bit wistful. "It's just that I always think of stars being people like Clark Gable and Joan Crawford."

Gracie knew she was famous, but she was careful never to take advantage of it. After we'd moved to Beverly Hills in the 1930s she wanted to bring our daughter, Sandy, up to San Francisco to see Aunt Clara. But instead of renting a car and driver, which we certainly could have afforded, she took a train. We argued about it, and she told me she didn't want people she'd known her whole life to think she'd become "full of herself."

To me, playing the Palace Theatre on Broadway

meant you were a star. Of all the thrills I've had in show business, playing the Palace for the first time was the most exciting.

We played the Palace for the first time in 1928. It was part of the deal with Keith-Orpheum. To celebrate I went out and bought myself a new pair of spats and a walking stick. All right, a cane. I wish I'd kept that cane. When I get old I may need it.

As usual, Gracie was very nervous before we went on. We stood in the wings, staring straight ahead. When the orchestra started playing our music—in those days it was a song titled "Crazy People"—I took her hand and led her into the spotlight. Nothing ever felt as good as the spotlight at the Palace Theatre. Well, almost nothing.

Actually, the Palace was a pushover for small acts like we were. Booking the Palace was tough, playing it was easy. The audience knew how important their response was to newcomers, so they rooted very hard for them; it was the headline acts that had better be good. Even the big stars rooted for newcomers to be successful—it was only after you were successful that they didn't like you. The competition on the bill at the Palace was often very tough. Al Jolson, for example, always left the water running in his dressing room so he wouldn't hear the audience applauding other performers.

A lot of stars demanded the number-one dressing room. So many people wanted it, in fact, that the management was constantly having it painted so that no one could have it. When the number-one dressing room at the Palace wasn't being painted, it was a weak show.

Opening night was Monday at eight-fifteen. That's when the critics came. We packed the audience with friends like Jack, Mary, Rena, Blossom Seeley, and Benny Fields, dress designer Orry-Kelly, Archie Leach—a handsome necktie salesman who was trying to break into show business with a stilt-walking act. He eventually changed his name to Cary Grant and after that was never much good as a necktie salesman. He was there, and Jesse Block and Eva Sully. I'll tell you how confident I was that we were going to do well. Before the show Benny Fields asked me, "We want to send some flowers up to Gracie. When should we do it?"

"Wait until after our second encore," I said.

Benny shook his head in disbelief. "Nattie, listen, you just can't go onstage with that lack of confidence."

Lamb Chops was a smash. We were a hit. And as I expected, the critics just raved about my performance: "The versatility of her delivery, the droll manner in which she offers to act, and her face expressions . . . are nothing short of marvelous."

"Miss Allen . . . your main worry is that the script be good enough for your talents."

At least my notices were as good as Gracie's dresses.

From that time on we played the Palace regularly. In 1930, we appeared on Broadway for seventeen weeks, a vaudeville record, nine of them at the Palace with Eddie Cantor and George Jessel, the other eight at Keith's Paramount, which was directly across the street.

After our third one-week booking at the Palace, Arthur Wolfe, who ran the place, offered to extend us a second week if Gracie would serve as the first Mistress of Ceremonies in Palace Theatre history. That meant she would have to introduce the other acts on the bill. I turned him down. In those days people bought a season ticket to the great vaudeville houses and came every week, so you couldn't do the same act two weeks in a row. We were stars, but we were stars with one basic act. And truthfully, I wasn't sure Gracie could face the audience alone.

A day or so after I'd turned down the offer, Gracie and I were having lunch with Jessel at Sardi's and told him the story. He immediately got Wolfe on the phone and accepted for us. Now all we had to do was find a new act in two days.

This was the first time Gracie was going to work alone since we'd teamed up, and we were both very nervous about it. We were so nervous, in fact, that we could have done a routine about it. "I'm nervous," Gracie would have said.

"And I'm nervous because you're nervous," I would have responded.

"And I'm nervous because you're nervous because I'm nervous . . ." We might have started a whole new career again.

Gracie opened the show by herself, walking on-stage with strings wrapped around each of her fingers to remind her "not to forget what I'm trying to remember." Each act she had to introduce, she explained, was represented by one string. By the time she came out to introduce the fourth act she was feeling so confident that she had decided to work the hard way, "without any strings."

It was a typical Palace bill. A roller-skating act, Sandy Lang assisted by the Emeralde Sisters, opened. Madie and Ray, the famed rope-twirling, dancing contortionists, followed. Ray was so good that his encore consisted of twirling his chewing gum. Then Charles Ahearn and his Millionaires Club

Orchestra did a nice music and comedy turn. A sultry black singer, Adelaide Hall, sang the showstopping "I Must Have That Man." The headliner, comedian Phil Baker, closed the first part of the show with an act that included heckler Humphrey Muldowney. During intermission a film short, *Jools*, was shown.

The great comedian Ben Blue, assisted by Demaris Dore, or "Hotsy-Totsy" as she was known, opened the second half of the show. Then Horace Heidt and His Californians, another comedy with music act, did their bit, and finally Gracie and I closed the show.

It's funny, this funny business. When we were starting out, we'd tried a finish in which we'd do a nice soft-shoe, pause to tell a joke, then dance a little more, tell another joke, and dance off the stage. It hadn't worked. At the Palace we decided to try it again. Maestro, if you please:

Dum-de-dum-de-dum, dum-de-dum-de-dum, "Tell me Gracie, how's your cousin?"

"You mean the one who died?"

"Yeah?"

"Oh, he's fine now."

Dum-de-dum-de-dum, dum-de-dum-de-dum . . . "Guess what, George, my sister had a brand-new baby."

"Boy or girl?"

"I don't know, but I can't wait to find out if I'm an aunt or an uncle."

Dum-de-dum-de-dum, dum-de-dum-de-dum . . . "George, my father fell down the stairs with three quarts of liquor."

"Did he spill it?"

"No, silly, he kept his mouth closed."

Dum-de-dum-de-dum, dum-de-dum . . .

The audience loved the finish, they loved our act, and most of all, they loved Gracie. If "superstars" had existed in those days, Gracie would have been a superstar. I think the finish worked because we were no longer simply Burns and Allen, struggling troupers. We were BURNS AND ALLEN, stars of stage, and soon to be stars of screen and radio. I'd mention television too, but we didn't know they were going to invent it, so we didn't plan on being television stars.

I admit those jokes in the finish were not our best material. But we only had a few days to write the act. I'll tell you, though, if they were good enough to close the show at the Palace Theatre, they are certainly good enough to finish this chapter: Music, please:

Dum-de-dum-de-dum, dum-de-dum-de-dum . . . "George, my brother the window washer lost his job."

"Your brother the window washer lost his job?"

"That's right. He was working on the twentieth floor, and when he got through he stepped back to admire his work . . ."

"And that's how he lost his job."

De-dum-bump.

3

"I don't want a husband with money and good looks and personality," Gracie used to tell audiences. "I'd rather have George. And I'm not the only one who feels that way about him. Plenty of women have told me how relieved they are that he's with me.

"I know there were a couple of people who thought he wouldn't be a good husband: Mama, Papa, Grandma . . . Grandpa . . . sister Bessie . . . Uncle Dan . . . Aunt Clara . . . the ice man . . . Schwab the druggist . . . the U.S. Senate . . . California . . ."

Marrying Gracie was the best thing that ever happened to me. I have a feeling she felt the same way—that marrying her was the best thing that ever happened to me. She called me Nattie and I always called her Googie. I started calling her that just after we'd gotten married. She woke me up in the middle of the night and asked me to make her laugh. This had nothing to do with sex. So I looked at her and said, in baby talk, "Googie, googie, googie." Look, when I was wide awake in the middle of the day my material wasn't great, so how much better could it have been in the middle of the night? I think that phrase probably came from the song "Goo Goo Googley Eyes," or maybe the song came from that phrase, but Gracie laughed and I began calling her Googie. From that night on, for the rest of our lives, even today, she's always been Googie to me.

❧

After headlining the Palace, Gracie and I were in demand in vaudeville houses across America. We knew we were good too; we must have been, because as soon as we were introduced at the Palace we could hear Jolson turning on the water in his dressing room. I'll tell you how stardom affected Gracie. Gracie's hobby was window-shopping. She loved to spend hours going from store to store looking at clothes, trying things on, and not buying. Probably the only difference success made to Gracie was that she could afford not to buy at much better stores.

I know Gracie enjoyed performing, but it was never her whole life. It was her job. The minute the show was over she was out of her stage clothes and out of show business. Not me, I was in show business whether I had my clothes on or not. Gracie was known as the least show-biz star in show business.

The only problem was that just as we were becoming stars, vaudeville was dying. No one could pin the rap on us, though. Everybody believes it was the movies that killed vaudeville. That's not true. Movies, vaudeville, burlesque, the local stock companies—all survived together. Then radio came in. For the first time people didn't have to leave their homes to be entertained. The performers came into their house. Gracie and I knew that vaudeville was finished when theaters began advertising that their shows would be halted for fifteen minutes so that the audience could listen to "Amos 'n' Andy." And when the "Amos 'n' Andy" program came on, the vaudeville would stop, they would bring a radio on-stage, and the audience would sit there watching the radio.

It's impossible to explain the impact that radio had on the world to anyone who didn't live through that time. Before radio, people had to wait for the newspaper to learn what was happening in the world. Before radio, the only way to see a performer was to see a performer. And maybe most important, before radio there was no such thing as a commercial.

Radio made everybody who owned one a theater manager. They could listen to whatever they wanted to. For a lot of performers, the beginning of radio meant the end of their careers. A lot of acts couldn't make the transition. Powers' Elephants, mimes, acrobats, seals, strippers, what could they do on the radio? What was the announcer going to say, the mime is now pretending to be trapped in a box? The seal caught a fish? You should see this girl without her fan? Gracie and I had the perfect act for radio—we talked.

That also made us right for that other new sensation, talking movies. There was no such thing as talking in the movies when I was growing up. If you talked, they threw you out of the theater. So we would silently watch the silent pictures. We used to go to Zyden's Theatre on the Lower East Side. Two kids could get in for a nickel. Actually, I saw my first "talkie" there. It was Mary Pickford starring in *Tess of the Storm Country*. It wasn't really a talkie, but Zyden and his son Jack stood behind the screen and spoke the lines for the actors in the movie. For years I thought Mary Pickford was a baritone.

Nobody really knew anything about the movie business in those days. For example, one of the biggest stars was a woman named Valeska Suratt. She was visiting a New York dance palace one night and the employee she was tangoing with told her he was leaving for Hollywood to be in the movies. She asked him his name, and when he told her it was Rudolph Valentino, Valeska Suratt said, "Well, the first thing you have to do is change your name."

That's about as much as anyone knew about the movie business.

❦

In 1929 Gracie and I were getting ready to sail to England for a twenty-six-week vaudeville tour. A few nights before leaving we were invited to a party for Jack Benny thrown by his agent, Arthur Lyons. During the party Arthur came over to Jack and asked him if he wanted to make $1800. Now, asking Jack Benny if he wanted to make money was like asking me if I'd like to sing a song. "For what?" Jack asked.

Fred Allen had been scheduled to make a nine-minute short film for Paramount at the Astoria Studios in Queens the following morning, Arthur explained, and he couldn't do it. "Take his place," Arthur said. "You get eighteen hundred dollars for nine minutes."

Eighteen hundred dollars for nine minutes? I started figuring it out. That was . . . that was . . . even with a fourth-grade education I knew that was a lot of money a minute. So when Jack said he couldn't do it, I told Arthur Lyons that Gracie and I were available.

Gracie didn't want to do it. She wasn't a movie actress, she said, then suggested, "You go and do it."

I told her the truth. "Listen, kiddo, if I go out there and I say, 'How's your brother?' and you're not standing next to me, that short is going to be a lot shorter than they think." Reluctantly, she agreed to do it.

The set was a living room. That was fine for Fred Allen, but all wrong for us. We did a flirtation act, we were supposed to be bumping into each other on a street corner. The theater audience knew we were supposed to be outside because we wore hats. Life was easier then—you wore a hat, you were outside. So we had a problem. It's hard to be surprised when you bump into someone in your living room, and we couldn't perform without our hats.

Coincidentally, the director was an old friend of mine from the Lower East Side, Murray Roth. At first I didn't believe he really was the director, but he proved it by commanding, "Lights!" and the lights on the set went on. After that, until I became God fifty years later, I thought the director was God.

Gracie and I finally worked out our bit. We walked onto the set and she started searching the room. She looked under the couch, in a cigar box; she lifted up a magazine. "What are you looking for?" I asked.

"The audience," she said.

I pointed to the camera. This was before cameras had red lights. "The audience is right there," I explained. "We're supposed to talk for nine minutes. If we can do that, we get paid eighteen hundred dollars. Can you talk for nine minutes?"

"Ask me how my brother is."

I knew my line when I heard it. "Gracie, how's your brother?"

Gracie began talking about her brother. My performance consisted of looking at my watch every few minutes. I was very convincing. At the end of nine minutes she was in the middle of a joke. I stopped her. "That's nine minutes," I said, "you can't finish that story." I looked directly into the camera and said, "Ladies and gentlemen, we just made eighteen hundred dollars. Say good night, Gracie."

Someone later told me that that short was avantgarde. I told them I didn't think so, I thought it was pretty funny.

That film allowed us to see ourselves performing for the very first time. I had no difficulty recognizing myself: I was the dapper fellow smoking a cigar standing next to Gracie. I thought I looked fine. Gracie was very upset by her appearance, though. She just didn't like the way she looked on screen. She never did, in fact, so she disliked watching her movies. I thought she looked great. To prove I was right, we had a meeting with the supervisor, as the producer was then known, and I asked him to tell her how beautiful she looked. "I'm not paying her to look beautiful," he snapped, "I'm paying her to make people laugh."

Well, if that was true, then he must have been paying me to look beautiful.

Paramount liked the short so much that they signed us to do four more at $3500 each. Too bad Benny passed on the first one, he might have had a career. In the next two years we made a total of fourteen short films. They were really just skits. I wrote most of the. I had to do something. The plots were very basic: Gracie was a nurse and I was a patient. Gracie was a salesclerk and I was a customer. Gracie was a manicurist, I came into the shop to get a haircut. Gracie was a taxi dancer, I was a sailor on leave. Finally we made one that was a complete change for us; I was the salesclerk and she was the customer. She came into my shop to buy an unbreakable vase, but I didn't know which vases were unbreakable. So she broke almost every vase in the place until she found one that was unbreakable.

Directors loved working with Gracie because she didn't need any direction. That made their jobs easy. They would scream, "Action," she would act, and we would all go home. What advice could a director have given her? Be more Gracie? Hit the line harder? Gracie was such a natural performer that the worst thing a director could have done was to tell her how to perform. I needed direction. I'd ask, "Where do you want me?" and they'd direct me to a spot out of Gracie's light.

Onstage, Gracie used the footlights to block out the audience. On a movie set, she simply ignored the presence of the camera. When we were making out first full-length feature, *The Big Broadcast of 1932*, there was a scene in which Gracie was supposed to be eating breakfast. So she ate breakfast. Today that would be known as "method acting," back then we just called it eating breakfast. But Gracie wasn't facing the camera as she ate, so one of the stars of the picture, a nice actress named Leila Hyams, whispered to her that the scene would play better if she "cheated," or turned slightly toward the camera. "Oh, I can't do that," Gracie explained. "This is the way I eat breakfast."

Gracie didn't love making movies, but after a while she didn't mind either. It was her job and she was a professional. She was on the set on time and knew her lines and my line. While we were making the shorts Paramount also signed us to a personal appearance contract, so we'd often be working on-stage in the same city one of our shorts was opening in. I know one of the greatest thrills Gracie ever had was playing at a vaudeville theater directly across the street from a movie theater at which our short, *Fit to Be Tied,* was playing. She stood in front of the vaudeville theater proudly admiring the movie theater marquee. To Gracie, movie stars were the real stars. We weren't' really movie stars, but we were in the movies and we hadn't paid to get in. "That's nice, isn't it, Nattie?" she said. And it was.

By the time we made our first full-length film we had become radio stars. We appeared on radio for the first time in 1929 in England, when they asked us to go "on the air" to promote our stage appearances. There was no national hookup in those days, so we'd do five minutes in London one, day, then the same five minutes in Blackpool a few days later, then the same five minutes in Brighton . . .

Making the transition to radio was very easy for us—we just did a portion of our act and cut the dancing. Performing on radio was not difficult; if you could read the words off a sheet of paper without rattling the paper, you could be a star. The real star on radio was the sound effects man. When a performer walked out the door, the sound effects man had to close the door. That was the toughest job in radio.

I knew Gracie would do fine on the radio because she was just as nervous before we went on the air as she was while she waited in the wings to go onstage. She suffered from mike fright even before they had a name for it. Her hands would get very cold and her skin would get very warm. When we were on the air I'd always stand near her and every once in a while I'd put my hand on her back just to remind her I was nearby. I'd keep a handkerchief in my hand, though, I didn't want to soil her dress. I think Gracie got her energy from her nervousness; if she hadn't been worried, I would have been very worried. But as long as she was nervous, I could be calm. We were a perfect team.

Big bands were the stars of early radio, but in the late 1920s a few major vaudeville stars proved that comedy could be successful "on the ether." After Eddie Cantor's show for Chase and Sanborn was a hit, sponsors began searching vaudeville for other acts that could make the transition.

Radio was controlled by the sponsors and their advertising agencies. Each show had a single sponsor and that sponsor's agency ran the show. Even though Gracie and I had been successful on radio in England, there were serious doubts that the public would like us here. We were asked to audition for Grape Nuts because their agency thought Gracie would make the perfect representative, but we were turned down when a top executive decided, "Gracie will never make it on radio. Her voice is too high." I didn't doubt the man knew what he was talking about. After all, commercial radio was about eight years old and he'd been working in the business his entire life.

Years later, after we'd become a big hit, I saw this executive at a party. We had a nice conversation, then I excused myself to get a drink. "Can you get one for me too, George?" he asked politely.

I'd waited years for this opportunity. "No," I said. "Go get it yourself. You thought Gracie's voice was too high."

Eddie Cantor gave us our first break. Actually, he gave me the break, he had Gracie on his show. We were sharing top billing with him at the Palace and he came into my dressing room and asked, "How about doing my show?"

"Great, Eddie," I said. "We'd love to."

He took a deep breath. "Uh, George," he said, "what I meant was I'd just like to have Gracie on alone."

That didn't offend me. I was Gracie's husband and partner, but I was also her biggest fan. I knew that with all my talents, the biggest talent I had was standing next to me. When movie producers wanted Gracie to work without me, I was completely supportive. And I'm sure that if anyone, anywhere, at any time, had ever wanted me to work without Gracie, she would have been supportive.

She was also very protective of my feelings. Once, for example, the wife of one of the writers on our show said haughtily, "I'll tell you one thing. My husband doesn't believe his wife should work."

Gracie thought this woman was putting me down. "That's very nice," she replied sweetly, "but it's a good thing for you that my husband doesn't feel that way."

So when Eddie Cantor wanted Gracie to appear on his show without me I had no objection, providing Gracie wanted to do it and he let me write the material they would use. As usual, Gracie was reluctant to do the show. Whenever we moved into a new medium, I had to talk her into trying it. When there was something I wanted her to do that she didn't want to, I'd tell her, "It's business, Googie." Most of the time she would agree to do what I asked.

I was standing a few feet away from her when Eddie Cantor announced with feigned surprise, "Why, Gracie Allen! Hello!" and Gracie made her first appearance on the radio in America.

"Mr. Cantor," she asked, explaining that she was doing an interview for a newspaper, "what do you intend to do when you're elected sheriff?"

"What sheriff?" Cantor replied. "President of the United States."

"Oh, but *you* can't be President of the United States," Gracie informed him, "because my father told me this morning he's going to be President of the United States."

"Your father?" Cantor played me almost as well as I played me.

"That's right. My father said that if I can get on Eddie Cantor's Chase and Sanborn Hour, he'll be President of the United States."

It was later on this program that Gracie's brother made his first appearance on radio. "My brother has this wonderful idea for coffee that he invented," she told Cantor. "A spoonless spoon."

"A spoonless spoon?"

"That's right. It's a spoon made of sugar. You can just put it in the cup of coffee."

"That's silly. You put it in the coffee and it goes to the bottom of the cup and then what happens?"

Gracie couldn't believe Eddie Cantor could be so dense. Who'd he think he was, George Burns? "Well, then," she explained carefully, "you take a regular spoon and you mix it up."

Apparently Gracie's voice wasn't too high, because right after the show NBC executive Mort Milman called and offered us $750 to appear on Rudy Vallee's Fleischmann's Yeast Hour. "How much?" I asked. I though he was kidding. I didn't know anybody got paid that much on radio.

"We can go to a thousand," he said, and I'm not puffing on my cigar. Two weeks later, I made my debut on American radio. Naturally, Rudy Vallee was thrilled to have me on his show. "Gracie Allen is certainly boric acid," he told his band leader, Ray Perkins.

"Boric acid?" Perkins asked.

"You know, soothing to the eyes."

Even with jokes like that, Rudy Vallee's Fleischmann's Yeast Hour was always in the Top Ten Crossley ratings, but then he had to be, there were only eight shows at the time.

Finally it was time to introduce me. "Oh, Rudy, tut-tut-tut," Perkins said. "But I don't understand why she lets that George Burns hang around . . ." How about that for an introduction? But it did pretty accurately describe the format Gracie and I would use on radio and television for the next thirty years. She was Gracie and I hung around.

On the Fleischmann's show Gracie told me that she'd been flying around in an airplane for nine months. I explained to her that that was impossible. "Didn't you ever hear of the law of gravity?"

"Oh, sure I did," she said, "but I went up before that law was passed."

Radio was being invented on a daily basis then, so I didn't know you couldn't dance on the airwaves. Gracie and I did what was possibly the first dance number on the ether. "We're dancing now," I told our listeners, "and right now Miss Allen is kicking the back of her head."

Claack! The sound effects man banged two wood blocks together. Believe me, dancing on the radio is every bit as easy as closing a door on the radio.

Gracie and I finished our appearance on Rudy Vallee's program with long excerpts from Dizzy and Lamb Chops. On one show we'd done about half our act; we still had half an act left and only twenty years to fill.

In those days advertising agencies didn't allow audiences in the studio during a broadcast because they were worried their laughter would spoil the show for listeners at home. Eventually some comedy shows like Ed Wynn, "The Perfect Fool," and "Baron Munchausen" began admitting audiences, but warned them not to laugh. If they'd have done that in vaudeville, I could have been a hit without Gracie.

Gracie was happy to work without an audience, but I missed hearing their response at the end of the show. In radio, you'd didn't know if the audience had liked you until you read it in the newspapers the next day.

The papers said we'd gotten applause. "The pair, for years known as a standard vaudeville act," a reviewer wrote, "did the same act they did in the visible theater, and the question was whether or not they would click on the air. . . . Any anxiety in this regard was quickly alleviated, however, when Miss Allen began to do her stuff, for the same sense of dumbness that you get from seeing her in the flesh came over the air and she clicked at once." In other words, Gracie had proved she could be just as dumb on the radio as she was in person. They couldn't say that about any other woman on radio, That was quite a compliment.

Since radio programs had only one sponsor, their advertising agencies tried to work the commercials into the context of the show. This was tough to do when the star of the show was a big band. So we were hired to do two four-minute spots on Guy Lombardo's WABC show for General Cigar. It was a perfect fit: Grape Nuts had almost hired Gracie because she was considered a nut; General Cigar wanted me because I was married to Gracie and she was considered a nut.

We joined the show on February 15, 1932, when the show was being heard over thirty-one stations. Eventually our contract was extended for thirteen weeks; we stayed almost a year.

Guy Lombardo promised listeners "thirty minutes of the sweetest music this side of heaven." We were supposed to do a brief routine and commercials for Robert Burns Panatellas. But since the show was only thirty minutes long, the orchestra had to keep playing while we did our spots. We weren't even playing second fiddle. At first we tried working behind a large screen that blocked out the musicians, but eventually we had to move into a different studio. It was while working with Guy Lombardo that we really learned how to work on radio. You do it very fast and loud enough to be heard over the music.

Radio introduced us to a much larger audience. A lot of people had read about us, but had never seen us perform. Gracie's illogical-logic clicked immediately. Women understood her. Men thought they were married to her. And everybody knew someone just like her.

By this time Gracie's character was fully developed. She did something that very few women did. She listened. And when she was asked a question, she answered it.

"Gracie," I asked her on an early Lombardo show, "how many days are there in a year?"

This is a relatively simple question. Every school kid knows the right answer. "Seven," Gracie said, as if it were a dumb question.

"Seven?"

"Seven. Monday, Tuesday, Wednesday, Thursday, Friday, Saturday, and Sunday. If you know any more, George, just name them."

Seven. You couldn't argue with Gracie's logic. Sometimes you couldn't understand it, but you certainly couldn't argue with it.

We worked with Guy Lombardo for almost a year, and when he left the show to go to another network at General Cigar Company offered us $2000 a week to do the whole show ourselves. As Gracie might have pointed out, in those days $2000 a week came to $104,000 a year.

We named our show "The Adventures of Gracie," and picked a nice tune called "Love Nest" as our theme song. We didn't put a lot of thought into that selection. I wanted to pick the National Anthem. That way every time we came onstage we'd have gotten a standing ovation. But we'd used "Love Nest" in vaudeville; it had a catchy tune and the title was right. Gracie and I were living in a love nest. Maybe I knew the lyrics once, but I don't anymore. Ask me about "When Frances Dances With Me," though. Jack Benny eventually got to hate his theme song, "Love in Bloom," but he had to listen to himself playing it on the violin. I still get a warm feeling whenever I hear "Love Nest," maybe that's because whenever I hear it I know I've got to be around somewhere. But believe me, if I'd have known I was going to have to listen to that tune for sixty years, I would have been a little more careful.

Do you have to pay a royalty for the National Anthem?

The gimmick that really made us major radio stars was the search for Gracie's missing brother in 1933. We'd been using Gracie's mythical brother as a character in our act for years. It was Gracie's brother who invented a way to manufacture pennies for only three cents. It was Gracie's brother who marketed an umbrella with holes in it so you'd be able to see when the rain stopped. It was Gracie's brother who first printed a newspaper on cellophane so that he could read it in a restaurant and still keep an eye on his hat and coat. And it was Gracie's brother who broke his leg falling off an ironing board while pressing his pants. Actually, as we discovered, Gracie's brother had been missing for years, but no one had noticed it because he'd left a dummy in his place.

Gracie's brother got lost when Stanley Holt of the J. Walter Thompson advertising agency and Paul White, a network executive, decided we needed an inexpensive way to publicize the fact that our show was going to move its broadcasting time from nine to nine-thirty P.M. Their plan was that Gracie would show up unannounced on other network programs, supposedly in search of her missing brother, and mention the time change.

The stunt began on January 4, 1933. Eddie Cantor was in the middle of a story when Gracie suddenly appeared and tearfully announced she was searching for her missing brother. A half-hour later Jack Benny was on the air when Gracie wandered in and explained, "I'm looking for my missing brother. Have you seen him?"

"Well," Jack asked, "what does he do?"

"He was going to go into the restaurant business, but he didn't have enough money. So he went into the banking business."

"Your brother didn't have enough money so he went into the banking business?" Jack also did my part very well.

"Yes. He broke into the banking business at two o'clock in the morning and was kidnapped by two men dressed as policemen."

Two days later Gracie and I were scheduled to appear with Rudy Vallee on NBC. The script was written, we were in the studio. But moments before the show went on the air NBC ordered Vallee to delete any mention of Gracie's missing brother from his script because they didn't want to give additional publicity to stars on CBS. So the script was trimmed and Gracie's missing brother really was missing from the new script. But when we went on the air, our friend Rudy Vallee "mistakenly" picked up the wrong script and asked Gracie about her brother. As soon as he did, a nervous engineer in the control room cut him off, and the entire NBC radio network went dead for four seconds.

Gracie hadn't even been in the radio business for a year, but she'd succeeded in knocking the second-greatest network off the air.

The fact that NBC had censored Rudy Vallee, even for four seconds, created a publicity bonanza for us. Suddenly, everybody in the country wanted to get in on the gag. No bit had ever captured the attention of the public as quickly as this one did.

Radio had only recently put large areas of the country in almost instantaneous contact with other areas, and this was the first stunt to take advantage of that capability.

Gracie walked in on "Guy Lombardo," "Mystery in Paris," "The Tydol Show," soap operas, dramatic shows. "Has anybody here seen my brother, George?" she would ask. Someone would say no, and she would respond happily, "Oh well, then bye-bye." In the middle of a tense drama set inside a submerged submarine a telephone rang, and someone on the surface asked the captain, "Is Gracie Allen's brother down there with you?"

One night Gracie appeared with the popular Singin' Sam, who offered to help in the search and asked what Gracie's brother called himself.

"Oh, you're so silly," Gracie laughed, "He doesn't have to call himself, he knows who he is."

"What I mean is, if your brother was here, what would you call him?"

"If my brother was here," Gracie pointed out, "I wouldn't have to call him."

Singin' Sam wasn't about to give up. "No, listen to me. If I found your brother, and I wanted to call him by name, what would it be?"

"It would be wonderful."

The stunt rapidly spread beyond radio. On Broadway, actress Grace Moore, appearing in *Du Barry,* responded to a costar's line asking where she'd been by ad-libbing, "I have just been out hunting for Gracie Allen's brother." Stores all over the country advertised, "Shop here. You'll find excellent bargains—and you might even find Gracie Allen's missing brother." In Congress, Speaker of the House Nicholas Longworth objected to a speech made by

Senator Huey Long, telling reporters, "It sounds like Gracie Allen's brother." *Time* magazine reported that famed big-game hunter Frank "Bring 'em Back Alive" Buck had joined the search. The catchphrase "You look like Gracie Allen's brother" became popular throughout the country, and comedians joked, "If an empty taxicab pulls up and no one gets out, that's Gracie's brother." Newspapers in several cities ran stories about men who had been arrested and were claiming to be Gracie's missing brother. And people all around the country warned friends, "If you see something on the ground, don't step on it. It might be Gracie Allen's brother."

We took full advantage of the publicity. We hired the Burns Detective Agency to search for him. Gracie was photographed at the Empire State Building, the Statue of Liberty, and Coney Island, looking for her brother. Wherever we appeared, she went to the lost and found department of the largest-circulation newspaper to see if anyone had turned in her brother. When we played a theater in Washington, D.C., she went to Griffith Stadium to meet Babe Ruth and his twin brother, telling reporters that she knew he had a twin brother because she'd read that Babe Ruth's double had won a game for the Yankees.

Within two weeks we received more than three hundred fifty thousand letters, some of them claiming to be from kidnappers who had Gracie's brother and warning that unless we paid a substantial ransom they would be forced to return him immediately. Our Crossley rating skyrocketed. Gracie's brother had become more famous by disappearing than I had by showing up.

About the only person who didn't enjoy the stunt was Gracie's real brother, George Allen, who was not missing and had never been missing. George had been living happily and quietly in San Francisco, working as an accountant for Western Pipe and Steel. When reporters discovered that Gracie really did have a brother, they descended on his home and office. Journalists followed him wherever he went. Photographers camped on his front lawn. This was one of those rare situations in show business when fantasy and reality got confused. Believing that quiet George Allen was really Gracie's fictional missing brother was like believing that Jack Benny actually was cheap.

Well . . .

George Allen was probably the most reluctant celebrity in America. Even though he had absolutely no talent, he received offers to appear in vaudeville and on radio programs. Advertisers wanted him to endorse their products. After a few weeks of this barrage, he wrote us a very sad letter, complaining, "Can't you make a living any other way? The newspaper people won't leave me alone. As it is now, I'm ashamed to go out into the street.

"I don't like being laughed at."

Finally he couldn't take it anymore. He disappeared. Newspapers were delighted to report that Gracie's missing brother really was missing, and that gave the story another boost. Gracie was not as close to George as she was to her sisters, but she certainly cared about him. She felt very badly for him, but there was nothing we could do about it. The stunt had simply gotten out of hand. Some of the things that people did during that time made me believe that Gracie really was the sane one among us.

It was literally years before people stopped asking

Gracie if she'd found her brother. And by then he'd returned to his home and job.

From vaudeville all the way through television, Gracie's mythical relatives were always close to us. As we often said, Gracie's family tree certainly produced a lot of nuts. Her mother, for instance, could read lips, and therefore could tell whenever Gracie's father was lying—when his lips were moving, he was lying.

And her sister Bessie could see with her tongue—for instance, she could see if the soup was too hot.

Then there was Gracie's cousin, Audubon Allen, the noted bird doctor, who cured a parrot of his stuttering, taught a hummingbird to sing the lyrics, and improved an owl's grammar by teaching it to say "whom."

And we both dearly loved her Uncle Otis, the politician, who once ran for the San Francisco City Council. Uncle Otis guaranteed that if he was elected he would make San Francisco a better place to live in—he would move to Los Angeles.

Gracie was always fond of her cousin Gallup Allen, the famous polltaker, who conducted a survey to find out how many people had telephones in their homes and discovered that 100 percent of all the people he called had phones.

Then there was the sad case of cousin Rush Allen, the bus driver who had an accident because he'd pasted all his safety awards on the windshield and couldn't see a thing. But he deserved those awards. I'll tell you how safe a driver he was. He was driving his bus from San Francisco to Sacramento when he lost his rearview mirror. Realizing how dangerous it was to drive without being able to see the traffic behind him, Rush turned his bus around and drove back to San Francisco, and that way all the cars that had been behind him were then in front of him.

Gracie had a nephew too. One day he had a terrible cold and went to the doctor. The doctor told him to take something warm, so he took the doctor's overcoat.

It was Aunt Clara's husband, Uncle Joe, who took up glassblowing as a hobby. "And every night," Gracie explained to me on the air one night, "Uncle Joe would sit on the back porch blowing glass . . ." When Gracie finished laughing at Uncle Joe's mistake, she told me that he'd blown a bottle around himself and been taken away by the milkman.

Gracie's character was the result of this heritage, and Gracie undoubtedly made her relatives proud when she tested Mickey Rooney's education on one of our shows by asking him to spell the word "to."

"T-O, t-o-o, or t-w-o," Mickey spelled.

Gracie was too smart for that. "Oh, no," she said. "You don't get three chances."

In real life, just like everybody else, our relatives were all completely normal people. I might have gotten my sense of humor from my Uncle Frank Birnbaum, for example. When I was growing up, Uncle Frank had a small butcher shop on the Lower East Side. One day a six-year-old kid came into the shop and said, "Mr. Birnbaum, would you like to buy a cat?"

"Business is bad," Uncle Frank told him. "I'll take half a cat."

My sister Mamie had a great sense of humor. Toward the end of her life I called her and asked, "How are you feeling, Mamie?"

"I'm ninety-three," she said, and hung up.

Gracie's Aunt Clara, who was married to Uncle

Joe the glassblower, was also quite a character. Clara collected pendulum chime clocks, and every hour every clock would go off. I stayed there once for a week. I never slept. Clara also had a pet parrot that someone had trained to say dirty words—but only to priests. This is true. Every time a priest walked past the house, that parrot would squawk, ''Go to hell, go to hell!''

Gracie and I were at my sister Goldie's house one day with our daughter Sandy and our granddaughter Laurie. Goldie served a turkey, and Laurie, who was probably less than a year old, pulled on the tablecloth and the turkey fell on the floor. ''Let her play with it,'' Goldie said, ''I've got another one.'' Then she went into the kitchen and returned with a second turkey. Goldie often cooked two of whatever she was preparing, then stored leftovers around the house. Leftover turkey would go under the bed, for example. One day I opened a closet and found a roast. I hadn't spent a lifetime as a straight man for nothing. ''Goldie,'' I asked, ''what's this roast doing in the closet?''

''The cupboard was full,'' she explained. And Goldie worked without a cigar.

Gracie's brother-in-law, Ed Myers, was an eccentric inventor. Among many other devices, Ed invented a machine that constructed cardboard boxes, a machine that separated gold from ore, and he figured out a way of pumping water over a mountain. The only thing Ed couldn't figure out was how to make money from his inventions.

Ed was married to Gracie's sister Bessie. Unfortunately, what happened to Bessie and Hazel and Pearl wasn't funny. As Gracie's sisters got older, they became senile. Eventually each of them had to be put in a rest home. That was the kind of pain Gracie never spoke about, even to me. But when you know someone as well as I knew Gracie, you can see how much it hurts. Gracie would go to visit her sisters whenever she could, but eventually they got so bad they couldn't recognize her. As Gracie got older, she began to worry that the same thing was going to happen to her. That thought petrified her. She even used to do basic memory exercises just to make sure that her mind was fine. Believe me, Gracie's mind was fine.

※

The search for Gracie's missing brother made our show one of the most popular programs on the airwaves. The show was so popular, in fact, that our scripts were translated into idiomatic French and two actors played Gracie and me on "Les Adventures de Grace et Georges," for which we received $300 a week royalty. It was truly incredible. When I'd started in show business there was no such thing as radio, and within two or three years we were among the most popular stars in the industry. We were so successful that I could hardly wait for someone to invent television.

Gracie never let fame and money interfere with those things that she thought were really important: our life together, our home and family, our friends, and decorating. Gracie was always funny that way. The biggest change we made was moving from a comfortable two-bedroom apartment in the Edison Hotel to a larger place in the Broadhurst and finally into a thirty-sixth-floor suite overlooking Central Park in the fashionable Essex House.

We had to move; we kept running out of rooms

to furnish. Gracie had exquisite taste, and she made sure that every place we lived in was beautifully furnished and had fresh flowers in every room. Some women love furs; other women love flowers. Gracie was one of those lucky women who loved furs and flowers. "Furs are my hobby," she once told an interviewer, but she wasn't happy unless the house was filled with flowers. She was the kind of woman who would see a very successful bank in a great location and decide, "That's a great place to put a flower shop."

After we became famous Gracie couldn't leave our apartment without being recognized. If people didn't recognize her face from our movie shorts and the numerous photos that appeared in newspapers and radio magazines, her voice was unmistakable. In real life Gracie's voice was about an octave lower than it was when she was performing, but as soon as she opened her mouth in public everyone knew who she was. Although we never tried to pretend that Gracie really was Gracie, her fans expected her to be as dizzy in person as she was on the radio. When she got into an elevator and told the elevator operator what floor she wanted to go to, for example, everybody else in the elevator started laughing. I couldn't get a chuckle with my best material; she got hysterics with "Six, please." Once, she went to Macy's to buy a rolling pin so our cook could make a pie. For some reason the women in Macy's thought this had to be a publicity gimmick. Why else would Gracie Allen be in Macy's buying a rolling pin? So they crowded into the housewares department to see what was going to happen. Gracie was so flustered by all the attention that she didn't even buy the rolling pin—instead she bought a $125 end table. That was ridiculous. How could the cook make a pie with an end table? I don't know why everyone thought the sight of Gracie buying a cooking utensil was so funny—they hadn't even tasted her cooking.

A lot of husbands appreciate their wife's cooking. I appreciated my wife's not cooking. She didn't do it to please me. In the kitchen, Gracie was a great comedienne. She couldn't cook. She couldn't even give the cook good instructions. Fortunately, she tried to cook for me only once after we were married. We were playing a date in Cleveland, and my brother Willie, who was writing for us, was sharing our suite. After a performance one night Gracie decided she was going to make spaghetti for us, using her mother's recipe for a hot white-pepper sauce. On the show we used to say that Gracie's mother made a fantastic cabbage layer cake, but Pidgie was actually a fine cook. As I later found out, the only significant difference between the white-pepper sauce Gracie made that night and the sauce her mother made was that Pidgie never cut the peppers before putting them in the sauce. Gracie cut the peppers. Willie took one mouthful and put down his fork. "George," he wheezed, as little flames shot out of his mouth, "you're her straight man—you have to eat this."

From that night on, either our cook made dinner, our daughter, Sandy, cooked, or we ate out. I didn't care. I'd rather have a bad cook who gets laughs than a good cook who doesn't.

Not that I would have known the difference between good cooking and bad cooking. Everybody develops certain tastes in childhood that stay with them throughout their life. Mine was ketchup. We were so poor when I was growing up that we ate ketchup with everything. Sometimes we even ate ketchup with nothing—dinner was just bread dipped in ketchup. So even when I could afford much better things, like food, I still liked to have ketchup with my dinner. Or, as some people might say, dinner with my ketchup. Gracie knew this so every night, no matter who we were having over for dinner, no matter how formal the occasion, she made sure that there was a sterling silver bowl of ketchup in front of my place at the table.

One of the many advantages of radio was that we could broadcast from almost anywhere in the country. In vaudeville, you had to be there; in radio, as Gracie might have said, you didn't have to be anywhere. That enabled us to continue working on the stage and making movies while we were doing the radio show. In fact, there were times when we were working with Guy Lombardo that we not only weren't in the same studio, we weren't even in the same state.

But Gracie loved being in New York because she was a night person. "I love everything that happens after five o'clock," she used to say. "Theater, opera, movies, nightclub shows, dinner, dancing, and card games. The only real fun I can think of in the daytime is shopping." So when we were in New York we went to the shows and the movies and the restaurants, we went dancing at the big ballrooms and the smart clubs, but the best times of all were the nights we spent at home with our friends.

It was quite a group: Jack Benny and Mary Livingstone, Jack "Baron Munchausen" Pearl and his wife, Jack and Flo Haley, Blossom Seeley and Benny Fields, Fred Allen and Portland Hoffa, Eddie and Ida Cantor, Goodman and Jane Ace, Harpo and Susan Marx and Eva Sully and Jesse Block. We called our little group The Home Folks because that's where we spent most of our time together, just talking, or playing cards, or performing for each other. I suppose it was during this time that I learned the true secret of a happy marriage. Obviously, sex is important. Being able to talk to each other openly and honestly is vital. A sense of humor is a necessity. You've got to be able to share. But if a man really wants his marriage to work, the one thing he has to remember is: Never play cards with your wife. One other thing too: If you're going to cheat on your wife, never play cards with your girlfriend.

That's it, that's the secret. You can solve every other problem. But a married couple that plays cards together is just a fight that hasn't started yet.

Gracie was a real games player; she loved canasta, gin rummy, and backgammon, and when we got together with our friends, the cards or the boards would always come out. If you ask the girls who played cards with Gracie what kind of player she was, they would tell you, "She was always so well dressed." We used to do a bit in vaudeville in which Gracie would show me a card trick, but she wouldn't use any cards. "Gracie," I'd tell her, "this is a very good trick. But don't you think it would be better if you used cards?"

"Oh, George," she'd admonish me, "I'm just learning the trick. I can't do it with cards yet." That's about the kind of player she was.

Once she decided to teach Ruth Henning, the wife of the great comedy writer Paul Henning, how to play gin. Paul Henning was one of our Gentile writers, and when I worked with him I always used a lot of Jewish expressions. He passed them on to Ruth.

Now, in gin, when somebody is beaten without scoring a single point, they say, "I'm blitzed." Ruth almost got it right, she laid her cards down on the table and announced, "I'm schmucked."

Maybe she was, too. Who knew what Gracie was teaching her?

I'm a cardplayer. Bridge is my game and I play it seriously. Not well . . . seriously. I still lose my temper sometimes when I'm playing—that's one of the only parts I have left to lose. Now, I also have this belief I can only get mad at people I love; if I don't care about them, why should I get angry? One day I was playing bridge with a new member of my club, the Hillcrest Country Club. He made a foolish move and maybe I overreacted and said some things I shouldn't have said. He got up angrily and promised, "Mr. Burns, I'll never talk to you again," then walked out of the room.

He couldn't do that to me. "Listen," I yelled after him, "you don't know me well enough not to talk to me again."

I did try to teach Gracie how to play bridge. Believe me, it would have been easier to teach her how to build a bridge. So we compromised, we never played cards with each other.

Eventually, when we got together with our friends, we'd put away the games and the entertainment would begin. At these sociables everyone got a chance to do whatever they wanted to do. For example, I'd announce that I was going to sing and all our guests would make a ring around the piano. But somehow I'd manage to fight my way through that ring and sing anyway.

Gracie did what she liked to do best, which was nothing. Gracie rarely performed at parties. Unlike some people in our marriage, she never needed the attention. But she was a great audience. She'd sit on a couch or in a chair, her legs tucked beneath her, and listen to every word. She had a high-pitched staccato laugh, a machine-gun laugh, *ha-ha-ha-ha*, that was just delightful. To me, it was the sound of someone having fun.

Gracie might have been the star on the stage, in the movies, and on radio, but in the living room, where it really counted, I was the star. In fact our friends often told me I was much better offstage than onstage. Gracie was my best audience. Not that there was too much competition for the job. And I'll be honest, she thought "Googie, googie, googie," was hilarious, so how tough an audience was she?

Just like Gracie's mythical relatives, my singing ability played an important part in our act. She called me "Sugarthroat," and claimed to love my voice. Once, on the show, I admitted to her, "Let's face it, Gracie, people don't appreciate my voice. It's old, out of date, extinct."

"No, it doesn't," she protested lovingly.

She used to compare my voice to the essence of a flower. One week we had Al Jolson on the show and Gracie complained that he had prevented me from singing. "He never gave people a chance to enjoy your fragrance," she said. "He kept the world from finding out how you smelled.

"In fact," she continued, "the real reason people like him is because for years and years he kept you from singing!"

This was another time when our act and our lives overlapped. My singing voice wasn't really much better in the living room than it was on the radio, it just had a little less static. But Gracie was as supportive in real life as she was while in character. I loved to sing at our sociables and I'd sing all my old favorites. Gracie must have heard me singing these same songs hundreds of times, and some of them weren't so wonderful the first time. But she always listened, always laughed in the right places—not like a lot of our friends—and she always applauded when I finished. I don't know that she ever really liked my singing; I do know she liked me.

Although Gracie never sang opera, as her mother had hoped, she did have a lovely voice. You couldn't call it haunting—my voice was haunting. She used to tell people her favorite instrument was a baton, and she once claimed to have thrown away a flute because it had holes in it. But in fact she could sing. I tried to convince her to sing on the radio show, but she really didn't want to. Finally she agreed to sing a few bars from a popular gimmick song, "I Want to Go Back to My Little Grass Shack in Kon-A-Ku-Lee, Hawaii." I suspect she agreed to sing that song because it was amusing and she wouldn't be upset if the audience had laughed. Nobody laughed, which was good and bad. It was good because it meant they liked her singing, it was bad because we were doing a comedy show. We got hundreds of letters asking Gracie to sing more often, and for years we ended the show with her doing a number.

In 1932 the country was in the middle of the Depression, but Gracie and I were doing great. That was all right. When the rest of the country had been doing great, I hadn't been doing so good. We were hosting one of the most popular shows on radio, our movie shorts were successful, and the movie companies wanted us to appear in full-length features. We were booked for as many live performances as we had time to fulfill. We were making as much as $10,000 a week.

Since I'd never really anticipated being successful, I was thoroughly enjoying every moment of it. For me, real life was show business, and our life offstage was only a time to prepare for our next show. To Gracie, show business was our job; real life was our marriage and our life together.

Obviously Gracie enjoyed the life-style that our success enabled us to lead, but I'm not sure she ever felt really comfortable with it. On some level Gracie never accepted the fact that she was a star. She was afraid it was all just temporary and something was going to happen and we were going to lose everything. For example, she always bought "on time," meaning we could pay for it over several months, even though we could have easily bought almost anything she wanted for cash. In fact, she never took the price tag off an item until it was totally paid for. Once it was paid for she knew that no matter what happened, we could keep it. Then the price tag came off.

I never did know why she was worried our success wouldn't last. The only thing I can think of is that she'd seen my act.

4

This is my favorite joke: In school one day the teacher asked three boys to stand up and tell the class what their fathers did for a living. The first boy stood up and said, "My father's a plumber."

"That's good, Tommy," the teacher told him.

The second boy stood up and said, "My father's an engineer."

"That's good, too," the teacher said.

Then the third boy stood up and said, "My father's dead."

"I'm very sorry," the teacher said. "What did he do before he died?"

"He went 'Oooowwww!' "

A lot of people ask me why I tell jokes about dying. Death is part of life, and it doesn't do any good to worry about it. In fact, I once knew a man who was so worried about dying that he had a heart attack caused by worrying about having a heart attack.

Gracie died in 1964, and I still go to Forest Lawn Cemetery once a month to see her. I stand in front of her marble monument and tell her everything that's going on in my life. I told her I was writing this book about her, for instance; evidently she didn't mind, she didn't say anything.

When the television program "60 Minutes" did a segment about me, I took their crew to Forest Lawn. "Imagine that, Googie," I told Gracie. "After all this time we're working together again." I don't know if she hears me, but I know that after speaking to her, I feel better.

Life and death were part of our life together. I don't mean onstage; I died a lot onstage. The first real heartbreak we shared was the death of Gracie's mother. Margaret Pidgeon, Pidgie, was a high-spirited, brave lady. In fact, I took my first airplane flight because she dared me to. We were vacationing on Catalina Island and a pilot was offering sight-seeing flights around the island in an open-cockpit biplane for $10. Pidgie wanted someone to go with her. Gracie couldn't go; she got all the laughs. I was expendable. So Pidgie and I squeezed into the rear seat and we took off. After we got several hundred feet up in the air the pilot yelled back, "If you want to know how fast we're going, put your hand in the air."

I didn't want to know how fast we were going. I wanted to know how soon we were going to land. But Pidgie immediately stuck her hand in the air. The wind nearly ripped it off. That's how fast we were going.

She had a bad heart. The doctors had warned her not to eat eggs because they contained cholesterol. "Let me tell you something, Pidgie," I said. "You love eggs, eat eggs. That way if you die, at least you'll die happy."

So she ate eggs and she didn't die, not for a long time. When Gracie and I were playing theaters on the West Coast, she often traveled with us. We were in Portland when she got sick for the last time. Our next booking was at the Golden State in San Francisco, and as soon as we got into town Pidgie went into St. Francis Hospital. We spent the next week running back and forth between the theater and the hospital, but Gracie didn't miss a performance. Twice the hospital woke us in the middle of the night and we raced down there, but both times Pidgie fought back.

She died while we were doing a Wednesday matinee. Gracie knew. Nobody had to tell her, she just knew. As soon as we finished the show we went to the hospital, but her mother had died before we got there. The doctors had been right, she'd eaten eggs her whole life and she'd died. Gracie cried and I cried and we held each other. What else can you do when someone you love says, "Oooowwww?" That's life.

Pidgie was buried in the Holy Cross Cemetery. When we got back to the house after the funeral, we discovered we were locked out. The front door had been locked from the inside. Maybe somebody slammed the door too hard when we were leaving, or maybe, as Gracie suggested, "Mama doesn't want us to go inside without her."

We hadn't performed for two days. But the night of the funeral Gracie wanted to work, and no one in the audience could have possibly known she had buried her mother that morning. Gracie was always a very private person, even in private. But no matter what was happening in our private life, in public she was always Gracie. She knew that the best cure for tears is laughter.

I think one of her greatest regrets was that Pidgie

never lived to see our two children. Both Gracie and I had been brought up in large families, and both of us wanted to have children. Gracie loved kids, and kids loved Gracie. Maybe it was because she was so small, maybe it was her childlike voice, but children usually treated Gracie as if she were just a kid wearing lipstick. After our show there were often kids waiting outside the studio for us, and Gracie would stop and talk with them. And inevitably, one of the younger ones would look up at her and ask, "So, Gracie, how old are you?"

Before we had our own kids, Gracie was especially close to her niece, Hazel's daughter Jean. Gracie and Jean would spend hours together, going through fashion magazines, cutting and styling Jean's hair, playing jacks on the kitchen table. As far as I know, Jean never got schmucked in jacks. Once we were visiting Pidgie, and Gracie decided that she was going to teach Jean how to bake a cake. This was like my teaching Jolson to sing. Gracie got the ingredients right, but accidently put the rack in the oven at an angle, so the cake came out lopsided. That didn't bother Gracie. She told Jean very proudly, "Now you know how you're not supposed to do it!"

When Jean was getting ready to go to college, she told her Aunt Gracie that she wanted to learn how to smoke cigarettes. Gracie thought that sounded like fun. "I've never learned either," she said enthusiastically, "so let's learn together." The two of them sat down at the kitchen table opposite each other and lit cigarettes. After a few moments of silence, Gracie asked Jean, "How do you feel?"

"Not so good," Jean admitted.

"You don't look so good either," Gracie told her.

"Neither do you."

Gracie thought about that, then decided, "Well, then let's not smoke anymore, okay?" They put out their cigarettes and ended that experiment.

Actually, that was not the last time Gracie smoked. On momentous occasions when our kids were young, Gracie would sweep downstairs to the dinner table, dressed like a silent movie queen in one of her beautiful silk kimonos, carrying an unlit cigarette in a long, long, long gold cigarette holder. After she sat down, the kids would beg her to light it, which she did with a big ceremony. Then she'd take a puff and blow the smoke casually into the air with an exaggerated savoir faire. And then she'd start coughing. She'd cough and she'd cough and then, just when we thought she was finished, she'd cough again. The kids thought that was the funniest bit they'd ever seen. Believe me, if I had known there were that many laughs in a cigarette, I never would have started smoking cigars.

Of course, the kids didn't know that Gracie never inhaled. She couldn't stand the taste of cigarettes. She really couldn't smoke without coughing badly.

I loved kids too, but having children of my own wasn't as important to me as it was to Gracie. I'd seen the kids of too many performers growing up in theater wings to want to raise my own children on the road. Gracie and I discussed it often, and when the radio show was a hit and we knew we were going to be able to stay in one place for a long time, we decided to start a family.

Gracie couldn't have children. We tried, but she didn't get pregnant. I never told her, but I was glad about that. She was such a tiny thing that giving birth might have been too hard for her. Maybe it wasn't even Gracie who couldn't have a baby, maybe it was me, but in those days if a couple couldn't have a baby everyone thought it was the woman's problem. What did we know? Science was a man standing outside in a thunderstorm flying a kite. Besides, men weren't supposed to give birth; any man who had had a baby could have played Hammerstein's for life. I figured it had to be Gracie who couldn't have babies, because I knew I was doing my part correctly. I'd been putting my cigar in a holder for years, so I knew how the whole process worked.

Now, if I'd have said that at a party, Gracie would have pursed her lips, raised her eyes, and admonished, "Now, Nattie, pleeeeasssee. . . ." That was our party routine. I'd say something risqué and she'd pretend to be embarrassed. Maybe she was embarrassed, who knows? I've told you, she was a great actress.

Adopting babies was a popular thing to do among showbusiness people in the 1930s. I was agreeable; Gracie wanted to have children and I wanted to make Gracie happy. But we just kept putting it off. We were on the road too much, the apartment wasn't big enough, we had a picture coming up, there was always something. Then one afternoon we had lunch with Wallace Beery and be brought along his adopted daughter. The kid did all the right things—she smiled at Gracie and laughed at my cigar. As soon as we got home, we called The Cradle, a Catholic foundling home in Evanston, Illinois, and ordered a little girl. "I love clothes and trinkets and I could spend the rest of my life shopping," Gracie told a magazine writer, "but if our daughter turns out to be not at all interested in finery, I'll let her go around reading philosophy books and wearing a sackcloth and ashes and I won't mind a bit.''

Possibly the only person as optimistic as an out-of-work actor is an expectant mother. And Gracie was expecting a phone call from The Cradle.

Onstage we used to do a nice bit in which I told Gracie, ''I'm a pauper.''

''Oh,'' she responded. ''Congratulations. Boy or girl?''

That's almost exactly what happened with us. Months passed before we heard from The Cradle. I knew I was going to be a papa, but we didn't know when and we didn't know for sure if we would be adopting a boy or a girl. I learned much later that it's only after you have a child that you become a pauper.

Finally, Mrs. Florence Walwrath, who started the home, called and told us that we could have a baby if we came to Evanston immediately. Grace and Mary Kelly were on a train to Chicago three hours later. I stayed in New York.

Mrs. Walwrath showed Gracie three babies to select from. How do you pick out a kid? How do you know which one is going to be tall and attractive and smart? How do you know which one is going to have a good disposition? How do you know which one is going to laugh at her father's jokes? The answer is, you don't, you can't. It's exactly the same chance you take as having a child naturally.

Gracie picked the smallest baby, a tiny five-week-old with great big blue eyes, and named her Sandra Jean. Sandra Jean Burns.

The Cradle offered to provide a nurse to accompany Gracie and Mary back to New York, but Gracie figured two grown women should be able to take

care of one small baby. And the two of them felt
very confident—until the baby sneezed. That's when
Gracie realized they were outnumbered. Neither one
of them knew what to do, so Gracie covered the
baby's body with her fur coat. Sometime during the
night, the coat slipped down and covered the baby's
head. When Gracie woke up and saw that, she
thought she'd smothered her daughter. Making a
lopsided cake was one thing, but smothering your
daughter a few hours after you've had her? She
grabbed the coat and watched helplessly to see if the
baby was breathing. The baby was fine—it was Gracie who was having trouble breathing. So she sat up
in the compartment the rest of the trip just watching
her daughter breathe.

I didn't get to pace up and down in a waiting
room; I had Grand Central Station. Believe me, I
was as nervous as any expectant father has ever been,
and I knew exactly when my baby was due. The
train pulled in on time. That was one of the rare
occasions when a train conductor delivered a baby.

Gracie was superstitious only when it came to
luck. She always claimed that she wasn't superstitious at all, but I suspect she had her fingers crossed
when she said that. She had decided it would be bad
luck for us to buy anything for the baby or prepare
the apartment before we actually got her, so as soon
as she got back to New York we had to run around
buying clothes, a crib, a bassinet, diapers, more diapers, and then more diapers. Has the man who invented disposable diapers won the Nobel Prize yet?

The first night we had Sandy at home Gracie asked
me if I wanted to change the baby. "Nah," I said,
"let's try this one out first." That was about as close
as I ever came to actually eating a cigar. I guess

Gracie was a little sensitive. But what did I know about changing a baby's diapers? Ask me about changing a line in a routine and I can do forty minutes. So we had a day nurse and a night nurse and a relief nurse from the beginning.

The thing about the baby that surprised me most was how much space something so small could take up. Our second bedroom, which had been my den, became her nursery. The kitchen was the operations center—that's where we kept her bottles, her milk, her formula, her jars of baby food, the piles of clean diapers, and some of the toys that overflowed from my former den. I don't know, maybe there were some babies who had more toys than Sandy did. Santa Claus's kids, for instance.

When Gracie had picked up Sandy, Mrs. Walwrath had said to her, "I guess we'll be seeing you again next year." Gracie didn't understand what she was talking about. Mrs. Walwrath explained, "You'll probably be coming back next year for a boy."

"Oh, no," Gracie protested. "Nattie and I have decided we only want one child. There's no way we're going to adopt another one. We just can't."

❋

Ronald Jon Burns was a very sick two-month-old baby when Gracie first saw him at The Cradle. As it turned out, Sandy was such a delight that we decided she should have a brother. I figured, how much more trouble could two babies be than one? Of course, I'm the same fellow who thought the Cherry Sisters could sing.

Gracie picked out Ronnie because he needed her most. Now, that sounds like a line written by a Hollywood press agent, but it's true. I've already admitted that I lie a lot. As Gracie said, if telling the truth was so easy, no one would remember George Washington. But this is true. The other babies they showed her were all chubby and healthy, and she knew there was a long list of people waiting to adopt chubby, healthy babies. Ronnie's crib was off by itself in a corner, maybe that's what first attracted Gracie's attention to him. He was by himself. She went over and looked at him. "He was so small," she told me when she finally brought him home, "and he followed me with his eyes when I moved, and I knew I had to take him."

He was premature, a nurse told Gracie, and for several weeks doctors didn't know if he was going to survive.

Since I'm telling the truth, I have to admit that Ronnie was an ugly baby. People say all babies look like Winston Churchill; Ronnie made Winston Churchill look handsome. Ronnie looked like a wrinkled little man with a funny-shaped head. "What do you think Nattie?"

I thought that if I was smart, I'd keep my mouth shut. "Look, you know I don't mind responsibility," I said, "but, Googie, why'd you pick a sick kid?"

"I just fell in love with his eyes. I know he's not well, but we can make him well. It's the same chance we would have taken if we'd had him, isn't it?"

Gracie was right. I looked him right in the eyes and he had me exactly where he wanted me to be. Paying the bills. "Googie, googie, googie," I said. That was the only line I spoke in baby talk.

I wanted to name him Allen Burns, after both of

us, but Gracie's favorite name for a boy was Ronnie. So we compromised, we named him Ronnie Burns.

Ronnie had a tough first year. For a long time he couldn't gain any weight, and his skin was so sensitive that we could only bathe him in oil and we had to wrap him in cotton. Gracie and our nurse, Rose Norris, spent a lot of time in doctors' offices. Gracie fussed over him like I worked on our scripts. But Ronnie was a smart kid, and once he figured how to grow, he didn't stop until he was almost 6′2″ tall and much better looking than Winston Churchill.

So we had our two kids, Sandy and Ronnie, and that was all we were going to have or my name wasn't George Burns. Actually, my name wasn't George Burns, but we still weren't going to have any more. I would have put my foot down, but if I had I would have stepped on one of their toys.

About a year after we'd adopted Ronnie, Gracie and I had Harpo and Susan Marx over for dinner. Next to the Bennys, they were our closest friends. And even though the character Harpo created never spoke, we had him as a guest on our radio show one night. The plot had Gracie hiring him as an investigative reporter for her gossip column.

"But, Gracie," I pointed out, "he can't talk."

"I know," she said. "Wouldn't he make a great congressman?"

During dinner we received our annual call from Mrs. Walwrath. She had a beautiful four-week-old little girl, she said, who looked just like Sandy and Ronnie. If we came to Evanston right away, we could take her home. "We can't," Gracie explained. "We've got our family. It wouldn't be fair to her."

Harpo and Susan had already adopted three chil-

dren. "Give me the phone, Googie," Harpo said,
getting up from the table. I guess he'd overheard all
he needed to know. "This is Harpo Marx," he told
Mrs. Walwrath, "and I heard you say you had a
little girl available for adoption. I can be on the train
tomorrow . . ."

After Harpo had completed arrangements to pick
up his new daughter, I asked him how many children
he intended to adopt. "We want to have one kid for
every window we have in the house," he told me,
"so that when we leave, we can look back and see
one of our kids in every window waving to us."

For a man who made his reputation by not speaking, Harpo Marx was a very eloquent man.

Even before our kids were old enough to understand what we were talking about, we told them that
we had adopted them; we had picked them out. We
never tried to hide it. When Gracie held them in her
arms, she would call them "My darling adopted babies." There had been a tremendous amount of publicity when we'd adopted the kids, and we didn't
want them to be confused or hurt when they went to
school and heard other kids tell them they were
adopted. We wanted them to know what the word
meant and feel comfortable about it. Even proud. In
fact, every few years, Gracie took the kids with her
to visit Mrs. Walwrath at The Cradle. Maybe the
stork brought other kids, but Ronnie and Sandy knew
they came from Mrs. Walwrath.

Once, when Sandy was about four, Gracie was
bathing her and she asked, "Mommy, who was my
real mommy?" Gracie could usually handle any
question the kids asked, but I could see that that one
hurt. As far as she was concerned, she was Sandy's
real mother. Gracie didn't know what to say. So I

took Sandy's hand and we went for a walk. "You're a very lucky little girl," I told her. "Most children have only one mommy, but you have three. You have your physical mother, you have Mrs. Walwrath in Chicago, and you have Googie. Now, Googie—she's your real mother."

Not too many days later, Sandy was in the tub and I heard her singsong, "I have three mothers. I have my physical mother, my Chicago mother, and my real mother." I suppose it wasn't as catchy as some of my songs, but I know it was high on Gracie's hit parade.

Gracie was a good mother. Because she worked she didn't have as much time to spend with the kids as she would have liked, but she tried to make up for it. When we came home from the studio or office, for example, she'd rush right into their rooms to play with them even before taking off her coat. And she insisted that the four of us sit down for dinner together in the den every night we were home.

If anything happened to the kids, she dropped everything else. When Ronnie was ten or eleven years old, for example, he went to camp on the Russian River, which is about seventy-five miles north of San Francisco. He was horseback riding and his horse threw him, snapping his arm in half. They rushed him to St. Francis Hospital in San Francisco. It was a very serious break; the doctors were afraid they were going to have to amputate his lower arm. The minute Gracie heard about it she called me and we raced to the airport. She was ready to charter a plane, but fortunately we caught the last regularly scheduled flight of the day. When we got to the hospital, they were operating on Ronnie's arm. The operation took five hours. Gracie and I sat and waited.

Gracie was wonderful in difficult situations. She was so tough. When the terrible things in life happened, like this, or like having to put Bessie in a rest home, she was always able to remain calm. It was the little things that bothered her. If we went to a restaurant and they forgot to peel a tomato or they prepared the wrong food, she'd get upset. She'd send her food right back. But when her son was undergoing a five-hour operation to save his arm, she was completely in control.

Ronnie was still under anesthesia when he came out of the operation, but we went into his room and sat with him. Gracie pulled her chair right next to the bed and held his other hand all night. Occasionally she would wipe his brow. And when he woke up the following morning, the very first thing he saw was his mother's smiling face telling him he was going to be all right.

Gracie lived in Ronnie's room for three days, until she was sure he was going to be well taken care of. Only then would she come back to Los Angeles to do the radio show.

Gracie was also a much stricter parent than I was. She was determined that her kids were going to have good manners. As soon as each of them was old enough, for example, she taught Sandy to curtsy and Ronnie to bow, and whenever they were introduced to guests she expected them to do just that.

I was a pushover if the kids said the magic word. The magic word was "Dad." Gracie didn't care if they said Dad, they still had to sit up straight, keep their elbows off the table, butter their bread on the butter plate, finish the food they were served, and speak only when spoken to. Once, I remember, Sandy didn't eat her breakfast. So Gracie packed it up and followed Sandy to school, and sat there until she'd finished eating. Basically, Gracie's rules consisted of "Watch Dad and don't do what he does." Both of them had a list of chores they were supposed to do, they had to practice the piano an hour a day, and they had to keep their rooms clean to earn their allowance.

It's a good thing she didn't make me follow those rules. I would have been broke. And truthfully, the rules didn't work any better in our house than they did anywhere else.

Gracie wasn't a parent who treated her house like a museum. When the kids were young she put away all her breakable trinkets, and they were allowed to touch anything except her makeup and brushes. And she had a lot of brushes. So naturally, the thing Sandy liked to do most was play with Gracie's makeup and brushes. Funny thing was that Gracie changed completely when Sandy made her a grandmother. When Sandy brought her little girls over to the house, Gracie prepared by putting fitted plastic zip-up covers on all the couches, the chairs, and even over the rugs.

There were three things Gracie wanted her children to be able to do: speak French, play the piano, and swim. In fact, she once told a newspaper reporter, "We're going to combine them, we're going to teach them how to swim in French." Maybe they learned French in school; all foreign languages were Greek to me. She made them practice the piano an hour a day, and when she was home she always listened carefully. Gracie had nearly perfect pitch and could hear the slightest mistake. Ronnie would be downstairs banging away and he'd hit a wrong note and suddenly, from the other side of the house, we'd hear Gracie yelling, "That's a mistake, dear. Go back over it."

We'd moved to Beverly Hills when the kids were still babies, and Gracie had a swimming pool built in the backyard. Gracie didn't like to spend time in the sunlight because of her fair complexion, and ordinarily, the closest she went to the water was looking at it from the deck of a cruise ship. But because it was so important to her that the kids learn how to swim, she took a series of private swimming lessons without telling anyone. Then one day she asked us all to come into the backyard, and as we watched, she dived into the pool and gracefully swam a complete lap. "See," she told the kids as she climbed out of the pool, "your mother can swim too." That was it, that was the only time I ever saw her near that pool.

I could swim. I did what was called the East River stroke, otherwise known as the "slap-overhand." I put my arms straight out over my head until the backs of my hands touched each other, then pushed out to either side. That was the safest stroke to use when swimming in the East River—every time you pushed to the side, you got the garbage out of the way.

We tried not to spoil the kids, and I don't think they were any more spoiled than any other kids who lived in Beverly Hills and had their own electrically powered miniature speedboat in their swimming pool. How could we not spoil the kids? We wanted to give them everything we hadn't had. And we could afford it. In Beverly Hills, for example, children's birthday parties were major social events. The newspapers covered them. We threw a small party for Sandy's fifth birthday and Ronnie's fourth. It was a typical kids' party: following the puppet show, two ponies were brought out for everyone to ride, then miniature toboggan slides were set up. Mickey Mouse and Donald Duck attended, along with the children of most of the stars in Hollywood. Our patio had been decorated to resemble a small Hawaiian city, and we served the usual children's menu: creamed chicken and ice cream molded to look like hula dancers.

So the kids were spoiled. How do you discipline kids who have their own boat in the swimming pool? Send them to their suite without dinner?

Gracie was the disciplinarian in our family, and when the kids misbehaved she made them leave the table after only one portion. Only once do I remember her spanking either one of them. Sandy was taking a bath and refused to get out of the tub. That sounds like Gracie Allen's daughter—the only kid in America who wouldn't get *out* of the bathtub. "Sandra!" Gracie yelled at her—she only called her Sandra when she was very angry—"get out of that tub, now!" Gracie usually kept her Irish temper well hidden, but once she found it, she lost it. This was one of those times. As soon as Sandy was dressed, Gracie put her over her knee and began spanking her with a hairbrush.

Unfortunately, she didn't get it quite right. She spanked Sandy with the wrong side of the brush. She hit her with the bristles.

Sandy was a lot like her mother, a feisty, independent little lady. For example, Gracie had fought very hard to get Sandy into the exclusive Marymount Academy, a Catholic school. In religion class one day somebody must have said something Sandy didn't like, because she stood up and told the nun teaching the class, "Excuse me, but there are other

people in the world besides Catholics, you know."
Maybe in the world, but not at Marymount. So we
got a letter from Marymount suggesting Sandy might
be happier in a different environment. What they really meant was that Marymount would be happier
with Sandy in a different environment.

Ronnie was more like me, a handsome charmer
with a wonderful singing voice. The difficulty in
punishing him whenever he did something wrong
was that he was always on your side. Once, for example, I bought the kids a very expensive set of
illustrated dictionaries. Within hours I found Ronnie
sitting on the floor cutting pictures out of the book.
I was furious. "Ronnie," I screamed at him, "what
am I going to do with you?"

Ronnie thought about that for a minute, then
sighed, and suggested, "Well, Daddy, I guess you'll
just have to kill me."

On another occasion he decided it would be interesting to stuff up the toilet with paper, then start
flushing. When Gracie and I got home from the studio there was probably two inches of water covering
the floor and downstairs carpeting. "Oh, Mother,"
Ronnie said before Gracie could say a word, "am I
glad you're home. Look what I've done. I've ruined
your carpet and I've probably ruined the whole
house." He shook his head and tapped his forehead.
"I just don't know what goes on up here sometimes."

A lot of people said the same thing about his
mother. Ronnie was a funny little kid, so maybe he
didn't inherit everything from me. When the kids
were young we took them with us to New York to
meet our friends there. Before we left, Gracie rehearsed them on the three questions she knew they

would be asked: How old are you? Where do you live? And, what kind of weather do you have out there?

When we got to New York we were ready to show off our kids. One of our friends asked Sandy, "How old are you?"

That was her question. "Four years old," she answered correctly.

Unfortunately, our friend then turned to Ronnie and asked him question number one: "And how old are you, young man?"

Ronnie didn't hesitate. As far as he was concerned, that was the second question—"Maple Drive, Beverly Hills, California."

When we adopted Sandy and Ronnie from The Cradle we agreed to raise them as Catholics. That never bothered me. I didn't go to synagogue; I went to the Hillcrest Country Club. Maybe if I had known I was going to grow up to be God, I would have felt differently, but I wanted the kids to understand and respect religion. So Gracie and I decided to raise the kids in the Catholic church and when they were eighteen let them make their own choice.

I learned a lot about Catholicism from Gracie. She was religious; she went to church regularly and wore a beautiful gold cross. Sometimes before we went onstage she'd make the sign of the cross. As long as our material was good, that seemed to help. I think one of the greatest moments of her life took place when we were in Italy and we were invited to meet the Pope. Pope Pius, I think it was. They asked Gracie and I if we wanted a private audience with His Holiness and I said, "No. What am I gonna tell the Pope? We just played the Jefferson Theater? That vaudeville is a great business? No, we'll go with everybody else.''

Gracie bought a new black dress and black stockings and about fifty strands of rosary beads to be blessed by the Pope for our friends in the States. Winnie Pearl, Jack Pearl's wife, was with us, and when we arrived at the Vatican we were escorted into a private room in which at least twenty other people were already waiting. Then we waited. And we waited. And waited. But when I looked around, I noticed that nobody else seemed to mind. Then I realized I shouldn't have been surprised, this is an entire religion based on waiting. They've been waiting almost two thousand years, what's a couple of hours?

Gracie was very nervous, at least as nervous as she was before going onstage, and she kept reminding me, ''When the Pope comes in, you have to get down on your knees. Remember, when he comes in, get down on your knees.'' She just didn't want me to embarrass her in front of God's agent. Believe me, we were waiting so long I would have gotten down on my knees if Benny Ryan had come in.

The door finally opened and a man wearing a red hat walked in. So I got down on my knees. ''Not now,'' Gracie hissed. ''That's just a Cardinal!'' How was I supposed to know? He had on a red hat and I knew he wasn't a porter.

The Pope's entrance was stunning. Maybe the Catholics know about miracles, and maybe they know about saints, but they've never received enough credit for what they know about show business. In my eighty-five years in the business, that was easily the greatest entrance I've ever seen. The Catholics know more about backlighting and indirect lighting than any stage manager. Believe me, if the religion thing doesn't work out so well, these people could have a very successful career in the legitimate theater.

There were three nuns in the room with us, and I watched them when the Pope came in. They'd waited almost two hours in this small room to see him, but when he arrived they lowered their eyes and they never looked at him. They just wanted to be in the same room with him. Then I looked at Gracie. She looked like a little girl, just innocence and love. She adored the Pope. I knew how she felt; I'd felt the same way the first time I met Al Jolson.

Someone had informed His Holiness that we were American radio stars and he blessed us in English. Maybe he'd heard the show and thought we needed his help. A few minutes later he made his exit. His exit was even more impressive than his entrance. Twenty-five minutes later I managed to get up off my knees, and we made our exit.

At home, we ate fish every Friday as Catholics were supposed to do. Being Jewish, I compromised, I wore a hat when I ate the fish, out of respect for my own religion and the fish's family. I would've made a great Catholic—I've always liked fish.

Sandy was just the opposite; she was raised Catholic and didn't like fish, so she used to tell people that she was a six-day Catholic—on Fridays she was Jewish.

Gracie made certain that the kids attended Mass at the Good Shepherd Church every Sunday morning. When the kids were old enough to go by themselves, we'd give them money for the collection plate and let them walk there. Only recently did I find out that they did go to Good Shepherd but they just didn't go inside. Instead, they took the money that I'd given them for the collection, threw it under a cactus in a park on Maple Drive, and went off to play, usually at Mervyn Leroy's house with his kids, Warner and Linda. I guess they didn't feel they were doing anything wrong by not going to church; they felt they were doing something right by not keeping the collection plate money.

I don't mind. The only thing I'm glad about is that Gracie and Jack Benny never found out. Gracie's feelings might have been hurt, and Jack could've cut himself badly on those cactus needles.

It couldn't have been easy for Sandy and Ronnie to grow up as Gracie Allen's children. When other kids taunted them by telling them that their mother was the dumbest woman in the world, they had to agree. Fortunately, they never had any difficulty separating Gracie Allen from their mother. Gracie Allen was the person who complained that people kept mistaking her for a child—they kept saying she'd lost all her marbles; their mother was the one who made them practice the piano.

Gracie was determined to expose her children to all types of culture. So in 1949, when we were booked into London's Palladium, she decided we were going to take the kids with us and show them Paris. Today they make funny movies about vacations like this one. We took the train from Los Angeles to New York. It was a four-day trip and we played a running game of canasta the entire time. It worked out pretty well—in four days Gracie won about $3.75 from Ronnie.

We sailed to England on the *Queen Elizabeth*. The first day out of port Ronnie decided to take a bath. Unfortunately, he forgot to turn off the water. Ever hear of anyone else having a flood on an ocean liner? We had more water in our stateroom than we were floating on.

As soon as we reached Paris, Gracie took Sandy to a fashion show at the House of Chanel. Now, taking Sandy to a fashion show was like telling me to watch the Milton Berle Show on television— neither one of us could use any of that material. Besides, Sandy was allergic to many different perfumes, so she sat sniffling and sneezing throughout the entire show.

Then Gracie decided we were going to take the kids to see the Folies-Bergère. As I said, she wanted to expose the kids to all types of culture, and vice versa. In those days the Folies was famous worldwide for its beautiful naked chorus girls. Nudity in the United States was outlawed; in our house I don't think Ronnie had ever seen a salad that wasn't fully dressed. So we sat down and the chorus girls came out wearing big smiles and I looked at Ronnie and his eyes were bulging out almost as far as mine. Gracie leaned over and asked him, ''How do you like the show, dear?''

Ronnie was a smart kid. ''Those are beautiful sets,'' he said.

''Yes, but how do you like the show?''

''And isn't the lighting great too?''

''But what about the girls?''

''Oh, they're not very funny, are they?'' A very smart kid. Finally, Gracie asked me to take the kids to see the famous art museum, the Louvre. So I took them to see the Louvre. She didn't say anything about taking them inside. Actually, I gave them my 5-Minute Tour. ''Here's the Venus de Milo, here's

Winged Victory, here's the Mona Lisa—and here's the back door.''

We flew back to New York. Because of bad weather, the flight took twenty-six hours. Gracie didn't mind at all, she won another $1.40 from Ronnie.

*

Sandy and Ronnie were just as good as most kids. But we still managed to survive. They put live baby frogs in Gracie's fingerbowls one night when we had guests for dinner, they released ladybugs and lizards in church, Ronnie did shoot a hole in the water heater with a .22, and he did rearrange the lightning rods on the roof so he could aim lightning bolts at the house of a kid he didn't like, but the problems we had were not really any different from those of almost every other household.

The kids were very understanding about their mother's headaches. If they came home from school and saw the curtains in our room were drawn, they behaved themselves. No running, no shouting, no playing loudly. They were good about it, even before they could fully understand the problem. We always had a dog when the kids were growing up, and everybody's favorite was a tough poodle Gracie had named Crepe Suzette, or Suzy as we called her. When Gracie's headaches got so bad she couldn't get out of bed, Suzy would sit on the end of the mattress, protecting her. Ronnie was one of the few people Suzy would let pass, though, and he'd go in the bedroom and tighten the bandana Gracie had tied around her temples to help relieve the pain.

The kids grew up too fast, literally and figuratively. One of the things that Gracie had always looked forward to was the day her daughter was big enough to wear some of her clothes. I think that probably happened on a Tuesday afternoon about quarter after three. Two hours later Sandy had outgrown Gracie's clothes. Sandy just shot past her mother, and by the time she stopped growing she towered over her. She was a big girl when she was still a little girl.

There was a period when Gracie and Sandy got along about as well as good scotch and chocolate syrup, but I guess that's true about most mothers and their daughters. Gracie wanted her daughter to be as feminine as she was; she wanted to take her shopping and buy her beautiful dresses and tie bows in her hair. Sandy preferred jeans, a shirt, and no shoes. The two of them had some tough times. Once, I remember, they were fighting about something, and Sandy picked up Gracie and carried her into our bedroom, then put her down, and left her there. And for a period of time they didn't even speak.

Not so surprisingly, as Sandy got older, Gracie got smarter, and the two of them eventually got along like . . . like mother and daughter. Sandy even named two of her daughters after Gracie. Her second daughter is Melissa Grace and her third daughter is Grace Ann, but Sandy calls her Jo-Jo, because she thinks it sounds just a little bit like Googie.

Neither of the kids wanted to go into show business. Maybe I pushed them a little, but they weren't the only kids in Beverly Hills to have an agent before they had a nurse. When they were old enough to behave themselves, or at least when we thought they were old enough to behave themselves, we'd take them to the studio to watch us do the radio show. But they told us they preferred to stay home and listen to us. We found out years later that that wasn't exactly true. What they were doing was reading the scripts beforehand so they'd know what our show was about if we asked them, then listening to a competitive show they liked better. Our rating in our own home was zero. I guess they figured they didn't have to turn on the radio to hear us.

As they got older and we made the transition to television, we began using them on "The Burns and Allen Show." Ronnie had some natural talent. As a kid, for example, he did an excellent penguin imitation. He turned out to be a handsome teenager and when Ozzie and Harriet Nelson's son Ricky helped raise the Nelson's ratings by attracting a younger audience, we made Ronnie a regular on the show. His character was named Ronnie Burns, and he played our son. The kid was born to play that role.

Ronnie also recorded several songs that sold reasonably well. It was obvious where he got his singing voice.

This is a very nice cigar I'm puffing on.

After working as an actor for eight years, Ronnie realized he didn't want to spend the rest of his life in show business. He knew how disappointed I would be when he told me, so he figured out an elaborate plan to break the news to me—he was going to tell Gracie and have her tell me.

One Friday night when I was at the fights, he took her out for dinner at a new restaurant Jerry Lewis had opened on the Sunset Strip. After they were seated he said, "Mother, I have a problem I hope you can help me with."

"What is it, dear?" she asked.

"I've decided I don't want to be an actor."

Gracie didn't even hesitate. "Don't look at me,"

she said immediately. "I'm not telling your father."

So Ronnie realized he had no choice and he did
the brave thing—he convinced my brother Willy to
tell me.

Sandy grew up to be a beautiful girl, but she had
absolutely no talent. It was pretty obvious where she
got that from, too. Her only talent was that she was
a beautiful girl. The first time she did the show she
played a waitress, and she was so good in that role
that we immediately elevated her to doing voice-
overs on our commercials. Sandy didn't care, she
had no desire to act at all. So when she was pregnant
and we wanted to make sure she had a little extra
money, we hired her dog to be on the show and paid
her as its handler. Now, that dog could act. He
played a dog and was very impressive. The dog got
$300 for the show, I believe, and Sandy made $150.
The dog earned that money, he knew all his barks.

One of the many things the kids taught us was that
children grow up faster than their parents. As far as
we were concerned, they were *only* sixteen or seventeen; they knew they were *already* sixteen or
seventeen. I guess the first time I realized that I could
no longer treat Ronnie like a little boy was when he
came home and told me that he'd gotten a speeding
ticket for going sixty miles per hour in a thirty-mph
zone. "Ronnie," I explained to him, "any fool can
drive sixty miles an hour. If you really want to impress
people, learn how to run sixty miles an hour."

Gracie and I knew that Sandy was no longer our
little girl when she called us from Las Vegas at four
o'clock one morning to tell us she'd just eloped.
Imagine how Gracie and I felt. Sandy was only sev-

enteen. What was she doing out at four o'clock in the morning?

The marriage actually wasn't a big surprise, because Sandy and her new husband had been planning to get married for some time. The thing that disappointed Gracie most was that she didn't have the opportunity to throw a big, beautiful, expensive wedding.

"She's only seventeen," Gracie protested.

"Where were you when you were seventeen?" I reminded her.

"That was different," she argued. "I was traveling with Larry Reilly."

"All right then," I said, "let's get Larry Reilly on the phone. We'll see if he wants to go on tour with Sandy."

"That's not funny, Nat." I'd certainly heard that complaint before.

Jack and Mary Benny's daughter Joanie and Marvin Mitchelson had gone to Vegas with Sandy and her new husband to be the witnesses. It figures that the witness at the wedding of Gracie Allen's daughter would become the best-known divorce lawyer in the country.

When Sandy and her husband finally got home, we were sitting there with Jack and Mary and our neighbors Tony Curtis and Janet Leigh. Gracie was so angry that she wanted to throw rice at the newlyweds, but I told her she had to take it out of the box first. Eventually, we all got over Sandy's marriage, including Sandy.

Gracie was sentimental about the kids—she even kept their baby teeth in a small, glass-topped table in our bedroom—but she was not one of those mothers who tried to hold on to her children. Sandy had

moved out of the house when she'd gotten married,
but Ronnie lived with us until he was twenty-one.
Gracie seemed very happy when he finally moved
out. "He's on his own," she kept telling me, and I
thought she was trying to convince herself. But the
day he moved out, she had the decorators in. Who
knew she'd had her eye on his room for twenty
years? Ronnie came home a week later and when he
went upstairs to his room, his room wasn't there
anymore. Gracie had converted it into her sitting
room.

Now that's a hint.

After Ronnie moved out, his mother insisted that
whenever he came for dinner he had to dress properly. That meant he had to wear slacks and a tie.
Gracie wouldn't even let him in the house if he was
wearing jeans and sneakers. It worked out fine—
Ronnie didn't come to dinner for a year and his
mother didn't yell at him. Finally, Sandy engineered
a compromise, and he was allowed to wear a turtle-
neck and sweater. But no frogs.

Sandy turned out to be very much like Gracie.
Only taller. Gracie never objected to my smoking
cigars. She knew how important they were to me—
if I didn't have a cigar, how would anybody know
when I'd told a joke? One of the first things she did
after we'd gotten together, though, was buy me a
cigar holder and tell me how to use it. The only rule
she made about my cigar was that I wasn't to get her
clean ashtrays all dirty with cigar ashes. We had two
lovely standing brass ashtrays in the living room,
and Gracie made sure they were always shining. I
wasn't permitted to use them for ashes.

"But they're ashtrays," I told her.

"Does that mean that you're supposed to make

them filthy? I'll get you an ashtray.'' And she'd go into the kitchen and get me an ashtray so that I wouldn't get the ashtray dirty.

Sandy never objected to my smoking cigars either. She thought I was pretty funny. One Sunday afternoon soon after she'd gotten married, Gracie and I went to her new house in Westwood. We were all standing in the backyard and I casually flicked my cigar ash on the ground. "Daddy!" Sandy practically screamed, "don't do that. I'll get you an ashtray." I didn't know whether to be proud of her for being just like her mother or angry at her for being just like her mother. So she went into the house and returned with an ashtray. Not using an ashtray for ashes was one thing—but the ground?

I understand how Gracie felt about her ashtrays—she was so proud of the home we'd built on North Maple Drive in Beverly Hills. When we'd adopted Ronnie we'd moved out of the Essex House into a huge triplex apartment in the Lombardy Hotel on Fifty-sixth Street. That place was so big it had two balconies. Two balconies. That wasn't really new for me; the one-room apartment on Rivington Street that I'd grown up in also had a balcony. Only we called it a fire escape.

One week after I'd signed a two-year lease on that apartment, we were offered roles in Bing Crosby's second movie, *The Big Broadcast of 1932*. Obviously my timing in real estate was as good as it was onstage. After *The Big Broadcast*, we went right into another movie and we never got back to the Lombardy. So, for the next two years, every time someone we knew was going to New York, we gave them the keys to the apartment. Believe me, if I had known we were never going to be able to use it, I'd have rented a much smaller place.

We were actually very smart. We moved out to Los Angeles before any of our friends had written jokes about how bad it was to live in Los Angeles, so we thought we loved it.

Practically the first thing Gracie did when we moved to Hollywood was find a church all the way on the other side of the city. Gracie didn't drive then, so every Sunday morning our driver would take her completely across town. It was probably a half-hour trip. When I asked her why she didn't go to a church nearby she told me she couldn't. "When I give confession," she explained, "I don't want the priest to know who I am."

She was the most popular woman on radio, she'd starred in fourteen successful movie shorts, her picture had appeared in practically every popular magazine, and she thought the priest wouldn't recognize her because she didn't live in the neighborhood. Gracie was quite a character, even when she wasn't.

Gracie was actually a very rare person in California—a native Californian. By the time we moved there, more of our friends from New York were living there than were living in New York. At first we moved into an apartment in Hollywood near the Paramount lot, then we rented a comfortable mansion that had been built by actress Pauline Fredericks.

This estate wasn't just bigger than the Lower East Side building I'd grown up in, it was bigger than the Lower East Side. It was the first time I knew a house could have wings. The dining room was so large it had two tables in it, so we ate breakfast at one and dinner at the other. That's the way I always behave when I have a dining room with more than one table in it. The huge pool had a mosaic tile bottom, porcelain dolphins at either end spouting streams of water, and an arched bridge crossing it in the middle. For a comedian with a haunting voice I was doing pretty good—I had a pool with a bridge crossing it.

Beyond the bridge were the gardens and the stables. Benny came over to the house soon after we'd moved in and I asked him if he wanted to see my stables. "Stables?" He couldn't believe it. "What do you need stables for?"

"Come on, Jack," I said, "you've known me for a long time. Do I really look like the kind of guy who would rent a house that didn't have stables?"

We had a party at that house one night, and among our guests was actor Herbert Marshall, who had a wooden leg. He was sitting at the bar, and as he got up, he tripped and broke his wooden leg. A group of us quickly picked him up, carried him to a car, and rushed him to a carpenter. It would be inaccurate to say he was plastered. Actually, he was glued.

I'll tell you how big that house was. We lived there three years, and several weeks after we'd moved out, Gracie and I were invited back to the Fredericks' house for a party. There were about one hundred fifty people at the party, which was held in the downstairs playroom. We lived in that place for three years; I never knew there was a downstairs playroom.

We had an opportunity to buy the entire estate, including the seven acres of Beverly Hills land, for $80,000. Gracie thought it might be a good investment, but I turned it down. I was from New York and I was a pretty hip fellow. I wasn't going to let these locals pull a fast one on me. And as it turned out, it's a good thing I didn't buy it. That land was beautiful, but they've practically destroyed it by putting larger houses and buildings on it.

Now I'm choking on my cigar.

Our house on North Maple Drive was already under construction when we bought it. When Gracie discovered it the cement foundation was already in the ground. But she wanted it, so we bought it. That was more than fifty years ago, and I'm still living in our house, so I guess she was right.

Gracie wanted the house because she thought the plans were absolutely perfect; and as soon as we bought it she started making changes in the plans. She knew exactly what she wanted. We added bedrooms, we added a patio, a swimming pool, and a separate game room-pool house. Gracie went over to the site as often as possible to check on the progress, and would return all excited about the fact that another wall had gone up or a floor had been laid down. Of course, what would have been exciting would have been a floor going up and a wall coming down. But by the time the house was done, Gracie was an expert in all the inside construction terminology, like "brick" and "two by four."

The house really was beautiful. From the front it looked like a movie set. It was white wood and brick, with more windows than Harpo Marx had children, and an elaborate canopied grillwork balcony running almost the entire length. Gracie had planted olive trees in the front yard and, in anticipation of our first harvest, I'd started drinking martinis. The newspapers described the house as a "palace" and claimed we had a swimming pool, private golf course, and tennis courts. We did have a swimming pool; the golf course must have been really private because I didn't know anything about it, and the closest thing we had to a tennis court was a warped Ping-Pong table.

We didn't need them—Gracie never participated in any sport that required getting up from a table. When we were building the house, her favorite game was backgammon, so we installed four backgammon tables. Socialite Hope Hampton had taught us how to play the game during a cruise, and after we'd bought four tables Gracie realized, "It's a good thing Hope Hampton didn't teach us how to play polo." Gracie told magazine writers that she was the family backgammon champion. That was absolutely true. At that time Sandy was five, Ronnie was four, and I rarely played. On that basis, Gracie was also the family heavyweight boxing champion.

She decorated the house with the assistance of Harold Grieve, one of the most famous interior designers of the day. Actually, that was her favorite sport. Gracie just loved elegant things, and the house was very elegant. It was soft and comfortable and beautiful, just like she was. The one thing she demanded was that we use only subdued colors, because she thought bright or loud colors might have something to do with causing her headaches.

The house was furnished with Georgian furniture, which I thought was appropriate, but we had plenty of Gracian things there too. Our close friend from New York, movie costumer Orry-Kelly, was a talented painter and we had his work hanging all over the house, next to Grandma Moses and Modigliani. Gracie's favorite painting was an Orry-Kelly Paris street scene that pictured nuns and prostitutes walking along, but the nuns were in the street while the prostitutes were on the sidewalk. Gracie thought this was scandalous, and she was so embarrassed by it that she just loved pointing out to visitors how scandalous it was. The house also had plenty of room for her collections of furs and hats, jewelry, Crown Derby china and matching Steuben glassware, and bibelots.

Gracie used to claim, "The only thing I like about winter is fur," and she had almost as many furs as hats. And Gracie had a lot of hats. Furs were her favorite possession and were probably the only thing she really splurged on. She had furs from animals that I'd never even heard of. She had a full-length mink coat, a hip-length silver fox for afternoon wear, and a white fox for the evening; she had an ermine coat, a white ermine cape, a black karakul trotteur, a sable cape and a black caracul cape. Imagine how many furs she would have had if we had lived in a climate where she needed them. I knew she'd bought another coat whenever she announced, "Nattie, would you like to see what you bought me today?" And even if I'd never seen a new coat, she got great pleasure from showing it off and telling our friends, "Nat bought this for me."

Buying gifts for Gracie was not difficult. Furs and jewelry were my job, but for her birthday, or holidays, or to celebrate a special occasion, Ronnie and Sandy and our friends would give her a piece of Crown Derby china or glassware. Eventually she collected twelve complete place settings, including several centerpieces, which she kept in a locked cabinet. We could have afforded to simply go out and buy a whole set, but it never would have had the meaning that this set did. This was a gift from the people who loved her, and the people she loved. Once, I remember, we had a mild earthquake while Sandy and I were alone in the house. We took one look at each other and then started running—toward Gracie's cabinet to make sure nothing had happened to that china.

Bibelots, or as we call them in English, chatchkas, are little trinkets. I suspect they're called bibelots because if they were called trinkets, or knickknacks, they wouldn't dare charge the prices for them that they do. Bibelots is a French word that, literally translated, means ''overpriced trinket.'' They're things like little carved horses, dancing figurines, tiny birds, the kind of objects people are constantly knocking on the floor or sitting on. They were not my taste, but I wouldn't dare complain about Gracie's taste: Hey, she picked me.

The house was completed just before Christmas in 1936. Christmas was Gracie's favorite holiday. She would do all her own shopping for presents, then she would bring them all into one room and wrap them herself. Gracie couldn't cook, and her gardening skills consisted of occasionally watering the flowers in the centerpiece, but she was an outstanding suitcase packer, she made very good lists, and she was a great package wrapper. Gracie could wrap as well as any salesgirl at Saks.

We always had a tall tree in the living room for Christmas, with dozens of beautifully wrapped presents beneath it. And on Christmas day the house would be filled with friends and relatives. It was a happy place. The day after our eating our first dinner in our new house, Christmas dinner, 1936, we left for New York. That was the only real home Gracie and I ever had, so naturally we left it as soon as it was finished.

Gracie did a wonderful job helping to design, decorate, and furnish the house. When it was done it was a nice home, it had everything I wanted in it: Gracie, Sandy, Ronnie, and a piano with sheet music in my key.

5

Our marriage was not at all like it was portrayed on radio and television. For example, we never had to worry about it being canceled because of poor ratings. And we didn't have a sponsor. And Gracie never hired Marlene Dietrich to stay with me when I was sick, never convinced Lana Turner to pretend she was in love with me, never sent me over to Rita Hayworth's house to pick up a magazine, never got Clark Gable to let me substitute for him in a movie, and never really made Frank Sinatra admit I had a better singing voice than he did.

Real life is like that sometimes.

Actually, one of the reasons that Gracie and I had such a good marriage is that we each had different responsibilities. I made all the decisions concerning our careers and our finances, while Gracie's job was to run the house, raise the children, and make sure we always had enough dresses, hats, and furs.

We rarely argued. I didn't care what Gracie did in the house as long as there was ketchup on the table, the soup was hot and the piano was tuned, and she was almost always willing to do whatever I decided was best for our act. On occasion I was accused of manipulating Gracie the way Edgar Bergen pulled Charlie McCarthy's strings. There was one big difference—Gracie was no dummy. When there was something Gracie didn't want to do, she could be very tough.

When there was a line in a script Gracie didn't think was right for her, she would wait until we were alone and tell me, "Nat, I don't like that line," and I'd say firmly, "It's a wonderful line, Googie, just do it," and she usually would. She would never argue with me in front of the cast and writers. Other married couples fought about paying the bills, we fought about whether a line like "Let's go into the Belgian building at the World's Fair and belch" was appropriate for her to say.

I'd usually win the arguments. In the end we would do whatever I thought was right. First, Gracie would tell me what I thought was right, then we'd do it.

Whenever she really wanted a change made in a script, I'd go into the office and tell the writers honestly, "You know boys, I was thinking about this line. It just doesn't feel right. Maybe we should change it." The writers knew that that meant Gracie hated the line and had refused to do it even after I'd threatened to sing on the show.

Only once in our entire career did she dislike an entire script. I don't remember what it was about, but after reading it she decided, "Nattie, I don't want to do this script."

"What's the matter?" I asked her. "What's wrong with it?"

"I just don't think it's funny. I don't think the jokes are good," she said.

I've always accepted criticism very well. "What

are you talking about?'' I said, beginning to raise my voice. ''This is one of the funniest scripts we've had all season.''

She was adamant. ''I'm sorry. I'm just not going to do it the way it's written. I'm just not going to and that's it.''

''What do you mean, you're not going to do it?''

''I know what's funny . . .''

''THIS IS FUNNY!'' I screamed. ''In fact, this is the funniest script we've ever had!''

She opened the script and pointed to a line. ''Here. Look at this,'' she said. ''What does this line mean? Why do I say that?''

''BECAUSE YOU'RE CRAZY, THAT'S WHY!''

She paused and glared at me. ''Do you mean me—or the character?''

Sometimes it would have been easier fighting over the bills. ''The character,'' I said. ''Who'd you think I meant?'' The next morning I went into the office and told the writers, ''You know, I was thinking about this script last night . . .''

Because Gracie made playing Gracie appear to be so easy, she never received the credit she deserved as an actress. One of the very few regrets I have is that Gracie never won an Emmy Award for her work on our television show, which she certainly deserved.

Other comediennes played dumb; on our show Gracie was dumb. When she wasn't supposed to know what she was doing, she didn't know what she was doing. And she didn't know it completely. Although Gracie was a natural actress, she worked at her craft and could dissect a performance as well as anyone I've ever known. One night, for example, I came home from the Friday-night fights that I always attended with Jack Benny and Harpo and Jessel, and Gracie was watching an actress named Cathy Lewis playing the role of Marie Wilson's best friend on the television show "My Friend Irma."

"How's the show?" I asked.

"Cathy Lewis is not Irma's friend," she said, summing up the problem with the script in one sentence. She meant that Cathy Lewis was taking laughs that Marie Wilson should have been getting, making the show less effective.

Sometimes Gracie would go out to dinner with our good friend Jack Langdon, who has run the office for more than thirty years. One of the many reasons Gracie loved Jack is that he would take her places she couldn't go with me. After dinner one night, for example, the two of them decided to do something daring. There was a burlesque house on Sunset named The Largo that advertised "15 Gorgeous Girls—One After Another," and Gracie convinced Jack to take her there. Now, the thought of Gracie in a strip joint is about as ridiculous as the thought of Jack Benny playing a philanthropist, but she really wanted to go.

The place was very dark and almost empty when they got there. The first girl was dressed in a yellow costume. She took off her yellow costume and received scattered applause. The next girl took off a blue costume and also received a poor response. The third girl got out of a green costume. Same thing. Gracie and Jack sat through six acts, and then she asked him, "How many more acts do they have here?"

"According to the sign outside," Jack told her, "nine more."

"Well, Jack, would you be terribly disappointed if we left now?"

"No, of course not, Gracie," he told her. "Anytime you want to go."

"I know we haven't finished our two-drink minimum."

"Don't worry about that," he said, then asked her why she wanted to leave.

"You know, Jack," she explained, "the girls are all very pretty, and they all have lovely bodies, but there's one thing wrong with their acts. They just don't have any sense of humor."

She was absolutely right, of course. Gracie always knew how to please an audience. So when she told me there was something wrong with a line or a script, I listened to her. No one was ever any smarter when it came to being dumb.

A lot of performers have difficulty living with their character. It killed Marilyn Monroe, for example. But Gracie made it work. She was always Gracie, whichever Gracie she was. There were two very distinct Gracies. There was the Gracie that I married: "She was a petite creature," famed mystery writer S. S. Van Dine wrote in his novel *The Gracie Allen Murder Case,* "and gracefully animated, with a piquant oval face and regular, sensitive features. Her eyes were large and brown, with extremely long lashes curling over them. A straight and slender nose lent dignity and character to a mouth made for smiling. She was slim and supple, and seemed to fit in perfectly with her pastoral setting."

And then there was the other Gracie that I married: "A most charming and astonishing young woman . . ." Van Dine also wrote. "A child whose spinning brain, much like a pinwheel, radiated the most colorful sparks, and whose spirit was as guileless as an infant's.''

It was Gracie's ability to make her character come alive that made her the most popular and successful woman in radio history, as well as a television and motion picture star. The character she created obviously struck a responsive chord in people. We got hundreds of letters every week from husbands claiming to be married to the real Gracie Allen, and office workers who swore they worked with the real Gracie Allen, and even people who happily confessed that they were the real Gracie Allen. Never have so many people boasted of being so silly.

Gracie became the national symbol of misunderstanding and ineptitude. The federal government even created a safety campaign warning Americans, ''Don't Be a Gracie Allen.''

Gracie had no choice. She was Gracie, the only woman in America who disappointed people by being smart. People loved the character, and they loved her. She was the only woman to be the central character of a radio program. She was the first woman to be the title character of a novel and movie, Van Dine's *Gracie Allen Murder Case*. And she later became the model for all the dumb women on television. Her catchphrases, ''George-Porgie,'' ''I'll bet you say that to all the girls,'' ''Oh, there you go again,'' and ''That's silly,'' became part of the language. And my line, ''Say good night, Gracie,'' to which she replied, ''Good night,'' was certainly one of the most famous catchphrases in entertainment history.

It's a show-business myth that Gracie replied to my request to ''Say goodnight, Gracie,'' by saying, ''Good night, Gracie.'' In fact, that's probably one of the most misquoted lines in theater history. Maybe she said it once, but I don't even remember that. She simply said, "Good night." There were many reasons for that, the main one was that I just never thought of "Good night, Gracie." And now that I've thought of it, from now on she will have said it.

❀

The key to our success was the radio show. The show ran for seventeen years. Of everything we did, radio was easiest. We stood in front of a microphone and read from a piece of paper. Gracie rarely saw her script until the night before the show was to be broadcast. She'd read it once before rehearsal, once during rehearsal, and then on the air. Sometimes Mary Kelly would stand in for her when the writers were working on the script. Gracie loved Mary, so if Mary had problems reading a line, when Gracie read the script she also had problems with the line—and then both of them blamed it on the line.

The only people who had difficulty in radio were the producers. They couldn't figure out what they were supposed to do. Early radio was run by Yale men. Everyone who graduated from Yale became either a politician or a radio producer. Apparently neither one required much of an education.

The producer of a radio show did nothing. He did less than I did. One day, for example, our producer left the show, and our sponsor's advertising agency, J. Walter Thompson, brought in a new Yale man to replace him. This new man thought he was supposed to do something. I don't know what they taught people in the Ivy League. He met with us the morning of the show and started explaining numerous details. Gracie was always polite to strangers, so she listened

I never knew Gracie's age. All I knew for sure was that she was born in San Francisco either before or after the 1906 earthquake. In this picture she's about a year and a half. © 1934 Paramount Productions, Inc.

Gracie never received credit for her acting ability. Here she's taking a bow onstage when she was about five years old. Or maybe she was much older and just playing a five-year-old. She was a great actress. © 1934 Paramount Productions, Inc.

Gracie began her professional career in an Irish dancing act with her sisters Pearl, Bessie, and Hazel. Even they put her on a pedestal.

At about age twelve Gracie dressed as a Spanish-Irish dancer for a recital. This was the Gracie that America loved: lace and ribbons, smiling shyly, and banging herself in the head with a tambourine. © 1934 Paramount Productions, Inc.

In our first feature film, The Big Broadcast of 1932, *Gracie played a secretary. I once asked her if she could read shorthand. "Sure," she said. "Listen. Curved line with a hook, straight line with a little thing on the end, cute little circle . . ."*

I know this is a posed photo because I'm showing Gracie how to do something. With our writers I helped put the words in her mouth, but when they came out they were all her own. Photo by Ray Lee Jackson.

The most successful gag in early radio history was the search for Gracie's mythical missing brother. Jigsaw puzzles were created with a missing piece— which looked exactly like her brother.

The Gracie Allen Murder Case *was the first feature she made without me. In that film she claimed to admire French children because they spoke a foreign language so well, was visited in prison by a friend and said she hoped she could return the favor, and created a great mystery of her own: what exactly was it that I did in our act?*

Gracie and I started on radio with Guy Lombardo and his Royal Canadians, and later we made several pictures with him, and them. Guy was actually related to every member of his band by tailor. Gracie is the one without the pocket handkerchief. © 1934 Paramount Productions, Inc.

We made our first trip to Europe in 1928 to play the London Palladium. By this time I'd acquired everything I would need to be successful: a walking stick, spats, cigarettes (for small laughs), and Gracie.

She was always Googie to me. © 1939 Paramount Pictures, Inc.

Jack Benny and Mary Livingstone, and friends.

From our family album: the Burns family at home. Ronnie is the kid without the ribbon in his hair. Sandy is the pretty one . . .

. . . Gracie and Ronnie on the observation deck of the Empire State Building . . .

I'm a pretty smart fellow: Once I found her, I was smart enough not to let her go.

The most successful woman in radio history. NBC

More photos from our family album: I think this was just before Sandy got married. Ronnie is the one without the necklace. CBS

. . . Upon our return from Paree . . . CBS

At the top, Gracie is with Ronald Reagan, James Cagney, and Danny Thomas, while below we're with producer Dore Schary, Danny Kaye, and Eddie Cantor.

to him as if he were actually saying something. Finally I stopped him. "Listen," I said, "don't get excited. Let me tell you what to do. At the beginning of the show, you just point at us and we'll start to talk. If we're talking too fast, pull your hands apart and we'll stretch it out. If we're talking too slow, make a circle with your finger, that means talk faster. And at the finish, if we're doing it right, point to your nose. That means we're on the nose. That's all there is to producing."

Yale men do not like to be told anything by people who didn't go to Yale. The closest I ever came to Yale was once I had one of their padlocks. But this man was a producer and he was going to produce. When the show went on the air he stood up and raised his index finger straight into the air and then, boom!, brought it down hard and pointed at us.

Unfortunately, when he brought his finger down he slammed it against the control booth window and broke it.

From then on he had to produce with his thumb. It didn't really affect the quality of our program. This was the most serious injury I ever heard of in radio. Radio just wasn't that tough.

Jack Benny invented the situation-comedy format used first in radio and later in television. Jack was the first person to have a repertory company of continuing characters interacting with each other. The primary group consisted of the star; his foil, who could be either a man or a woman; the announcer, who was actually part of the cast; the band leader; and sometimes the vocalist. Our original format was a variation of the flirtation routine we did in vaudeville. Gracie and I were both supposed to be single, and she was being pursued or was pursuing either me or the orchestra leader or the announcer or one of our guests.

The orchestra leader was an essential character in early radio. We had several different band leaders after Guy Lombardo left, including Paul Whiteman, Ray Noble, Artie Shaw, and Meredith Willson. Meredith later wrote *The Music Man,* and there is no truth to the rumor that he based it on my career, no matter how hard I tried to spread it.

Artie Shaw never pursued Gracie. Artie Shaw was married to Lana Turner when he was working for us, and as pretty as Gracie was, nobody was going to believe he was cheating on Lana Turner with her. No one besides Gracie. Artie was actually one of the most dedicated musicians I've ever known. His contract read that his band would play for two minutes and thirty seconds every half hour. One week we were a little long in rehearsal and I asked him to cut five seconds—he followed me home in a taxicab begging me not to cut those five seconds.

At one time Artie Shaw wanted to hire a talented trumpet player from Chicago to work on our show, but Caesar Petrillo, the head of the musician's union, refused to give him the necessary waiver. While that was going on I picked up the paper one morning and saw a big story announcing that Lana Turner was leaving Artie Shaw. I felt awful for him. When I saw him at work that afternoon I put my arms around him and said, "Artie, what can you do? That's life."

"Oh, it's okay, Nat," he sighed. "If I can't get the trumpet player from Chicago, I'll get someone from around here."

And people thought Gracie was the dumb one.

We changed the format in the early 1940s. The show had been in the top ten since we'd started, but we were gradually losing our audience. When a rating suddenly drops three or four points, that means the competition is doing something special against you. But when the rating loss is progressive, a half point, a point, that means the audience is turning off the show. We were losing a half point, a point each week, and I couldn't figure out what was wrong.

It was making me crazy. I couldn't sleep nights. Gracie didn't seem to be very concerned about it. A few years earlier she'd told a reporter that the one thing she wanted to do more than anything else was retire and stay home with the kids and at Saks with the salesgirls. I knew she was at least partially serious about that. Fame just wasn't important to her. Besides, Gracie always believed our success was just temporary, so our falling ratings didn't surprise her. It had taken almost fifteen years, but she knew it wouldn't last.

I went to the experts at that show-business mecca, the Hillcrest Country Club, for their advice. Jack Benny told me Gracie wasn't laughing enough. Eddie Cantor said Gracie was laughing too much. George Jessel thought we weren't doing enough double routines. Jolson turned off the water. Nobody suggested that I sing.

Finally the answer came to me in the middle of the night. "Googie," I said, shaking her, "are you awake?"

"Wha . . . what's the matter, dear?"

As long as she wasn't sleeping either, I could talk to her. "I know what's wrong."

"That's nice, Nat," she said in a groggy voice. "What's wrong with what?"

"The show. I know why our ratings are dropping. Our jokes are too young for us. Everybody knows that we're really married and have the kids. But on the show you're still flirting with everybody. Let's tell them we're married.''

Maybe that discovery wasn't as important as uncovering the secrets of the atom, but Albert Einstein never had to worry about his ratings. At the beginning of our next show I told the audience that in real life Gracie and I had been married for a long time and had two wonderful children, Sandy and Ronnie, and that from that moment on we were going to be married on the show. ''Well,'' I concluded, ''I think I see my wife coming now.''

We were the only couple in radio history to get married because we had to. And evidently we were funnier married than single, because our ratings began to improve. We stayed among the top shows on the ether until quitting radio for television in 1950.

The plots of our shows were very simple. Either Gracie had misunderstood something—for example, I was going to sing for the Army Air Force and they wanted to give me some vaccination shots, and she thought the Army Air Force wanted to shoot me for singing—or she was trying to help me or someone else accomplish something or resolve a problem. On one show I was supposedly running for a spot on the Beverly Hills City Council and she was trying to help me get the support of her club, the Beverly Hills Uplift Society, so she went to Lana Turner for assistance.

''Lana,'' she pleaded, ''I need your help.''

''What is it?'' Lana asked.

''Well, you see, I'm married to George Burns . . .''

''Oh, you poor kid.''

Another week we were reminiscing about how we'd started in vaudeville and had gone to Al Jolson to ask for a job. Jolie mistakenly thought Gracie was a ventriloquist and I was her dummy.

"But's he's not a dummy," Gracie protested, "he's a real man. He's George Burns."

Jolson couldn't believe it. "Are you trying to tell me that he has blood and muscles, and that he walks and talks and makes love like other men?"

"No," Gracie explained, "I'm trying to tell you he's George Burns."

On another show she decided to help Mickey Rooney; she wanted to adopt him because she was certain he hadn't gotten a proper education. Mickey told her that he had received a degree in geometry and a degree in Latin.

"Oh, yeah?" Gracie challenged. "Say something in geometry."

Mickey thought about that for a second, then stated, "Okay. Pi R square."

"Ah ha!" Gracie exclaimed. "There's proof you haven't had a good education. Everybody knows pie are round!"

We had several continuing characters on the show, among them Gracie's overweight and underattractive best friend, Tootsie Sagwell, who Gracie was always trying to help find a husband. On a typical show she urged Tootsie to run for Queen of the Fleet against Hedy Lamarr. She had the two of them stand next to each other, then decided, "Just as I thought. There's no difference in your faces. Your eyes and ears and nose and mouth are the same."

Tootsie was thrilled. "Really?"

"Yes," Gracie said. "I counted them carefully."

The announcer was a continuing character who worked the commercials into the show. Before Harry von Zell joined us, we worked with Bill Goodwin, who played a handsome young bachelor who dated most of the beautiful women in Hollywood. One week Ronald Reagan appeared on the show. "Uncle Ronnie," as our kids called him, was a close friend who often came to dinner with his wife, Jane Wyman. In fact, Ronnie was one of Hollywood's most attractive men, and on our show he and Bill Goodwin got into an argument about who was the most debonair. They agreed to let someone who knew absolutely nothing about good romantic technique decide. Guess who?

"Now," Ronnie Reagan told Gracie, "forget you're married to George Burns."

"But it takes time to forget something like that," she said loyally.

"Well . . ."

"That's long enough."

Reagan began. "Ah, Gracie, you're lovely," he said romantically. "Beautiful . . . enchanting. I kiss your hand."

And then he kissed her hand, loudly, four or five times. The most important thing about a radio kiss is that it had to be loud.

"All right, all right," Bill Goodwin interrupted impatiently. "Now it's my turn!"

Gracie laughed. "You'll love it, Bill. It tickles."

Probably our most popular character, besides Gracie, was Mr. Postman, played by Mel Blanc, who advised listeners sadly at the end of each appearance, "Remember, keep smiling." Mr. Postman hated his wife. That was his character—he hated his wife. Mr. Postman used to get a lot of fan mail. Once he told Gracie that his wife had fallen into the ocean and he had been very worried because there were sharks in the water. But fortunately, he reported, they all survived.

All Mr. Postman wanted to do was get rid of his wife. "But in all these years," Gracie pointed out to him, "I've never heard you say you hated her."

"You're right, Mrs. Burns," he agreed. "I haaatttteeeee her!"

He was very jealous of Bill Goodwin. "Oh, Mr. Goodwin," he said, "I envy your gay, romantic life. Always a different girl. Believe me, once you marry, the glamour is gone."

"Really, Mr. Postman?"

"Yes. What a mess at night. Wrinkle creme, foundation creme, chin strap, curlers . . ."

As usual, Gracie was there to help. "But Bill wouldn't have to give all that up just because he got married."

We didn't have guest stars on the show the first few years we were on the air, but then we began attracting the biggest names in the business. Among the people we had on the show were Clark Gable, Eddie Cantor, Jolson, Charles Laughton and Elsa Lancaster, Rita Hayworth, Betty Grable, Lana Turner, Veronica Lake, Hedy Lamarr, Dorothy Lamour, Marlene Dietrich, Lucille Ball, Charles Boyer, Shirley Temple, Bea Lillie, Cary Grant, Ronald Reagan, Frank Sinatra and, every time his rent came due, Jack Benny.

We knew most of these stars socially, and when they were on the show Gracie was always friendly and gracious, but guarded. Even with our regular cast she was always proper, but rarely personal. Gracie was just a very private person. She always had gifts for everyone on holidays and remembered their birthdays, but the only member of our cast she ever became close to was Bea Benadaret, and even that never went beyond the studio.

Bea was an extremely talented actress who played several different character parts for us on the radio show and eventually became Blanche Morton, our next-door neighbor, on both the radio and television show. Both Gracie and Bea loved gossip, and each of them had their own sources. Gracie got most of her stuff from Orry-Kelly, who knew all the best dirt in show business. I don't know where Bea got her information. The two of them would sit together at the back of the studio whispering tales and laughing as loudly as I ever heard Gracie laugh.

No matter who was on the show, the plot always revolved around Gracie's illogical-logic. It was Gracie's mind that made the show work. For example, one week she complained, "I read in the papers that the Los Angeles police are hunting for a Chicago gangster. But why do they want one from Chicago? Can't they be satisfied with a hometown boy?"

On another show she asked Cary Grant to come over to our house. "You said you needed to see me about something important?" he asked Gracie.

"Won't you sit down?" she suggested politely, indicating the couch.

"Yes. But what is it?"

"It's a couch."

When British comedienne Bea Lillie was on the show, she was conspiring with Gracie about something and decided, "I'll call my butler and tell him not to expect me for dinner."

"Save your voice," Gracie offered. "Use the telephone."

We never tried to be sophisticated. The only rule we followed was that we would only use jokes that were funny. If people wanted jokes that weren't funny, they could listen to our competitors.

Our guests always played themselves on the show, and scripts were written specifically for them. The elegant James and Pamela Mason, for example, actually raised purebred cats, so when they appeared on the show Gracie claimed, "My husband is a cat fancier too."

"Oh, really?" Pamela asked. "How many do you have?"

"Just one," Gracie replied. "In this country we're only permitted one husband."

Pamela persisted. Fortunately, our guests always persisted. "Well, what is your method of raising cats?"

"Same as yours. Put both hands under their belly and lift."

"Mrs. Burns," the suave James Mason interrupted, "I appeal to you . . ."

"You certainly do," Gracie admitted, "but I still don't want any more cats."

Because of Gracie's mike fright we did the show without an audience for the first few years. We even taped paper over the glass in the studio doors to prevent people from looking in while we were on the air. Actually, doing a live broadcast in front of an audience was considered very daring, and many performers besides Gracie refused to do it. To me, going into show business with my talent was brave; standing next to Gracie in front of an audience was easy. But if Gracie couldn't work with an audience in the studio, I couldn't either. "When we were working in vaudeville," I explained to reporters, "we never invited people to come up onstage to watch us make the audience laugh. So why should we do it in radio?''

But by 1933 vaudeville was dying, maybe because we never invited people to come up onstage and watch us make the audience laugh. We were playing a week in Shoreham, Washington, and the Loew's Fox chain asked us to help bolster ticket sales by allowing anyone who bought theater tickets to also attend a live broadcast of our radio show. I thought it was a good idea. Gracie didn't want to do it.

"It's business, Googie," I insisted.

"Pass the salt," she said.

We were doing four live shows a day in the theater. This was before radio programs were taped for later transmission, so we were also doing our once-a-week thirty-minute radio show twice, first for the East Coast, then again three hours later for the West Coast. When local newspapers announced that theater-ticket stubs could be exchanged for tickets to our first live broadcast before an audience, we sold out our theater shows. As it turned out, many people who bought tickets to the Fox didn't even bother going to the theater, they just exchanged their stubs for tickets to the broadcast.

That made sense to me because there was such a big difference between the way we performed in the theater and the way we did our radio show. In the theater we stood directly in front of the audience and recited our lines. When we did the radio show we stood behind microphones and read from scripts. So it was easy to understand why people preferred attending a radio broadcast rather than a live show.

We did the broadcast from a thousand-seat studio in the Willard Hotel. It was packed for both shows. We rigged footlights in front of the mikes so Gracie wouldn't be able to see the audience, and we asked everyone attending the show not to laugh or, more importantly, applaud our jokes. Having an audience applaud a joke is about as satisfying as smoking an unlit cigar.

At the conclusion of our first show we found out that people in the rear of the studio couldn't hear us. That problem was solved with a slight technical adjustment—we spoke louder.

After that night we regularly did the show in front of an audience. I'd stand centerstage, facing straight ahead; Gracie would stand at my left, at a right angle to me, so she didn't have to look at the audience. She always wore a hat during our broadcasts and was continually taking it off and putting it back on, primarily so that she would have something to do with her hands.

Gracie also worked behind an oversized microphone that kept her partially hidden from view. She never conquered her mike fright, and I think the only thing she liked about making the transition to television was that we didn't film the show in front of an audience.

She certainly wasn't the only performer to suffer from mike fright. Clark Gable couldn't read his lines unless he was sitting down, and he always had an unlit pipe clenched between his teeth. Tony Martin was our male vocalist, and the first few years he was on the show he couldn't sing unless he had his saxophone around his neck. Bing Crosby wouldn't sing unless he was wearing a hat. Harriet Hilliard Nelson always turned her back on the studio audience when singing. Both Rudy Vallee and Edward G. Robinson constantly tugged on their earlobes. And Jack Benny couldn't perform unless he had a cigar in his hand. Even then the man was stealing my material.

Gracie's mind was made up by a group of very talented writers that included my brother Willie, John P. Medbury, Paul Henning, and Harvey Helm. When I had hired Paul Henning, he'd written his mother that he was going to be writing comedy for George Burns. "That's very nice for you, dear," she wrote back, "but who writes for Gracie? She has all the funny lines."

Maybe I should have hired Henning's mother.

I'd meet with the writers the day after we finished one show to decide what the following week's show would be about, then each of the writers would go home and complete an entire script. Finally we'd get together again and hammer out the script we would use on the air. And except for the crying, screaming, and occasional threat's to rip out each other's hearts, it was very easy.

Once the script was finished we usually followed it very closely. We rarely ad-libbed. Gracie considered herself an actress rather than a comedienne; instead of saying funny things, she said things funny. Offstage she never told a joke, although once she did confide to Carol Channing, soon after those flashing "walk" and "don't walk" signs had been put up in Beverly Hills, "I was crossing the street and the sign kept warning, 'Don't walk, Don't walk . . .' so I ran!"

Only twice in the seventeen years we did the radio show did we have to forget the script while we were on the air. One night the lights in the studio went out, and once Gracie accidently dropped her script on the floor, scattering all the pages. In both instances I reacted the same way: I stepped right over to her, put my arm around her waist, and asked, "So, Gracie, how's your brother?"

She immediately replied that he had joined the Navy but was having trouble, because every time they ordered all hands on deck he put them there and people kept stepping on them. Or something like that.

Radio just wasn't that difficult.

Although it took Gracie only a day and a half each week to do the show, being Gracie was a full-time job. By the time Gracie was thirty years old she was one of the four or five most famous women in the United States, and accomplishing that had required a tremendous amount of work. Today, because of television, a person can become an overnight success just by being successful with the right person overnight. It used to be much more difficult. It took talent, or at least a different kind of talent. Once there was a time when there was no "Johnny Carson Show," or network news, and if a person wanted to be an overnight success he or she had to work a lot of nights.

While we were doing the radio show the first few years, we continued working in variety theaters—we never knew when the radio fad was going to end—and we began making movies. Gracie also made numerous personal appearances: she started six-day bike races and christened ships and buildings and appeared at charity events before huge crowds in places like Yankee Stadium and Madison Square Garden. She was always available for newspaper and magazine interviews, endorsed products, and even guest-starred on other radio programs like "Information Please," dazzling experts with her knowledge of mythical flying creatures, and "Screen Guild

Theatre,'' on which she played a dramatic role opposite James Cagney. With the help of our writers, who picked out the words and put them in the correct order, Gracie wrote a newspaper column, magazine stories, and even two short books. She also created ten surrealistic paintings that were exhibited at some of the finest art galleries in the country, appeared in concert at the most respected music halls, and ran for President of the United States against Franklin Delano Roosevelt—all in addition to running the house, raising the children, and making sure we never ran out of dresses, hats, and furs.

Gracie did everything necessary to make her character popular. We were very fortunate that being dumb was a talent adaptable to every popular medium. In newspapers, for example, Gracie and I often appeared in the photo-comics, a combination of photographs and illustrations with clever captions. One, I remember, pictured Gracie and me standing in front of an illustrated storefront, and I was asking, ''Where are you going?''

''To have my fortune told,'' she said, pointing, presumably, to the place where her fortune-teller would be found.

In the second panel I took my hat off and asked, ''By a palmist?''

''No, by a mind reader,'' she replied, pointing to her head, presumably the place where her mind would be found.

In the final panel I had both my hat off and my arms crossed as I suggested, ''Well, don't let them charge you more than half price.''

In the comic strips I got the funny lines.

Actually, I did some of the best acting of my career in the photo-comics. I acted like I knew what I was doing.

Gracie eventually got her own syndicated advice and philosophy column entitled "I Always Say—Sez Gracie Allen." The kind of in-depth advice she offered included, "A young boy shouldn't be given up for hopeless just because he's lazy, surly, and good for nothing. Don't be discouraged by those things— maybe he's just trying to be like his daddy."

And, "Education is worth a whole lot. Just think— with enough education and brains the average man would make a good lawyer—and so would the average lawyer."

And, "It's foolish to bet on a horse without talking to him first. I know it seems silly to ask a horse who's going to win a race—but it's no sillier than asking anyone else."

Of course, anyone who would take advice from Gracie deserved it.

The success of that column was followed by a short book Gracie wrote, with the assistance of Paul Henning, for Campbell's Tomato Juice, entitled, *It's Murder—But It Could Be Worse*. I've read the book. The title's wrong.

I wrote the introduction, in which I reminded readers, "All I know is that if Gracie should accept a penny for her thoughts she'd be a professional idiot." A lot of husbands would have been delighted to get paid for insulting their wives like that, although I suspect many of them would have done it for free.

Gracie didn't write the material supposedly written by Gracie Allen, just as she really wasn't the dizzy dame she played on the radio, but it was her ability to create a believable character that made everything else work. Nobody could have done that job better, or been more delightful about doing it, than she was. And it wasn't an easy job. How many people have a job that requires them to say silly things every day? Besides politicians? But Gracie was always cordial to the public and always tried to cooperate with the press. I never saw her refuse to sign an autograph or shake somebody's hand, and the only publicity request I ever saw her turn down was a photographer's suggestion that she pose in front of an insane asylum. She thought that idea was in very poor taste. To Gracie, that was like asking Mae West to pose in front of a whorehouse; it missed the whole point of the character. She just wouldn't do it. What could I do, tell her she was crazy?

One of the reasons that Gracie was able to do so much publicity is that she never took it personally. She believed it was the character people wanted to interview and photograph, not the actress. As far as she was concerned, doing this was all part of the act. I still don't believe she ever completely understood that it was the person they were interested in.

One thing I always found amusing was that Gracie was promoted as being the nitwit of the networks, America's most scattered brain, yet she was constantly receiving requests for her to endorse products. People may have thought she was dumb, but for some reason they wanted to buy products she recommended. And she endorsed products from bath salts and perfumes to muffin makers and wedding gowns. One New York beauty salon even offered a Gracie Allen facial, in which the client was supposed to lie down on an incline board so that all her blood ran to her head. This supposedly increased blood circulation to the face, which improved skin appearance. They named it after Gracie, however, because it also caused extreme dizziness.

I know that one thing she regretted about our success was the complete loss of her privacy. Gracie was so famous she couldn't leave the house without attracting a crowd. Women identified with her and wanted to talk to her or get her autograph. Gracie almost always went out with friends, or, when her heart started getting bad, with her nurse, and when the crowds got too big it was that person's job to go up to her and say loudly enough for everyone to hear, "I'm sorry, Miss Allen, but you have to leave right now. They're waiting for you at the studio." Gracie would shrug her shoulders, apologize to her fans, and leave quickly.

Even our home wasn't always private. Unlike most motion picture stars, whose fans seemed to feel were unapproachable, everyone believed that Gracie was their friend. Quite often someone would ring our doorbell and explain that they were just visiting and couldn't go home without saying hello to Gracie or getting her autograph for their dumb cousin. This is a nation of dumb cousins. Sometimes people wouldn't even bother ringing, they'd just stroll into our backyard, expecting to be welcomed. I suppose they felt since they let us into their homes, we should let them into our home. Neither Gracie nor I liked this, but we both understood that people meant it as a compliment.

Gracie was terrified that because of our fame someone would do something to our children. After the Lindbergh baby was kidnapped we had an elaborate silent alarm system connected directly to the police department built into the house. Gracie also taught the children to scream "Police! Police!" if anyone they didn't know approached them. Sandy didn't quite understand; she thought Gracie wanted her to yell "Please! Please!"

That alarm system was always a problem. One button was hidden in a coat closet, and several times guests reaching into the closet to get their coats accidently summoned the police. Another button was hidden behind a painting in Sandy's room, and once, when she and Ronnie were playing, she kicked the button. As Sandy might have said, the please came instantly. And they were not pleased.

🌿

Of all the promotional events Gracie participated in, of all the interviews and stories and photographic sessions and personal appearances, the three stunts that were the most successful were Gracie's art exhibition, Gracie's celebrated concert tour, and Gracie's campaign for the presidency.

Gracie had absolutely no artistic ability. The only straight line she could draw was a curve. Nothing she drew looked like anything recognizable. In 1938, surrealist art was very controversial. Nobody really understood what surrealism was, and since nobody understood what Gracie's paintings were either, they had to be surrealist. She claimed to have done ten paintings, and we were able to convince the prestigious Julian Levy Gallery on East Fifty-Seventh Street in New York to sponsor a one-woman exhibition. We charged twenty-five cents per person admission and donated all proceeds to the China Aid Council for the Chinese Relief Fund.

Gracie's paintings were most accurately described by their titles: "Man With Mike Fright Moons Over Manicurist," "Dogs Gather on Street Corner to

Watch Man-Fight," "Toothless Mouth Munching on Tuneless Melody," "Keg-Lined Can Sinking a Couple of Hard Putts in No-Trump," "Behind the Before Yet Under the Vast Above the World is in Tears and Tomorrow Is Tuesday," "Man Beholds a Better Mouse Trap and Buys a Mohair Toupée," "Gravity Gets Body Scissors on Virtue as Night Falls Upside Down," and "Eyes Adrift as Sardines Wrench at Your Heart Strings." Gracie ran out of titles before running out of paintings, so two of them were officially titled, "Untitled."

A well-known expert examined them and declared that they were legitimate works of Art, but Gracie protested angrily that she'd done them by herself.

Normally I'd be puffing on my cigar, but the new federal law mandates that I provide a no-smoking section in this book.

Gracie said they were surrealist. Julian Levy said they might be surrealistic, but that they certainly weren't surrealist. Julian Levy and Gracie got along very well—nobody knew what either of them was talking about.

I knew they were satirical. The paintings, not the people.

The exhibition was a tremendous success. The opening was covered by reporters from every national news service and every New York newspaper, radio station, and photo syndicate. Transradio Press, a national radio-news network, covered the event live. *Look* magazine ran one of the paintings on its cover and three more full pages inside. The *Herald-Tribune* did a color feature in its Sunday magazine section. The opening-night party was a major New York social event, and the gallery was packed with celebrities. Gracie spent much of the night posing with her paintings. Believe me, the opening night party lasted longer than it had taken her to do the paintings.

At the party a reporter asked her if the paintings were for sale. "Sure," she told him, "if they don't want to charge me too much for them."

Another reporter wanted to know why she had chosen surrealist painting "as an expression of her subconscious."

"What made Maine and Vermont vote for Landon?" she replied.

There was a rumor that she had done the paintings in the dark, but she denied it vehemently, claiming, "Someone's trying to make me look silly."

That was ridiculous. It took me, four writers, a producer, the William Morris Agency, a publicity man, a secretary, and a major public relations firm to make Gracie look silly.

The exhibition was so successful that it was extended a third week and received worldwide publicity. After closing in New York, it toured fifty cities over six months, proving that you may not be able to fool all of the people all of the time, but you certainly can fool a lot of them for a short period of time.

Ironically, when the show was at the American Art Congress in Los Angeles, someone stole one of the paintings—a crime that was reported in the Los Angeles *Times* right beneath a report that thieves in Binghamton, New York, had broken into an automotive repair shop and stolen the owner's artificial leg. In Gracie's case the thief obviously had a sense of art appreciation—he returned the painting the very next day.

Compared to her painting ability, Gracie was an

extremely talented musician. She had learned how to sing and could actually play the piano a little. When Paul Whiteman was the conductor on our show, his arranger wrote "The Concerto for Index Finger," featuring Gracie performing a piano solo. Gracie's part in "The One-Finger Concerto," as it became popularly known, was to play the scale with her index finger and hit the wrong final note. Paul Whiteman would then play that note correctly, and the entire orchestra would play until they reached Gracie's solo again—and again she'd play the scale with her index finger and hit the wrong last note. The piece ended with Gracie playing the scale correctly to the last "do," and finally hitting it right, causing the entire orchestra to stand up and start cheering.

It was a nice little bit. When we did it on the show the audience loved it, and Gracie began receiving invitations to perform the concerto in public. She eventually appeared at the Hollywood Bowl, several music halls in other cities and, finally, at Carnegie Hall. Gracie Allen at Carnegie Hall. She went further by hitting the wrong note with one finger than I did in my entire musical career.

The real secret of Gracie's performance was that she wasn't even playing. There was another pianist backstage playing the notes while Gracie faked it for the audience. It took a professional musician to play it wrong correctly. So the truth is that Gracie made it to Carnegie Hall by not playing the scale with one finger. Of course, nobody came to those concerts to hear her playing the piano, they came to see her playing the piano. That was another thing Gracie and I had in common: nobody ever came to hear me make music either.

How many real musicians can fill a major concert

hall by pretending to play the scales incorrectly with their index finger? The art exhibition was successful and the piano concerts were popular because Gracie was an excellent satirist. Gracie was an observer of people's behavior and was able to imitate and exaggerate their actions. Nobody really cared if she could paint, or play the piano: what the audience wanted to see was her interpretation of the modern artist's pomposity and the concert pianist's somber attitude. Because Gracie never did anything malicious, because she never told a joke to hurt anyone, she was able to poke fun at people without making fun of them.

These stunts worked because of Gracie's talent. It wasn't as simple as walking onstage and not playing the piano. Very few performers could have not played the piano as well as Gracie did. They worked because when she went out on that stage, in her mind she was a concert pianist. She took the role seriously, which is why the audience thought it was so funny.

It was one thing to put her name on a thin book and claim she'd written it; playing the piano incorrectly required performing. It was unlike anything Gracie had ever done, or not done, and I think I was more nervous about it than she was. I remember standing backstage with her at the Hollywood Bowl when she did it in public for the first time. When the time came for her solo, what could I tell her? Go out there and don't play well? I'll tell you the truth, I wasn't sure how well Gracie wouldn't play. This wasn't doing a stand-up routine with me, this was straight acting. I gave her a little kiss and she marched out to centerstage, faced the audience and bowed, and successfully became one of the world's worst concert pianists.

❦

Gracie was good as a painter and excellent as a concert pianist, but she was best as a politician. Gracie's presidential campaign of 1940 attracted as much attention as the search for her missing brother had seven years earlier. Since that time several other comedians, some of them show-business performers, have run for the presidency, but Gracie was the first comedian to do it seriously. Or the first performer to do it comically.

We rarely did topical humor on the show, although Gracie once claimed she was going to run for the office of the governor of the State of Coma, claiming to have been there for many years. We were a domestic act; Fred Allen and Will Rogers were the social commentators. Occasionally we would do a joke about a politician, but that was tough to do because in real life they were funnier than we were. Actually, what we tried to do was provide relief for people from the fact that millions of them were on relief. Probably the most political thing we'd done was a series of broadcasts for the government to publicize and explain the National Recovery Act, an industrial code that provided protection for the worker, including the creation of a minimum wage.

"Look here, Gracie," I told her. "This means that women will be getting men's wages."

"Don't be silly, George," she corrected. "My sister Bessie has been married to three men and never got their wages."

"Gracie, the NRA . . . do you know that the gov-

ernment will see that everyone in this country is going to be paid a living wage?''

"It's a good idea. They should be paid living
wages because wages aren't very good when you're
dead.''

Imagine how confused the country must have been
to have needed Gracie Allen to explain the economic
recovery.

Although the history books fail to record it, the
1940 presidential campaign pitted Democratic President Franklin Roosevelt against Republican Wen-
dell Willkie as well as against the candidate of the
Surprise Party: Gracie Allen.

Gracie's presidential campaign began on the show
as a gag that was supposed to run for two weeks.
She announced that the American public had been
laughing at political candidates for years, so why
shouldn't she run? Her slogan was, "Down with
common sense, vote for Gracie," and she claimed
that she had a real chance of winning because "half
of all the married people in this country are
women.''

When the gag caught on we extended it a few
weeks, then Gracie began making unannounced appearances on other radio shows like "Dr. I.Q." and
"Jack Benny's Jell-O Show," just as she had during
the search for her brother. On "The Texaco Star
Theatre," Ken Murray asked her which party she
was affiliated with. "Same old party," she told
him—"George Burns.''

Fibber McGee and Molly told Gracie they'd heard
that several other candidates intended to run for the
White House, and asked her if she'd heard about
those rumors.

"They're not true," she told them. "I'll be run-

ning the White House and I don't intend to take in
any roomers.''

It was the participation of the Union Pacific Railroad and the city of Omaha, Nebraska, that turned
this stunt into an event. To promote the release of
the movie *Union Pacific* a year earlier, the railroad
and the city had staged an Old West festival called
Golden Spike Days, during which the men of Omaha
grew beards and everyone wore traditional western
costumes. Golden Spike Days had been such a successful tourist attraction that Omaha had decided to
repeat it. The Union Pacific Railway offered to provide a campaign train for Gracie for a whistle-stop
tour, and Omaha volunteered to host her nominating
convention.

The plan was to have her board a campaign train
in Los Angeles and make a series of speeches en
route to Omaha, and when she got there she would
inaugurate their new coliseum. I thought it was a
great idea. Gracie had been stumping the country for
years; this was an opportunity to do it in person. She
didn't want to do it. She didn't think she could do
it. Gracie disliked making speeches, even to small
groups, and certainly didn't want to make a series
of them. I thought it was too good an opportunity to
turn down, and I did everything I could to talk her
into it. Only when her sister Hazel and Mary Kelly
and our entire writing staff agreed to come along on
the train did she decide to try it.

And then I began worrying that maybe she
wouldn't be able to do it. This was a far more elaborate event than standing in front of some paintings
or not playing the piano; this required her to make
as many as twenty speeches to thousands of people
from the rear platform of a caboose. I'd seen her

do so many difficult things, I'd talked her into doing so many difficult things, that it just hadn't occurred to me that she might not be able to do it. Maybe this was too much; maybe this was too physically draining for her. I didn't know and I was concerned.

Neither Gracie nor I were interested in politics. Gracie read the newspapers every day and knew what was going on in the world; I knew the words to "Red Rose Rag." Gracie had her own opinions about current events, but she was never vocal about them. We never publicly supported any political candidates or made fund-raising appearances for them, although we were often asked to. In those days show-business people concentrated on show business, while politicians concentrated on giving people the business. Performers never ran for office, although some of the people who ran for office turned out to be performers.

The only politicians Gracie ever cared about were the Kennedys. Not because she agreed with their policies—maybe she did—but because they were Irish Catholics. Gracie was very proud of her heritage, and the thought that an Irishman could be President of the United States absolutely thrilled her.

Gracie's campaign for the presidency began when First Lady Eleanor Roosevelt invited her to Washington, D.C., as the guest of honor of the National Woman's Press Club. While in Washington, Gracie promised that if elected she would change the D.C. to A.C. so that her clock would work. She also visited the Capitol and was taken to the statuary hall echo spot, a place where a person speaking in a very low voice can be heard forty or fifty feet away. As reporters listened, Gracie whispered to Mary Kelly, "Is my nose shiny?"

Her campaign began seriously . . . well, her campaign began, when she returned to California. Her campaign song, "Vote for Gracie," was published and she held her first press conference.

"Vote for Gracie," the song began, "vote for Gracie/ She's the best little skipper in the land. Vote for Gracie, vote for Gracie/Won't you please give this little girl a hand.

"Even big politicians don't know what to do/ Gracie doesn't know either. But neither do you, so, vote for Gracie to win the Presidential racie.

"A hundred million strong, that's right, you can't go wrong/ Vote for Gracie and keep voting all day long."

At the press conference Gracie announced that her first official act as President would be to settle the California-Florida boundary dispute. She also promised to give the East Coast a rebate of 25 percent of California's climate, and absolutely refused to eradicate the national debt, pointing out that we should be very proud of it because it's the biggest in the world. When asked her opinion of the Neutrality Bill then being debated in Congress, she stated flatly, "If we owe it, let's pay it." She also told reporters that "if elected, I will do what Mr. Dionne did when the nurse told him he was the father of quintuplets. I'll demand a recount!" Walter Winchell decided that her promises were not nearly as funny as those being made by the Democrats and Republicans.

The whistle-stop tour began on May 9, 1940, with the train whistle rigged to play the opening bars of "Vote for Gracie." Nothing like this had ever been attempted before, so we were all quite apprehensive. We didn't know if anyone would actually turn out to greet the train, and I had no idea how Gracie would react to the pressure. If the stress caused her to get a migraine, we would have to curtail much of the tour.

When the train began to slow down outside Riverside, California, our first scheduled stop, Gracie decided she couldn't do it. She was just too nervous. I sat with her and tried to calm her down, but she really wanted to cancel the whole thing. It took all of her friends to convince her to make this first speech and then see how she felt about it, and I agreed that if it didn't go well we'd cancel the rest of the stops and go directly to Omaha.

More than three thousand people were waiting for the train when we arrived in Riverside. And when Gracie stepped onto the rear platform, standing right above her campaign slogan—a kangaroo holding a baby in her pouch and declaring, ''It's in the bag''— they gave her a huge ovation. That seemed to help her relax, but she was still unusually hesitant as she began reading her campaign speech. ''As I look around and see all these trusting and believing faces shining up at me with love and respect,'' she told the hushed crowd, ''tears come into my eyes. And do you know why? My girdle is killing me.'' The laughter from the crowd really calmed her down. In the speech Gracie promised to provide old age for people with pensions, advocated bigger farms ''so asparagus can grow lying down,'' and welcomed foreign relations, ''but they have to bring their own bedding!''

In conclusion, Gracie declared, ''The reason we need a woman in the presidential chair is to pave the way for other political jobs for women, such as lady senators and lady congressmen. And anybody knows that a woman is much better than a man when it comes to introducing bills in the house.''

The train stopped in thirty-four cities and towns on the way to Omaha. In Las Vegas we rode in a long torchlight parade—they made me drive an ox-cart. In the parade held in Salt Lake City they made me drive a midget racing car. During the torchlight parade in Cheyenne I had to drive a stagecoach. Gracie was running, but I was getting exhausted. At nearly every stop schools were closed and stores held sales in Gracie's honor, which I thought was particularly appropriate. Along the campaign trail Gracie was given boxes of oranges, Colorado trout packed in ice, doughnuts, a lamb, a rabbit, a pig, even a descented skunk to symbolize her opponents, a beautiful Indian war bonnet, several carved trophies and hand-woven rugs and blankets.

A total of more than two hundred fifty thousand people turned out to meet the train. Gracie shook countless hands and kissed hundreds of baby girls, explaining, ''I won't kiss male babies until they're over twenty-one.'' As the train got closer to Omaha, Gracie had become a presidential candidate, just as she had become an artist and a musician. She gave her speech forcefully and confidently, waving her hands to emphasize a point and even making her promises sound convincing. I was incredibly proud of her. It was amazing to me that she could do this. To me, she was always a fragile little girl who might fall over if the wind blew too hard. I found it hard to believe that she could control large crowds, but she was so good at campaigning that she probably could have become President—if it hadn't been for Roosevelt and Willkie.

Fifteen thousand people were waiting in a light rain to greet the Surprise Party candidate when our train arrived in Omaha. Her speech to the crowd was broadcast nationally on the NBC radio network. When Omaha Mayor Dan Butler asked her to "Call me Dan," she refused, explaining, "Everybody knows you can't say Dan on the radio."

In Omaha Gracie was given the Indian name Chief Wau-La-Shja-wa, which supposedly meant "She who says funny things." A contingent of state troopers was assigned to escort our group, just like real candidates, although I'm not sure how seriously they took their jobs. One morning a racket in the hotel hallway woke me up at two A.M. When I went outside I found Gracie's sister Hazel teaching a line of state troopers how to do the Irish reel.

On May 17, eight thousand cheering delegates nominated Gracie for the office of President of the United States. There was no nominee for Vice President, Gracie didn't want any vice on her ticket. After being officially nominated, Gracie was carried onto the floor of the coliseum on a sedan chair by twenty bearded men—a claim not even President Roosevelt could have made. The main theme of her acceptance speech, during which she kept tugging at her hips, seemed to be, "My girdle is killing me."

After the convention Harvard University announced it was endorsing Gracie, but few other institutions supported her. On election day Franklin Roosevelt won a landslide victory over Willkie and Allen, although Gracie received several thousand write-in votes and the city of Menominee, Michigan, nominated her for mayor.

Gracie was actually a pioneer among political candidates—she was probably the first politician to write a book about the lessons she learned on the campaign trail. Among the advice she offered in *How to Become President* was, "Don't go around offending people just because it can be done sitting down," and, "If you're running for office you should try to remember faces, even if you don't want to call them names," and, finally, "God is said to love the poor because he made so many of them, and we politicians should love them for the same reason. . . . But rich people have feelings which should be respected. Even stockbrokers vote, especially if it doesn't rain on Election Day and the Yankees are playing out of town."

Proceeds from the book, which was published by the Gracie Allen Self-Delusion Institute, were used to settle her campaign debts. Those debts came to about $36.75, mostly for dry cleaning after my ox-cart ride.

❦

Gracie never considered herself a satirist, but of course she was. In fact, if anyone could have parodied a satirist, she would have been the one. She was a successful painter and musician and politician, but there was still one role she played that even I found difficult to accept: cook. As part of a series about the favorite recipes of radio stars, a magazine included Gracie's recipe for mutton curry, and wrote, "This versatile comedienne is never too busy to don an apron and go in the kitchen . . . to persuade the cook to allow her to mix the batter for George's waffles. . . . She believes that the kitchen should be a laboratory charmingly equipped for creative endeavor.'' Of course, the same thing could have been said about Dr. Frankenstein's laboratory.

Gracie as a painter? Sure. A concert pianist? Why not. A candidate for President of the United States. I could even accept that. But a cook? Now, that was ridiculous.

6

In radio we had to create pictures with our words. We talked about characters and places and events and left it to our listeners to imagine what they looked like. They didn't have that limitation in motion pictures. In the movies they could show the audience anything they wanted to. They could create anything that could be imagined, from King Kong to the Garden of Eden to a flight to the moon. So naturally the first feature film we were asked to appear in, *The Big Broadcast of 1932,* took place at a radio station.

I talked Gracie into making full-length pictures. I knew she was capable of doing anything she wanted to do in show business, and the opportunity was there, so I convinced her to make one movie. If she didn't enjoy it, I promised, I wouldn't try to talk her into doing another one. In all we appeared in fourteen feature films together and she made three more without me.

Before we signed for *The Big Broadcast* they asked us to do a screen test. That meant we had to stand in front of a camera and talk. The fact that we'd made fourteen shorts in which we'd stood in front of the camera and talked made no difference. At that time Gracie had naturally black hair. It was a lovely color for her cream complexion, but on black and white film it looked very dark. The studio hair stylist asked her to lighten it, which is how Gracie became a blonde. If they had had color film in those days she could have kept her black hair, but since they had only black and white film, she had to become a blonde. Gracie didn't mind at all; that allowed her to sit in the hairdresser's chair gossiping while still being able to claim she was working.

But other than her hair color, she was an absolute natural on the screen. Gracie was a director's dream because they didn't have to direct her. That was important, because many directors were not directors. In Hollywood's early years the studios were terrified that a director would shoot all the scenes and not be able to put them together to make a movie. So they often hired people with technical expertise rather than creative skills to direct pictures. The picture might not turn out very well, but at least the studio would be able to release it. These directors knew absolutely nothing about working with actors, so if an actor hit all the right marks, they'd scream professionally, "Print it!" If an actor said all the right lines, "Print it!" If an actor did the whole scene without falling down, "Print it!" So the best thing that could be said about a lot of those early pictures was that the actors didn't fall down.

Except the Marx Brothers, of course. If they didn't fall down they had no picture.

Gracie and I actually once made a picture directed by a German who spoke almost no English. This saved a lot of time on the set because nobody knew what he was talking about. The only thing he said that everyone understood, and he said this often, was, "Dis scene mitout sound." M.O.S., Gracie used to call this, mitout sound. Years later, when Sandy began working on our television program, Gracie used to suggest to her that she do her scenes M.O.S.

Gracie and I turned out to be very good film actors. Gracie played Gracie and I didn't fall down. Usually we were typecast, we played Burns and Allen. Screenwriters had an easy time writing for us. In our first few pictures they wrote the dialogue for all the other characters until we entered, then they instructed: Burns and Allen do four minutes here. That's what they wrote for us: Burns and Allen do four minutes here. Then, later in the script they wrote: Burns and Allen do four minutes here. So writing parts for us was easy. In those first feature films we probably appeared on screen for less time than we had in the shorts, so I knew we had to be film stars because we were getting paid much more to do a lot less.

We wrote our material for those pictures, and that created a problem. The shooting schedule usually provided a full day for us to do a complete scene, but because we were used to doing shorts, we could film our whole bit in two hours. Then everybody would stand around wondering what to do to fill the remainder of the day before they could go home. Hollywood was so accustomed to dealing with temperamental stars who took much longer than scheduled that they just didn't know how to deal with actors who finished too quickly.

But Gracie came to the set prepared to work. She was always on time and knew her lines as well as everybody else's lines in her scenes. In fact, her lines were often so complicated that she depended on the other actors in the scene to give her the correct cues. If they asked the right question, Gracie could answer it wrong. But if they asked the wrong question, or asked the right question but used the wrong words, Gracie would be lost. She wouldn't know where she was in the script. The most important thing about this was that it kept me working: another one of my many skills was that I knew how to ask Gracie the right questions correctly.

Being a movie star at that time meant being temperamental. Movie stars would do anything for publicity, including refuse to work. In fact, the more some actors didn't work, the bigger stars they became. Not that that would have worked for me; it was when I worked that people got upset. Gracie was probably the least temperamental star in the business. I remember only two things she ever objected to. In 1934 we were making *We're Not Dressing* with Carole Lombard, and Paramount brought in a successful New York banker to produce the picture. Just before production began, Carole's stand-in was fired, and Carole threatened to quit the picture unless the girl got her job back.

"Let me get this straight," the banker said. "You're making one hundred thousand dollars for this picture and she's getting thirty-five dollars a week, and you're gonna quit if I don't bring her back?"

"Exactly," Carole said.

The banker brought back the stand-in.

Later that same day I went into his office and explained that Gracie suffered from migraine headaches, and her dressing room had been painted the wrong color. "She won't use that dressing room unless it's repainted powder blue," I said.

"And if we don't repaint it?"

"Then we'll have to walk."

"Let me get this straight," the banker said. "We're paying you seventy-five thousand dollars for this picture and you're gonna quit if we don't paint your dressing room powder blue?"

"Right."

"Mr. Burns," he asked, "have you ever been head of a company?"

"Nope."

He stood up and put on his hat. "Well, you are now." Then he walked out of the room and returned to the sanity of New York banking. The new producer had our dressing room painted powder blue and Gracie was very happy.

The second thing Gracie objected to was having to sing the song "Lookie, Lookie, Lookie, Here Comes Cookie," in the 1935 Paramount film *Here Comes Cookie*. The premise of this picture was that Gracie's millionaire father wanted her to pretend that the family had lost all its money so that a Spanish fortune hunter would lose interest in Gracie's sister. To accomplish this deception Gracie turned the family mansion into a home for out-of-work vaudevillians. Trick bikeriders, hillbilly bands, knife throwers, acrobats, jugglers, tumblers, a fortune-teller, flamenco dancers, drummers, a performing bear, a monkey act and a bird act, a trained dog and a trained seal act moved in and started rehearsing day and night. The film opened with the butler discovering Gracie cowering under her bed because, she explained, "Somebody told me to read Dr. Jekyll and hide."

So it's easy to understand why Gracie thought this song was too silly for her to sing. It certainly would have ruined a class picture like this one. But I thought it was a pretty good song. I talked her into singing it and it became a popular hit. Unfortunately, it's not too popular now.

Incidentally, I tried to get the role of the trained seal for my old partner. He barked for the part, but they hired a younger, sexier animal. It's one of the old show-business axioms, no matter how successful you've been, there's always a younger and sexier seal coming along.

We had no difficulty making a successful transition to feature films. I was just as popular in full-length movies as I'd been in vaudeville and on radio. "Gracie Allen is at her best in 'Here Comes Cookie,' " a New York critic wrote about us.

" 'Many Happy Returns,' is the nuttiest picture that has struck Broadway in a good long spell," another critic wrote about that 1934 movie.

"Chief contributor to the laughter of 'College Swing' is Gracie Allen," *The Hollywood Reporter* said, "who has grown up in school because she's never been able to pass an examination. When she inherits the school she proceeds to revamp it on more modern and swingier lines. Gracie sings a song, 'You're a Natural,' by Frank Loesser and Manning Sherwin, and she dances an Irish reel . . . all with marked success. Partner George Burns is in too . . ." Look, I was good, but even I didn't think I was that good.

Gracie enjoyed being in movies, although she didn't particularly enjoy making them. Making movies may not require any heavy lifting, but it's still hard work. Gracie's lines were particularly difficult to remember because they were so confusing; they even confused her before she made nonsense out of them. And she had to be on the set for makeup at six-thirty in the morning, sometimes after having done the radio show the night before. But probably the most difficult thing of all for her was sitting on a movie set and waiting. Waiting two thousand years for the Lord is one thing; waiting six hours for a temperamental actress to be satisfied her hair was in place was much tougher. Gracie hated wasting time, but she really hated wasting time doing nothing on a movie set when she could have been doing something important, like shopping. Between takes she'd usually stay in her dressing room reading. She read everything, but she loved philosophy and trashy novels. I always figured that reading one helped her understand the other.

More than anything else, I think, Gracie found making movies to be very boring. There just wasn't enough for her to do. Making them, not watching them, she never got bored watching movies. Gracie was a big movie fan. She never liked to watch herself on screen because she was never satisfied with her performance, but she liked almost everything else. She liked sad movies best. Sad movies made her cry, and that made her very happy. The sadder the movie, the more she cried, the happier she was.

The thing Gracie liked best about making pictures was that it enabled her to work with movie stars. She was in awe of movie stars. It never occurred to her that if she wanted to see a real movie star all she had to do was look in the mirror. Well, first she'd have to push me out of the way, then look in the mirror. But during our career in the movies we worked with everyone from Crosby and Benny and

Bob Hope to Carole Lombard, Bela Lugosi and W.C. Fields.

Although Gracie knew she was absolutely nothing like the dizzy character she portrayed, she still seemed surprised to discover that her favorite movie stars were also different from their screen images. She was always telling me things like, "You know, Robert Taylor isn't anything like he is on the screen," and, "Can you imagine, Bela Lugosi is so nice." Of course, it wasn't difficult for Lugosi to be nicer in person than he was on the screen. If you met him and he didn't take a bite out of your neck, he was nicer than he was on the screen.

Gracie was so scandalized by the things Carole Lombard would do that she loved spending time with her. Carole Lombard was pretty and funny and, as my mother might say, she had some mouth on her. Carole would start to say something to the director and Gracie would whisper to me, "She's not really going to say that, is she?" And after she'd said it, Gracie would say, "She didn't really say that, did she?" And finally, as soon as possible, Gracie would call Orry-Kelly or one of her friends to report what Carole Lombard had said. "And then she called him an old bastard," Gracie would quote her, then quickly add, "Oh, I didn't say that, Carole did."

We made several films with W.C. Fields and eventually became good friends. But the first picture we made with him, *International House,* was only our second full-length feature and we were both intimidated by him. We'd report to the set in the morning and he'd be sitting in a corner with his script memorizing his lines for the day's shooting. "Good morning, Mr. Fields," I'd say and he'd just grumble something in response. Gracie was thrilled to find out that he was just as nice in person as he was on the screen.

In the movie Gracie and Fields did a scene in which she played a waitress serving him breakfast. She had the last line in the scene, then exited, leaving Fields sitting there. Fields wanted to finish the scene with a line or a piece of business, but nobody could suggest anything that he liked.

Then I had an idea. "Look," I suggested, "you've got a cup of coffee, a glass of water, and a martini on the table. As soon as Gracie leaves, why don't you drop two cubes of sugar in the water, stir the coffee, and drink the martini."

Fields stared at me coolly, then nodded in agreement. "You know," he said, "this is the first time I ever liked a straight man."

While we were filming a scene for that picture one afternoon, the entire set started shaking violently. "Everybody be calm," Fields directed. "Just be calm."

"Quake!" a technician screamed. "Quake!" Then everybody started running, with Fields leading the pack.

Gracie's sister Bessie was visiting the set that day and I grabbed her hand and we ran outside. As soon as we got out of the building I began looking for Gracie. I couldn't find her. I figured she was still inside, so I ran back into the building. She was standing very calmly inside a prop elevator.

"What do you think you're doing?" I screamed at her. "C'mon outside!"

By the time we got back outside Fields was nervously reassuring everyone, "Don't be nervous, don't be nervous."

Gracie realized I was furious with her. "What's

the matter, Nattie,'' she asked. "When there was an earthquake in San Francisco they always made us stand under a doorway or something firm so that nothing could fall on us.''

"That's right, Googie, that's what you're supposed to do. But you were standing in a fake elevator. The only thing over your head was the heavy klieg lights.''

It took her a few seconds to comprehend what I was talking about, and when she did, she started giggling, covering her mouth with her fingertips. "Oh my,'' she said, "I guess I wasn't very safe at all, was I?''

She was some wonderful character.

In *International House* I played a doctor and Gracie played my nurse, which was, of course, another significant change for us. Early in the movie the great character actor Franklin Pangborn arrived at my office and asked Gracie, "To what do you attribute your smartness?''

"Three things,'' she answered smartly. "First, my good memory and . . . and the other two I forgot.''

Aaaah yes, as Mr. Fields would have opined, a truly significant change.

The picture both Gracie and I enjoyed making the most was *Damsel in Distress*, a musical comedy starring Fred Astaire based on a P. G. Wodehouse story. RKO asked Paramount to lend us to that studio for this movie, and we really wanted to make it. It was the first film Astaire had done without Ginger Rogers in several years; the musical score had been written by George and Ira Gershwin—it was the last complete score George Gershwin had written before his death—and featured such wonderful songs as "A Foggy Day,'' and "Nice Work If You Can Get It,'' and it was to be directed by George Stevens. Paramount agreed, but before RKO signed us for the film they wanted us to dance for Fred Astaire and get his approval. That made me a little nervous. I was only a slightly better dancer than a singer, and Astaire might well have been the greatest hoofer who ever lived. I knew Gracie could stay close to him; I wasn't sure I could.

Then I remembered a vaudeville team named Evans and Evans who used to do a popular act in which they danced with whisk brooms. I didn't know how good I'd look trying to keep pace with Fred Astaire, but I knew I'd be great compared to a whisk broom. So I invited one of the Evanses to come to California to teach the whisk-broom dance to me and Gracie.

We spent hours in our backyard next to the pool learning the dance. Not only did we get very good at it, we ended up with the cleanest pool deck in Southern California. When we demonstrated the dance for Fred Astaire, he not only hired us, he thought the brooms were so good he also put them in the picture. So Gracie and I ended up teaching Fred Astaire how to dance.

As we signed our contracts, all I could think about was how good this was going to be for our careers. Dancing with Astaire to music by the Gershwins, directed by George Stevens in a story by Wodehouse, playing real characters rather than doing four-minute segments as Burns and Allen. Not bad for two vaudeville comics. Gracie thought it was unbelievable too—the worst dancer in her family starring in a Fred Astaire movie.

Astaire was as nice as his screen image. In the picture we had to do an elaborate sequence that took place at an amusement park, during which we danced on a whirling turntable, over rolling barrels, down a slide, and finally in front of funhouse mirrors that distorted our images and cut off our bodies above the knees. Trying to dance on that turntable was like trying to dance on a rapidly spinning record. It was very tough and I think Fred was concerned about making Gracie and me comfortable. So on the first day of rehearsals, as Gracie trailed him around the turntable, he suddenly slipped and fell. I don't know if he did it on purpose or not, but I do know that Fred Astaire fell down more gracefully than I danced. Gracie helped him get up and we went back to work. But after that we were no longer worried about making mistakes—if Fred Astaire fell down, what could anyone possibly expect from Burns and Allen?

He worked incredibly hard to make it look so easy. And he was such a great dancer that when he finished rehearsing, the crew would give him an ovation. We worked as hard as we'd ever worked before just trying to keep up with him. The dance at the amusement park was one of the most complex scenes ever filmed, requiring countless retakes. Gracie never complained, never said a single word; I think she was still amazed that the worst dancer in the entire Allen family was performing with Fred Astaire.

By the end of the day we were exhausted. For a while we went to the screening of the dailies, the showing of the film we'd just shot, but one night I looked over at Gracie and she had fallen asleep. I'd never seen her fall asleep in public before, even when I sang, so from that night on we always went right home at the conclusion of the day's shooting. That was probably the first time I realized that Gracie couldn't do everything.

Gracie did four or five dances with Fred Astaire, including the whisk-broom number, and made her sisters proud. Don't take my word for it, not while I'm holding a lit cigar, but *Time* magazine wrote, "Far more facile as an Astaire partner (than Joan Fontaine) is, of all people, rumpish Radio Dunce Gracie Allen." And a New York newspaper critic wrote, "Gracie and George go into several dance routines with Mr. Astaire, matching him step for step in one of the liveliest and merriest sequences in the picture. The gadgets . . . of the fun house are employed in one of the most unusual routines invented for the cinema. Miss Allen, moreover, is extremely pretty, and is quite as fetching, in spite of her loony sayings, as some of the glamour girls who could be mentioned."

At least I got better notices than the whisk brooms.

When the film came out, RKO suggested that theater owners promote it by putting mice in a cage in the lobby and advertising, "These waltzing mice are trying to imitate Fred Astaire and Burns and Allen doing 'The Fun House Dance' from *Damsel in Distress.*"

❦

I picked the films we would make. For example, I decided we would appear in *College Humor,* and *College Holiday,* and *College Swing.* For two people who never went to college, Gracie and I spent a lot of time on campus. When we were making *College Swing* with those crazy college kids, Bob Hope and Betty Grable, we announced the last annual Gracie Allen Award for Ingenuity. "Any smart boy can graduate from college if his grades are high enough,'' Gracie explained. "The really deserving boy is the one who gets his diploma, his 'skin,' with the lowest possible grades.'' So rather than giving a sheepskin, we gave a bearskin to the boy graduating from an American college with the lowest grades. We received thousands of entries; we probably would have gotten many more, but a lot of contestants got the address wrong.

I also turned down a lot of pictures. I turned down an offer to costar with the Marx Brothers in *Duck Soup*. I told them that I wanted to be in a picture about food, we would have done *Tortilla Flat*.

Speaking of food, in 1938 mystery writer S.S. Van Dine had published *The Gracie Allen Murder Case*, featuring his famed detective, Philo Vance, as well as Gracie and me. Gracie publicly claimed that she could never understand why a man would spend a year writing a novel when he could buy one for only two dollars, but privately she was very pleased by the compliment. When Paramount decided to turn the book into a movie, I suggested they eliminate my character. Nobody argued. *The Gracie Allen Murder Case* became the first film Gracie made by herself, although I was on the set with her every day.

In a master stroke of typecasting, she played Gracie Allen, the dizzy niece of the owner of a perfume company who becomes involved in a murder case when an employee of the company is accused of killing Benny the Buzzard. With Gracie on the case it really was murder for Philo Vance, or Fido, as she called him. She had all the answers. For example, although the victim had been murdered elsewhere, his body had been found in a nightclub.

"Why would the killer bring the body here?" a

police detective wondered, until Gracie pointed out, "They have a wonderful floor show."

At one point this police detective tries to explain to the other cops on the case exactly how much help Gracie has been to him. "This Allen dame is driving me crazy," he says. " 'The man was shot. The knife was found alongside him.' Who do you think poisoned him? 'Nobody, he hung himself.' How do you know he hung himself? 'The gas jet was wide open.' Was there much gas? 'He was cut from ear to ear.' Was he bleeding? 'Every bone in his body was broken; he'd been in the water for fourteen hours. The worst case of dandruff I've ever seen.' Was he dead? 'Well, if he wasn't he told me a lie.' I'm telling you, she's driving me crazy."

Or, as the police detective replied when Gracie announced she was going to plead temporary insanity, "You should."

After playing Mrs. North in the 1941 film *Mr. and Mrs. North,* Gracie made a brief appearance in *Two Girls and a Sailor* in 1944, performing her "One-Finger Concerto." That was the last movie she made, and I had to talk her into doing even that small bit. She had always disliked having to get up while it was still dark outside so she could rush to the studio and spend all day inside waiting, and after that picture she told me quite firmly that she didn't intend to make any more movies.

I told her that if she didn't want to make any more movies, she wouldn't make any more movies. But I didn't say a word about television.

I understood how she felt. We certainly didn't need the money, she was already one of the most famous and beloved women in America, and she was involved in many other things that were more important to her than making movies. The radio program was still among the most popular programs on the air, the kids were growing up, Saks was constantly receiving new shipments of merchandise, and in addition to making numerous appearances at military camps and hospitals, she was an active member of an American Women's Volunteer Service.

A couple of nights each week she would put on her AWVS uniform and join other women in making sandwiches and driving up and down the coast distributing food and coffee to coast watchers. Everyone in California was worried that Japanese submarines would try to land saboteurs and spies on our beaches, and it was the job of these men to make sure that didn't happen. In addition to entertaining the troops, Gracie's real contribution to the war effort was letting someone else drive when they made the deliveries.

The AWVS did an excellent job and Gracie was proud to be a member. But I have to admit, I thought she looked real cute in her snazzy uniform and little cap. Maybe that's a sexist remark, but at my age talking about it is about as close as I can get to the real thing.

The soldiers loved Gracie. She wasn't exactly a pinup, she was more of a glue-up. But as she often reminded me, nobody laughed at Rita Hayworth the way they laughed at her. For a while we wrote a weekly letter to Gracie's mythical brother, who was supposedly in service for the duration. The letter was posted on bulletin boards at nearly every military base in the country, and in response soldiers wrote us thousands of letters describing the humorous things that happened to them in the service. Most of the letters were very short. I read so many of them that it wasn't until years after the war that I realized "damn Sergeant" was two words.

※

Gracie never missed making movies. She didn't even want to appear in home movies. I think that after a while the one thing she wanted to get out of show business was to get out of show business. I know that the main reason she kept working was to keep me happy. She didn't need it, she'd accomplished everything she'd set out to do; she had head-lined the bill at the Palace and she'd had her picture on a lobby card outside the San Francisco Orpheum Theatre. I think what she really wanted more than anything else was the one thing we'd never had time to have together: a normal life.

When Gracie wasn't working she loved spending time with friends. She loved that even more than shopping. Even more than shopping at Saks. Even more than shopping at Saks for furs! Gracie had more friends than anyone in Hollywood. Everyone who met her adored her. She had the gift of making peo-ple feel they were very special to her, even while she was revealing very little of herself. In other words, she was a great listener. Maybe the role she enjoyed playing most of all was hostess, because there always seemed to be a crowd at our house for dinner or a party.

We threw a lot of parties. At the beginning of every party Gracie would stand by the door and per-sonally greet every guest. She made a point of re-membering everybody's name and a few personal things about them, so that everybody felt like they were a special guest. I made a point of remembering to order the ice.

I got the opportunity to sing at our parties. That's probably why we threw a lot of parties. One night, I remember, we had a party for about one hundred people in the backyard. There was always some reason for our parties. Planting season had started, the new fall outfits had arrived at Saks, the reason was never important. The usual group was at this party; the Cantors, the Bennys, Blossom Seeley and Benny Fields, Block and Sully, Jolson and Ruby Keeler, Flo and Jack Haley, Orry-Kelly, Cary Grant, Jessel. We had a great piano player that night. If you have a good piano player, guests will fight to get up to entertain. Of course, that was often the only way they could get me to sit down.

I never asked our guests to sing at our parties. I thought that was rude—if they wanted to sing let them throw their own party. But on this night, after I'd sung five or twelve of my favorite old songs, Jolson stood up and asked, "Nat, mind if I sing a song?"

How could anyone turn down the greatest entertainer who ever lived? "Go ahead, Jolie," I said, "but only one."

"Nattie!" Gracie scolded, "please . . ."

It was too late. Jolie was so insulted that he grabbed Ruby Keeler's hand and practically pulled her out the door. I ran right after them, right out the door, singing.

Undoubtedly the biggest party Gracie and I ever threw was in honor of Mary Livingstone's birthday and the new house she and Jack were building in Beverly Hills. It was such a wonderful party that I even let other people perform. We covered the swimming pool with a portable dance floor and thousands of gardenias, erected a huge tent in the backyard, and invited two hundred fifty people, among them Ginger Rogers, Edward G. Robinson, Eddie and Ida Cantor, the Don Ameches and Joe E. Browns, Dolores and Bob Hope, Robert and Betty Young, the Pat O'Briens, Cesar Romero, the Ed Sullivans, Louella Parsons and Doc Martin, the Marx Brothers and their wives, Ray Milland, Joan Blondell and Dick Powell—practically anybody in Hollywood looking for a free meal.

Gracie worried more about this party than she usually did about the show, probably because the party was more important to her. She wanted it to be absolutely perfect, and it was pretty close, but I was paying for it so I was going to sing anyway. It took twelve tentmen, four truckers, a draper, and two janitors to erect the tent and the false flower-gardens we installed for the evening. The cake was a perfect replica of the Bennys' new home, which in fact was a replica of our new home, complete with shrubbery, trees, and even a porch light. Mary amused guests by walking around all evening asking, "Who ate my living room?" That was actually pretty funny for Mary. She must have brought along a writer.

We hired a seven-piece orchestra and several acts to entertain our guests, including a dress designer who opened the show by bringing out several models in lingeries and proceeding to dress them. Worst finish I ever saw in show business. After the paid entertainment was done, our guests began performing. Groucho Marx, Harry Ruby, and Bert Kalmar sang the famous "Doctor Quackenbush." Fanny Brice as Baby Snooks sang "Dainty, Dainty Me." Ethel Merman rattled the tent by singing "With You on My Mind." I sang several songs. When finished singing, Ted Lewis asked, "Is evvvvv—rebody happy?" and everybody was. Blossom Seeley sang "After You've Gone." Finally Jack Benny, who had served as master of ceremonies, decided to sing. Jack rarely sang in public, and with good reason. But he was in such a wonderful mood this night that he decided to make an exception. So as he opened his mouth and the first notes came out, I shouted loudly, "Waiter, check please!"

"Nattie—please!" Gracie shouted.

Too late. Jack couldn't stop laughing. That ended his singing career.

On rare occasions Gracie would perform at our parties. Gracie almost never drank, but every once in a while she'd have more than one, then she would ask songwriter Sylvia Fine, Danny Kaye's wife, to play the piano for her, and would stand up and dance the hula. Gracie could do all the new dances, she could rhumba and she could samba, but the dance she liked most was the hula. She first saw it done when we went to Honolulu in 1939 to make a film, and as soon as we got back she organized a small group to take hula lessons at Dick Powell's house. She was very good at it, too, so good that I think it would be fair to say that Gracie was the finest Irish hula dancer in Beverly Hills.

❧

Dinner was always a big social occasion, either at our place, a restaurant, or someone else's house. Gracie and I spent an awful lot of wonderful nights together. We lived down the block from Louella Parsons and her husband, Doc Martin, and they often came over for dinner. They were both very religious and they often brought priests with them. Doc always liked to drink, and one night I thought he'd had too much and I said, "You know, you might have to operate in the morning. Maybe you'd better quit."

"Are you kidding?" he protested. "I'm so sober I could jump right over your bar without touching a single one of your glasses."

That's a tough etiquette question: Does a good host let his guest jump over his bar?

"You don't have to do that," I said. "I'll give you another drink."

"No, watch," he told me, backing up into the living room so he could get a good running start. I will say this for him: the very next day he replaced every single broken glass.

Rosemary Clooney and José Ferrer came to dinner another evening. Before we sat down, I mixed a round of martinis. I put crushed ice in the glasses, then stirred some gin and vermouth. José Ferrer said, "That's no way to make a martini."

"No?" I said. I'd been making martinis for a long time, but maybe there was a better way. "How do *you* make them?"

"Give me the biggest snifter you've got," he said, moving behind the bar. He poured some gin and vermouth into a glass, but didn't add any ice. Then he began gently rocking the glass. Eventually he added just a little ice. It took him, and I'm not smoking my cigar, exactly forty minutes to make the martinis.

Maybe a month later Gracie and I went to his house for dinner. When we got there he asked me if I wanted him to mix me a martini. "No, you'd better not," I said. "I'm scheduled to play Vegas in two weeks."

Actually, I liked José Ferrer. We had a lot in common. He was married to a singer, Rosemary Clooney, but when we went to his house, he got up and sang all night.

After we got to know W.C. Fields, he would occasionally come to the house for a fine repast. Bill Fields and Gracie liked each other a lot, and he really enjoyed making risqué remarks and watching her blush. It was well known that whenever Fields went to someone's house for dinner, he wore a four-pocket vest with a small bottle of gin in each pocket, in case of emergency. His host not having a supply of his brand was considered an emergency. Gracie always made sure we had a full supply of his brand. The first time he came for dinner, I took his coat and told him he wouldn't need his vest, we'd stocked as much gin as he could drink.

Hearing that, he opened the front door and shouted to his chauffeur, "Clarence, my good man, take the vest. I shall be getting my libation from another source."

We were very close friends with Ronald Reagan and Jane Wyman when they were married. In fact, the only time Gracie's headaches prevented her from doing the radio show, we asked Jane Wyman to play her part. We'd see them so often that our kids called him Uncle Ronnie. Whenever we got together, Janie would sing and Ronnie would discuss politics. I didn't pay any attention to him; I wasn't interested in politics, I was interested in harmonizing with Jane Wyman. Looking back on those days, there is only one thing I regret: if Gracie and I had known Ronnie was going to become President of the United States, we wouldn't have served meat loaf so often.

I can't remember who our guests were for the

worst dinner we ever served, but I remember the dinner. We were sitting at the table waiting for our butler to serve when we heard the cook screaming at him in the kitchen. Gracie tried to avoid unpleasant things, so she ignored the screaming and began speaking louder.

Finally our butler came out of the kitchen, carrying a beautifully garnished serving tray. That was it, just garnish on a serving tray. He'd completely forgotten to put the meat on the tray. When he leaned over to serve me, I got a whiff of the alcohol on his breath, and it became obvious why he'd forgotten the meat.

"Didn't you forget something?" I asked him.

He puzzled over that question for a minute, then realized what I was talking about. "Oh, excuse me," he said, and moved over to serve Gracie. He thought I meant he was supposed to serve the women at the table first. It was only after he'd picked up the serving fork and noticed he had nothing to stick it into that he understood what I meant. Then he started laughing, and then he tried to stop laughing, and the more he tried to stop laughing the harder he laughed. He laughed all the way back to the kitchen, and when the cook saw him laughing, she started screaming at him again.

Later in the evening I made the mistake of asking him to serve me some seltzer. He did manage to find the seltzer bottle. It was the old-fashioned type with a spritzer. He tilted the bottle over my glass and pressed the trigger—splashing the seltzer out of the glass into my face. He was so horrified he could barely laugh.

One of the advantages of being known as comedians was that whenever anything went wrong at our house people assumed we were doing it on purpose. As far as our guests that evening were concerned, Burns and Allen were putting on a show just for them. It was sort of discouraging to realize that even my butler got more laughs than I did.

Without doubt Carol Channing and her husband, Charlie Lowe, were responsible for the most memorable dinner we ever had at the house. Both Gracie and I believed the two greatest actors in show business were Alfred Lunt and Lynn Fontanne. They were Broadway stars, members of the Actors Guild and the Players Club, and they had to do only one show a night; while we belonged to the Friars Club and had to do at least two shows. Gracie considered them the gods of the theater. Whenever they opened on Broadway we sent them flowers, and we tried to see every show they did. But we didn't dare go backstage to meet them. We just didn't feel comfortable about that. So, in fact, we'd never met them.

One Saturday we were having a small dinner party for ten people, including Carol and Charlie. Lunt and Fontanne were ending a national tour in Los Angeles, and early that afternoon Charlie phoned and asked Gracie's permission to bring them to dinner. Bring Lunt and Fontanne to dinner? Gracie wondered if we had time to paint the house. She started getting dressed even before she'd hung up the phone. She literally started getting ready about three in the afternoon, putting on her makeup, then taking it off; putting it on, taking it off. She wanted to look perfect.

What we didn't know, of course, was that Lunt and Fontanne were just as nervous about meeting us as we were about meeting them. While Gracie was playing with her makeup, Lynn Fontanne was trying to decide what to wear. By seven o'clock she had tried on every dress she had with her and was starting again. Finally, she later told us, she took two quick shots of scotch and put on the first dress she grabbed.

Meanwhile, at our house, Gracie was trying to figure out what she could talk to them about. She didn't think we would have anything in common. "It'll be fine, Googie," I insisted. "Don't worry about it." What else could I tell her? Tell them we just played the Jefferson Theatre? Finally, her makeup was fixed, the table was set, our other guests had arrived, and the bell rang. Gracie was even more nervous than she was before facing an audience, but we went to answer the door together. Alfred Lunt was standing directly in front of her when she opened it.

"Good evening," she said, as coolly as a queen.

"I'm glad you're dizzy," Alfred Lunt replied, "because boys like dizzy girls."

"And I'm glad you're glad," Gracie immediately responded, "because I like boys."

"And I'm glad that you're glad that I'm glad . . ." Alfred Lunt continued.

Gracie joined in, "I'm glad that you're glad . . ." The two of them went into the living room, his arm around her shoulder, laughing as if they'd been friends forever. I followed with Lynn and Carol and Charlie.

When we went into the dining room to sit down for dinner, Gracie realized she'd been so nervous that she'd forgotten to add two places at the table for the Lunts. She handled it so well, though. She looked at the table and said, "Oh, dear, how silly of me. I've forgotten to set places for Nattie and myself.''

We didn't always eat at home. We were often invited to our friends' homes or ate at clubs like the Trocadero, the Brown Derby, Chasen's, the Mocambo, and Ciro's in Los Angeles, or "21" and The Stork Club in New York. Once, when we were working in a show with Eddie and Ida Cantor and Georgie Jessel in Chicago, we were all invited to dinner at Al Capone's home. Fortunately, we were free that night. Believe me, we were free that night.

Capone had a beautiful house and about a dozen of the biggest butlers I'd ever seen. There were about twenty people at dinner, and after we'd finished eating Capone asked if anyone felt like entertaining. Twenty hands went up. I don't think it would be accurate to say that our routine killed our audience.

Gracie fulfilled a lifelong fantasy one night at Ciro's when we had dinner with Charlie Chaplin. Chaplin was very quiet, he just laughed at all the right places. At dinner, Capone was funnier than Chaplin.

I remember one night when we had dinner at The Stork Club with the Prince of Wales, who'd just given up the British throne to marry a divorced commoner, Wallis Simpson. We actually had very little in common with the former King of England. He'd never even heard of the Jefferson Theatre. We didn't even have anything in common with the commoner. I'll tell you, Al Capone was funnier than the Prince of Wales too. I told Jack Benny stories. As I later reminded Gracie, at least I had the good sense not to ask them what it felt like to be canceled at the Palace.

I think I'd better light another cigar.

Gracie and I spent a lot of time with Georgie Jessel. One night, I remember, we met him for dinner at a restaurant, and by the time we got there he'd already had too much to drink.

"What's the matter with you, Georgie?" I asked. "How come you're drinking so much?"

"Didn't you hear the news?"

"No," I said. "What news?"

"Norma Talmadge left me."

"Georgie," Gracie said patiently, "Norma Talmadge left you twenty years ago."

"I know," he agreed, "but I still miss her."

Norma Talmadge had run away to Florida with a doctor. As Jessel often told us, he'd been so upset that he'd gotten a pistol and flown down there to fight for her. When he found them, he'd taken a shot at the doctor. He missed, but the bullet hit a Japanese gardener working more than a block away. In court, the judge asked Jessel, "How can you aim at a doctor and hit a gardener working on the next block?"

"Your honor," Jessel explained, "I'm a comedian, not Buffalo Bill."

In Romanoff's one night Gracie and I were having dinner with the Cantors, the Bennys, and Jessel and his date. When the check came, Jessel grabbed it and said, "Let me take care of it."

Jack Benny applauded.

"That's not necessary, Georgie," I said. "It's too expensive. Let's just split it four ways."

"No, I insist," he insisted.

"He insists," Jack Benny said. "Don't embarrass him."

But when Jessel took out his wallet to pay the bill he discovered that he didn't have enough cash. This was long before the existence of credit cards. So he asked me to lend him $90.

"Georgie, listen," I repeated, "why don't we just split it?"

"Absolutely not," he said. "I said I was going to pay the check and I'm going to pay the check. Now are you going to loan me ninety bucks or not?"

And that's how it cost me $90 to be treated to dinner by Georgie Jessel.

❧

Gracie would do almost anything to help a friend. When Mary Kelly was having problems, for example, Gracie hired her as radio's first, and only, stand-in, then later hired her as a secretary with nothing to do, and had her move into our house. When a man she had worked with in vaudeville was sick and broke, she had me hire him as our mailroom supervisor in New York—and we didn't have a mailroom in New York. When our doctor, Rex Kennamer, wanted to see *My Fair Lady* at the absolute peak of its success, she convinced the theater manager to break every fire law by putting a folding chair in the aisle so that he could sit next to her. When Blossom Seeley was having a tough time late in life, she'd write asking for assistance, and Gracie would always send a check—although she couldn't understand why, if Blossom needed money, she'd spend six cents on an airmail stamp asking for it rather than sending it first class for three cents. She even made sure we always found small parts for Larry Reilly, who wouldn't give her a billing in vaudeville. But she was no pushover. She may have been a little reserved, even a little shy, but she never allowed anyone to be rude to her or to take advantage of her good nature.

Gracie had some enemies. She had a mental list of people she didn't like and, as she used to explain, "When someone gets on my list it's very difficult to get off." Actress Myrna Loy was at the top of the list. Actually, Gracie was a big fan of hers until an afternoon in 1935 that we spent with Marion Davies at William Randolph Hearst's famed castle, San Simeon. I'll tell you how big that place was—Hearst had three bridges over his swimming pool. Gracie and Marion were talking, and Myrna Loy came over and interrupted Gracie in the middle of a sentence without apologizing.

"Myrna," Marion Davies said correctly, "do you know Gracie Allen?"

"Yes," Myrna Loy replied. "I've met her." Then she turned and walked away. So she was now at the top of the list. Later, Gracie told me, "Now, whenever I watch the 'Thin Man' pictures, I only watch William Powell."

Vaudeville comedian Frank Fay was also on the list. We were headlining a bill with him, and at the end of the show, the three of us came onstage to take a final bow. I was standing between them, and Fay made several extremely complimentary remarks about Gracie's talent, but then, as both of them leaned forward right in front of me, he said in an exaggerated stage whisper, "But where'd you find the man?" The audience thought it was very funny, but Gracie thought Fay was being rude to me, so he made the list.

Gracie liked actor Pat O'Brien, but when he was drinking he was on her list. Gracie was extremely sensitive about Irish people who drank too much.

One of the saddest things in her life was the fact that Mary Kelly couldn't overcome her drinking problem. Eventually Gracie had to ask Mary to move out of our house, because she was worried about leaving her there with the kids when she was drinking. When Mary was married, her husband had tried to help her stop drinking. He used to search the house every day for alcohol. Unfortunately, he hated bottled water, and Mary used to replace the water in the bottle with gin and put it where he'd never find it—in the front of the refrigerator. Certainly Mary's drinking contributed to her early death. Pat O'Brien was an Irishman who liked to drink. At a testimonial dinner one night he got drunk and unruly and said some things that embarrassed Gracie's friend Louella Parsons. So when Pat O'Brien was drinking he was on the list.

The difficulty with being on Gracie's list was that most people didn't know they were on it. Gracie never liked to say anything unpleasant about anybody, so she kept the existence of this list very private. That way the people she didn't like wouldn't get mad at her.

Without doubt, our best friends in the world were Jack Benny and his wife, Mary Livingstone. Well, at least Jack was. We saw or spoke to them practically every day. Jack would often stop by our house on his way home after work, or they came for dinner, or the four of us went out together or traveled together or even worked together. Both Gracie and I loved Jack very much. I still think about him often and miss him alot.

He was going out with Mary Kelly when I met him, he and Gracie had already become good friends, and he was just starting to have some success in vaudeville as a monologist. He'd come onstage and ask the audience, "How is the show up till now?"

The orchestra leader would respond, "It's been great."

Then he'd say, "Well, I'll change that."

He was creating his character as America's stingiest man even then. He would tell audiences, "I took my girl to an expensive restaurant the other night and she got to laughing so hard she almost dropped her tray." Or, "I used to go out with a girl whose father was so stingy that when he put a penny in the weighing machine he'd put rocks in his pocket so he'd get more for his money." In reality, though, Jack was really a generous man.

We became close friends almost instantly. Jack and Gracie had a little thing they would do. Jack would say to her, "I hope I live up to your expectations, Gracie."

She would casually wave her hand at him and respond, "Oh, Jack, I'm sure you will, on account of I'm not expecting very much."

Onstage Jack Benny had more nerve than anyone in show-business history. His biggest laughs came from staring at the audience and saying nothing. The longer he said nothing, the harder the audience laughed. It was impossible for the audience to dislike his jokes, because he never told any. Jack could get more laughs without saying a single word than I could get with an entire routine. For example, I'd say to Jack, "Jack, what do you think about my singing?"

And Jack would fold him arms, stare out at the audience and say,

❀

I wish I could have said nothing like that.

Another thing I admired about Jack Benny was that he thought I was the funniest man in the world. I could make him laugh so hard that he would literally fall down and start pounding the ground with his fist. Obviously, that was very embarrassing to him, so I tried to do it only when we were in public. Then I would tell people not to be concerned, he was just having a fit.

Whenever I did anything to Jack, Gracie would pretend to be shocked, upset, and embarrassed. "Nattie, please don't," she'd say, or just warn me, "Nat-tie!" But that was her role in our relationship, and I know she enjoyed playing it just as much as Jack and I loved playing our parts.

Actually, I didn't have to do anything to make Jack Benny laugh. He made himself laugh. During dinner one night, for example, he started laughing for no apparent reason.

"What are you laughing about?" I asked. "I didn't say anything."

"I know," he said, trying to catch his breath. "I know. But you didn't say it on purpose."

I wouldn't have done that, that was his act.

I never told Jack a joke. Never. I used to break him up with my ad libs. For instance, he met me at Hillcrest one afternoon and complained, "I didn't sleep at all last night."

I asked, "How'd you sleep the night before?"

"Oh, the night before I slept great," he said.

"Good. Then try sleeping every other night."

One summer Sunday afternoon Gracie and I and Jack and Mary went to a music recital in someone's backyard. On the way there Gracie warned me to behave myself with Jack. So just as the singer was introduced, I leaned over and whispered to Jack, "Gracie wants us to behave ourselves this afternoon. So whatever you do, when the singer opens her mouth, don't start laughing." Now, how could Gracie blame me for what happened? Was it really my fault that Jack started laughing even before the singer began and we had to leave the recital?

I really didn't have to do very much to get him started. We were at the Friday night fights and I was sitting on the aisle. I bought a soft drink from a vendor and handed it to Jack, telling him to pass it along. He passed it to the next person, who passed it to the next person—in fact, it was passed down the entire row because nobody had asked for it. I didn't say a word, but I noticed Jack watching the soda as it passed from hand to hand. Only when it reached the last person in the row, who looked at it, shook his head, then handed it back to the person who'd given it to him, did Jack realize what I'd done.

Most people don't laugh that hard at fights.

Jack just made it too enticing for me to resist. He did it to himself. Okay, maybe I helped a little. We often ate at Dave Chasen's restaurant, for example, and one night Jack decided, "Let's get Dave Chasen to pick up the check tonight."

I could see this one coming. "How do we do that, Jack?"

So could Gracie. "Com'on, boys, please . . ."

"We're probably his best customers," Jack continued, "so after dinner I'll call him over and tell him, 'Dave, if George Burns pays this check I'm never coming in here again.' Then you say, 'And if Jack pays this check, *I* won't come in here again.'

You know Dave, he'll say, 'Fellas—stop fighting,' and he'll pick it up.''

Gracie knew exactly what was going to happen. She glared at me, warning me that I'd better not do what she knew I was going to do, but she didn't say a word. So after dinner Jack called Dave Chasen over to our table. "Dave," he said, "if George Burns gets this check, I'm not coming in here again." Then Jack looked at me. I smiled at him and took a long puff on my cigar. I looked at Dave Chasen and smiled. Never said a word.

Jack pounded the floor so hard that he almost dropped the check.

I was always doing little things that broke him up. I'd be driving a car and I'd see him, so I'd stop and roll down the window and call him over—as soon has he came over I'd roll up the window and drive away. That gag worked so well I only did it to him eight times. Whenever we were speaking on the telephone, I'd hang up on him in midsentence. One night we were at the Friars Club and I noticed he had a small piece of white string on his tuxedo jacket. "I'm sorry, Jack," I said as I took it off his jacket and put it on mine, "but I left my piece of white string at home. You don't mind if I borrow yours, do you?" I wore it for the rest of the night, and every time he looked at me I'd point to the string proudly and he'd burst out laughing. The next morning I put the piece of string in a little box and had it gift-wrapped, then I returned it to him with a thank-you note.

Jack pounded his own floor.

The worst thing I ever did to him took place at a party at his house. It was a lovely party, there were about one hundred fifty people there, and everybody seemed to be having a good time. But Jack took me aside and said nervously, "I don't think the party's moving."

"Sure it's moving," I told him. "Everybody's talking and drinking."

He actually started to get angry. "I'm in show business too, you know. I know if a party's moving. This one isn't."

What could I do? Tell him to take his pants off and put on a stupid hat? Absolutely. "You want to liven it up a little," I said, "here's what you do: go upstairs and take off your pants, put on one of Mary's big hats, then come downstairs in your shorts playing your violin."

That appealed to him. "You think that'll make the party move?"

"Oh yeah, sure." What else could I say? Trust me? Me? As soon as Jack went upstairs I got everybody's attention and said, "In a few minutes Jack is going to be coming downstairs in his shorts, wearing one of Mary's hats and playing the violin. When he does, don't pay any attention to him. Just ignore him completely."

A few minutes later Jack appeared at the top of the stairs, wearing his shorts and one of Mary's wide-brimmed hats, playing the violin. And everybody ignored him. It took him only a few minutes to realize he was dressed in his underwear and a woman's hat, playing the violin and being ignored by one hundred fifty people. And then he realized I'd done it to him again.

Jack pounded the floor. When he caught his breath, he looked at me and said, "*Now* the party's moving."

Onstage Jack Benny was a quiet riot. Nobody

could make me laugh as hard as he could. But he could never make me laugh offstage. And he tried, he tried very hard. In fact, Jack would make the ultimate sacrifice in his efforts to make me laugh—he would spend money.

In 1949 Gracie and I were appearing at the Palladium in London, and Jack decided he would fly to England to surprise us. We were having a small party in our hotel room when the phone rang and an "overseas operator"—we later discovered it was Janie Wyman, who was appearing in a show in there, calling from another room—informed us that Jack Benny was calling from America. I should have realized something was going on; the call wasn't collect.

Jack and I had a pleasant conversation, then he asked me to hold on. While I was holding there was a knock at the hotel room door. Gracie answered the door and discovered Jack standing there, grinning broadly. He saw me standing there holding the telephone. I just looked at him and said calmly, "Okay, you tricked me. As soon as I'm done with this phone call I'll start laughing." Then *he* started laughing. He thought the fact that I didn't laugh was one of the funniest things I'd ever done.

Jack and I may have been comedians—at least Jack was a comedian—but what happened to us in 1938 wasn't funny. In fact, it was criminal. Jack Benny and I were arrested for smuggling jewelry. Usually, when a husband buys a present for his wife, nobody makes a federal case out of it, but in this case it led to the most embarrassing thing that ever happened to me and Gracie. It really shook up Gracie.

We were having dinner at "21" one night with a charming man named Albert Chaperau and his wife.

She was wearing an unusually wide diamond bracelet. I admired it, and told them that I'd love to buy
one just like it for Gracie because it would cover
part of the scar on her arm, enabling her to wear
dresses with shorter sleeves. "I'll tell you what,"
Chaperau said. "I'll sell you this one." So while we
were sitting at dinner I wrote out a check for $2000.

Even for "21" that was an expensive dinner.

When Mary Benny heard that I'd bought Gracie a
diamond bracelet from Chaperau, she asked Jack to
surprise her with a gift. The particular surprise she
wanted was a pin Chaperau had that Jack bought for
$350.

What none of us knew was that the jewels had
been smuggled into the country. Several months after we'd bought the bracelet and the pin, Chaperau's
German maid got very upset about some anti-Nazi
remarks he'd made and reported him to the Customs
Bureau. After a brief investigation, Jack and I were
charged with possession of smuggled property.

Gracie did not make a very good gangster's moll.
She was mortified. This wasn't a cute show-business
gag, this was real. There was a distinct possibility
that Jack and I might have to serve some time in jail,
to serve as an example for other people. I offered to
promise not to buy Gracie any more jewelry, but
they insisted on prosecuting me anyway. I think, on
some level, Gracie felt that she was responsible for
all of this. That was Gracie: when something bad
happened, she would figure out a way to make it her
fault. A show wasn't too funny, a movie didn't make
a lot of money, the worldwide Depression, somehow
Gracie felt she was to blame.

I didn't think we'd go to jail, but I was worried
that our sponsor would cancel the radio show. Spon-

sors were extremely sensitive about bad publicity, and having the host of the show arrested might be considered bad publicity. What was I going to claim, that they serve Maxwell House in the jail every morning?

Benny and I hired the best criminal lawyer in Los Angeles. Our defense was that we didn't know the jewels were hot . . . smuggled. But under a strict interpretation of the law we were guilty. We did have the loot in our possession. So on the advice of my attorney I pleaded guilty to a misdemeanor in Federal Court.

The judge sentenced me to one year and one day in prison. Few things have ever shaken me up as much as hearing that sentence pronounced. Most husbands get a kiss when they give their wife a present, I got a year and a day in the Big House. But then the judge added, "I shall suspend execution of sentence during good behavior."

Sentencing took place in New York City, and I was glad Gracie had stayed in California. She was so upset by the entire matter, who knows what she would have thought when she heard the judge mention execution?

Eventually I paid almost $15,000 in fines, plus a large fee to my attorney. Jack paid $10,000. The maid received an $8500 reward. Walter Winchell reported in his newspaper column that I had been convicted of smuggling and had lost my citizenship. What'd he think they were going to do, send me back to the Lower East Side? Gracie and I were both furious, and I called him and threatened to sue him for libel if he didn't immediately retract that statement. So the following Sunday night he said on his radio show, "The newspaper columnist who reported that George Burns had lost his citizenship was mistaken.'' Of course, he never identified that columnist.

After Jack and I had paid our fines, the jewelry was returned to us. Gracie refused to wear the bracelet. She finally just gave it away; she never wanted to be reminded of my criminal career.

Not only was Gracie embarrassed, but when our contract with our sponsor expired it was not renewed. The William Morris Agency was able to find us another sponsor, but for substantially less money. In fact, after paying our cast and the band, we were just about breaking even on the show. It took us an entire season to prove that my conviction had not affected our popularity, and to get our salary back up to the level it had been before I bought Gracie a present.

❋

Quite often while Jack and I were doing something together, Gracie was spending time with Mary Benny. Professionally, Mary was known as Mary Livingstone, but her real name was Sadie Marks. She'd been working as a salesclerk in the stocking department at the May Company in Los Angeles when she met Jack, and they were married not long after Gracie and I had gotten married. I always thought Jack had married her because after Gracie and I were married he was afraid he'd have nobody to play with.

I've spent my whole life trying not to say bad things about people who couldn't defend themselves, particularly people who have passed away.

Oh, it's times like this when I really wish Mary was still alive.

Mary wasn't a bad person, she was just difficult, a little jealous, and insecure. She didn't want to have better things than her friends had, particularly Gracie; she wanted to have the same things, but more of them. And bigger.

Gracie rarely told anyone how she really felt about Mary, but one night she whispered to Jack Langdon, "Mary Benny and I are supposed to be the dearest of friends, but we're not. I love Jack and I can tolerate Mary, but there are some things about her I don't like. Every time I get anything new, she has to go out and get the same thing. Once I bought a pair of boots that I really loved and I showed them to her and she went out and bought six pairs of exactly the same boots. She always has to have more than I do. So I can't show her anything at all, and I don't think that's a good friend, do you?"

"No," Jack agreed.

"You're absolutely right, it isn't. But if you tell anyone I've said anything against Mary, I'll just say I didn't say it, and they'll believe me instead of you, so I'm safe."

That was Mary Benny, or "our Mary" as her friends lovingly referred to her. She was the complete opposite of Gracie. Gracie was very easy to please, she had everything she wanted, while Mary wanted everything she didn't have. When Gracie and I took an apartment in the Essex House, for example, Mary convinced Jack to rent a larger apartment there. When we built our house in Beverly Hills, Mary convinced Jack to build exactly the same house, using the same architect and the same builder, but a larger version. When Flo and Jack Haley put in a 45′ × 20′ swimming pool, Mary installed a 60′ × 30′ swimming pool. When I gave Gracie a fur coat, Mary made Jack give her a fur coat. Whatever anybody else had, that was what Mary wanted. Once, when Jack was playing the Capitol Theatre, a voluptuous young girl came in wearing a three-dollar shirtwaist—a blouse. This girl's figure would have made any blouse look good, but Mary decided it was the blouse that made the girl look good. A swimming pool, a fur coat, a great figure—when Mary wanted something, she tried to buy it. So she sent the girl out to buy a dozen blouses for her exactly like the one the girl had on. The only figure it changed was Jack's bank account.

The girls always used to kid Mary. Once, Gracie and Flo Haley switched the label on a hat they'd bought at Bloomingdale's with the label on a much more expensive hat they'd bought at Bonwit's. Then they asked Mary which one she liked better. Mary examined both of them carefully, looked at the labels and said, "The one from Bonwit's, natch."

Even more than possessions, though, I think Mary was envious of the attention Gracie received. When Gracie's heart started going bad she would occasionally have a fainting spell in public. Naturally when she did, everybody made a big fuss and came running to help her. So one day when Gracie and Mary were on one of their Saturday-afternoon shopping excursions, Mary fainted. Maybe she was having a problem—Mary was always on a diet—but when the ambulance came to take her to the hospital, she asked the driver to go past I. Magnin's department store so she could see what they were showing in their windows.

Gracie was very excited about Mary's fainting spell, because the ambulance driver let her ride up front and work the siren. She thought that was terrific. "I was riding way up high," she told me, "and I saw Beverly Hills like I've never seen it before!" That was Gracie too: she could head the bill at the Palace, costar with Fred Astaire, even run for President, but the thing that really got her excited was riding up front in an ambulance.

In their own way Gracie and Flo and Eva Block and Susan Marx and the rest of their little group loved Mary. They accepted her for what she was. If anyone else criticized her they would leap to her defense—but they never hesitated to remind her that sometimes she demanded too much. Flo owned the beauty parlor they all went to. They used to call it Flo Haley's House of Correction, and everybody from Lady Astor to Betty Grable went there. Sometimes Mary would come in and, no matter how busy everyone was, demand immediate attention. Apparently, demanding immediate attention in a beauty shop is about as nervy as trying to sing at my house. So whenever she did, Flo would pretend to be holding a pair of stockings over her arm and ask, "Excuse me, Mary, but do you have a pair of these in beige?"

Mary worked in Jack's stage act, on his radio show and, occasionally, on his television program. I think Mary Benny was one of the most talented performers in the business.

I'm puffing, I'm puffing.

I've often wondered if Jack knew Mary had very little talent. I think he must have, because Jack was the finest judge of talent I've ever known. I think maybe Gracie felt a little sorry for Mary because she knew how much Mary wanted to be a star. She told me once, after we'd been married for years, that just after we'd gotten married Mary had come to her and said, somewhat critically, "Gracie, I've been meaning to talk to your about your entrance . . ."

"What I wanted to say to her," Gracie told me, "was, 'You're telling me about my entrance? I was born on the stage and you've been working two months.' That's what I wanted to tell her."

"But what'd you say?"

"I just smiled," Gracie admitted. "I didn't say anything."

Maybe it was because both Gracie and I loved Jack so much, and Mary really did run Jack's life, but Gracie was always loyal to Mary. Whenever we traveled, for example, Mary refused to leave her hotel room the first night in town. It didn't matter where we were, she'd put on her robe and call room service. I remember once we were in New York and a large group was getting together for dinner. Mary refused to go and somehow convinced Gracie to stay with her. I walked into Jack's hotel room and there were Jack and Mary and Gracie sitting at a table eating a room-service dinner. Gracie knew exactly what I was thinking, that she should be with me, but the expression on her face was clear: I have to be here. She saw it as a test of loyalty. As usual, she passed that test.

About the only thing Gracie wouldn't do for Mary was lie. Mary used to exaggerate, and she would try to intimate people into backing up her exaggerations. For example, she might say, "I was driving along Sunset and this other car almost crashed into me. You remember that, Gracie, you were with me."

Maybe some people would have agreed, or at least avoided a direct answer. Not Gracie. "I think you're mistaken, Mary," she'd say. "I wasn't with you."

Mary tried often to include Gracie in her tales, but each time Gracie corrected her, and Mary finally gave up.

Jack was intimidated by Mary. I knew that. Everybody knew that. Maybe we didn't understand why, but we knew it. Jack and I were having lunch at the Brown Derby one day and I ordered bacon and eggs and he ordered cream of wheat.

"What're you ordering that for?" I asked. "I thought you hated cream of wheat."

"I do," he admitted. "I really want bacon and eggs. But Mary says it's bad for you—she wants me to eat cream of wheat."

"Let Mary eat cream of wheat," I told him. "You eat bacon and eggs."

"You think I should?"

"Jack, you can't let Mary run your life like that."

"You're right," Jack said, sitting up straight. And he changed his order to bacon and eggs. After the meal, when the waiter arrived with the check, I told him to give it to Jack.

"Wait a second," Jack protested. "Why should I pay the check?"

"Because if you don't," I threatened, "I'm going to tell Mary you ate bacon and eggs."

If a person is very lucky, he has one best friend in his life. I had two, Gracie and Jack.

I'd give almost anything to hear Jack pounding the floor one more time.

7

By the late 1930s one of the biggest jokes on radio was television. On our show, for example, I told a wonderful joke and nobody laughed. "Maybe I'd better wait for television before I tell that joke again," I said.

"Oh, no, dear, don't wait," Gracie answered. "Television won't help you any." Then everybody laughed.

Radio was so popular that nobody believed it would be affected by television. We all thought television was a clever gimmick, but the screen was so small that the picture could barely be seen, and even when it could be seen, the quality was very poor. Of course that didn't matter too much because there was nothing to watch anyway. The top-rated program was a test pattern.

One of the first things they broadcast was a baseball game in New York between the Brooklyn Dodgers and the Cincinnati Reds. The picture was so bad that viewers couldn't even see the baseball. Watching a baseball game without being able to see the baseball took some of the enjoyment out of it, but the game still received about a 35 rating. That meant that 35 of the 50 sets in existence were watching.

Everyone working in radio believed it would be too tough to do a regular show on television. On TV, we heard, actors had to work without scripts. That meant, as the great comedy writer John P. Medbury pointed out, "You certainly couldn't do a show every week. There just isn't enough time to write, rehearse, memorize, and broadcast."

I disagreed. "Oh, I could do it," I boasted. "I'd just have to give up a few of the things I really enjoy doing so that I could devote all my time to work. You know, things like eating, sleeping, and breathing."

Even I thought I was kidding.

Within two years after the end of World War II, television screens had gotten so big that viewers could see the baseball, and suddenly TV became very important. Hundreds of people owned sets. Bars installed them so patrons could watch sports events, and radio ratings began dipping. It became obvious that Gracie and I would either have to make the transition to television or open a bar.

Major radio stars like Jack Benny, Fred Allen, and Amos 'n' Andy were preparing to make the move, and I wanted to do it too, but I knew Gracie had no intention of competing with baseball. She had settled into an orderly life and was very content. Her career took up only a few days a week and didn't interfere with the things that really mattered to her. She was already talking about retiring from show business, and I had to try to talk her into starting a whole new career.

I did it only because I wanted to make Gracie happy. Gracie was happiest when I was happy. I knew that doing a television show would make me happy. Therefore, I was doing it to make Gracie happy. Nice, huh?

"Absolutely not," she said when I told her that CBS wanted us to develop a show for the network. "Nattie, I've always done everything you've asked, but this is one thing I won't be pushed into."

"I'm not going to make you do anything you don't want to do," I promised. "But before you make your final decision, just listen to me. Television is here to stay, there's no use pretending it isn't. Just make one TV test, that's all I'm asking. Let's just see what it looks like. I'll shoot you from every angle so you can see the worst that can happen."

She knew me well enough to be suspicious. "And if I don't like it?"

"I'll never mention it again," I said.

Then I puffed on my cigar.

The first decision that had to be made was what kind of format to use. Everybody in radio was scrambling to find a framework that would work on television. We all knew one thing that wouldn't work—standing in front of a microphone and reading from a script. Unfortunately, that's what we were best at.

I remembered an old vaudeville act called Parker and Brown. They wanted to do a sketch that was a little different from anything anybody else was doing, so they borrowed $900 and bought two life-sized dolls that looked just like real babies. The sketch was about how hard it was to find a decent apartment. At the end they finally find a place they can afford, but the landlord tells them they can't have it if they have children—so they shoot the two kids. Eddie Darling, who was then the manager of the

Palace, like everything about the act except the finish. He suggested that instead of shooting the kids they do a song and dance. "But, Mr. Darling," Parker said. "Everybody in vaudeville finishes with a song and dance."

"That's right," Darling said, "and everybody in vaudeville's working except you two."

Eddie Darling gave them pretty good advice: give the audience what they want. Our audience knew who Gracie and I were. Gracie was a lovely, charming woman who decided if they didn't do something to cut down the high cost of living, she would have to do without it, and who asked, when informed that the country had a $2,000,000 deficit, "Why don't they get a cheaper one?" And I was the guy who stood next to her.

I met with CBS Chairman Bill Paley at the Brown Derby restaurant in Los Angeles to outline the format we would use. We agreed that Gracie would play Gracie. That meant she couldn't play Gracie playing another role—a waitress, a nurse, or a secretary, like she did in the movies. She had to play the same character the audience had grown to love. And I would play the guy who stood next to her. My major contribution to the format was to suggest that I be able to step out of the plot and speak directly to the audience, and then be able to go right back into action. That was an original idea of mine; I know it was because I originally stole it from Thornton Wilder's play *Our Town*.

As I later found out, one of the big reasons that Gracie didn't want to go into television was that she was worried about me. I was already in my midfifties, and she was concerned television might be too tough for me. I remember one week we had a very young Bob Fosse on the show as a guest. In rehearsal one afternoon he showed me some quick-steps, and I showed him some quicker steps, and before I knew it, we were going at it pretty good. Gracie had been sitting in the back of the studio, and she looked up and saw me trying to match steps with a twenty-year-old hoofer. She stood right up and ordered loudly, "Nattie, you cut that out right now!"

After Gracie agreed to do the show, I took several writers, including my brother Willie, and our announcer, Bill Goodwin, to Palm Springs for a week to devise a real format. We eventually decided that Gracie and I would play Burns and Allen, two performers, at home, and that I would be able to step out of the plot and speak directly to the audience, and then be able to go right back into the action. All my writers had seen *Our Town* too.

It was a very innovative concept. Nothing like it had ever been done on television before. Of course, television was so new that if an actor burped, everyone agreed it was an innovative concept and nothing like it had ever been done on television before.

Fred Allen, who was never able to make the transition to TV, once told famed humorist Goodman Ace that he should have used our format. "I should have done exactly what George Burns did," he said, "then I could've had a television career."

Maybe, but I don't know what his wife would have said if he had married Gracie.

On October 12, 1950, the band started playing "Love Nest" and "The Burns and Allen Show" went on the air live from New York City. I was standing alone at the corner of the stage, and I began by introducing myself: "Hello, everybody, I'm George Burns, better known as Gracie Allen's husband . . . I've been a straight man for so many years that from habit I repeat everything. I went fishing with a fellow the other day and he fell overboard. He yelled, 'Help! Help! so I said, 'Help? Help?' And while I was waiting for him to get his laugh, he drowned.''

Then the curtain opened to reveal our set. It was a typical suburban house, but most of our exterior brick wall had been cut away to reveal our living room. When I stepped out of the action to speak to the audience, I actually had to step over a few bricks that represented the wall, but when I was involved in the action I used the front door.

The interior of the house was decorated just like a real house in 1950—we had no television set. Gracie had often complained, ''Supposedly I've been on the radio for seventeen years, but I listen to the radio all the time and I've never heard me.'' Times had changed, now she could complain she couldn't watch herself on television because we didn't have a television set. In those days TV programs were very true to life—the actors listened to radios. One reason that our set was so realistic was that Gracie helped decorate it. If a propman or set dresser had selected the wrong dinnerware or set the table incorrectly, Gracie would change it. Gracie was very meticulous about her ''home,'' whether it had walls or not.

For a brief period after we started doing the television show, we continued doing the radio show. The radio show took up a tremendous amount of time and energy, but I was reluctant to give it up until I was convinced that viewers really could see the baseball.

Our cast was the same on television as it was on radio: Gracie and I played Burns and Allen, Bill

Goodwin played our handsome, amorous announcer.
And Hal March and Bea Benadaret played Harry and
Blanche Morton, our neighbors and best friends. Our
son, Ronnie, joined the cast a couple of years later,
and he played with girls.

The shows were loosely structured. We usually
had more plot than a variety show but less than a
wrestling match. The real importance of our plots
was that it was cheaper to have them than to hire a
guest star. We rarely had guest stars on the show.
Our plots were very simple: Gracie puts a dent in
the car. Gracie's aunt comes to visit. Gracie wants
to convince me to go on a trip with the Mortons.
Gracie thinks a surprise party planned for Harry
Morton is for me. Here's a good one: Gracie and I
have a fight. It's amazing that we could come up
with such innovative ideas with only five full-time
writers.

At first we borrowed from radio, interrupting the
plot for a singer to do a brief number. Our stories
were so flimsy that nobody even noticed when we
interrupted them for a song. The only real action in
the show was Gracie cleaning the house. Just like
when we were making movies, when Gracie was
supposed to be doing something, she actually did it.
During a conversation on one show, for example,
she was supposed to be sewing a lace border on a
handkerchief. After we'd finished, our director, Fred
de Cordova, showed me the handkerchief—with its
perfectly sewn lace border. When Gracie had "business" to do, as these actions are called, the business
became more important to her than the jokes.

From our first episode the show worked so well
that I could almost hear the water running in Jolson's
dressing room. During the eight years we were on

the air we had three different actors playing Harry Morton, famed radio announcer Harry von Zell replaced Bill Goodwin, Gracie and I suddenly gave birth to an eighteen-year-old son, we added a swimming pool and a large kitchen, and even a "magic" television set that enable me to keep ahead of the plot by seeing all the action going on in other parts of the house. But none of that really mattered. Gracie was the whole show. The show was successful because she was able to make her character come alive on television. This was the same Gracie that audiences had loved in vaudeville, on radio, and in the movies. The only difference was that this time the audience could see how that Gracie really lived when she wasn't performing in vaudeville, on radio, or in the movies. The audience knew Gracie so well that I once did an entire monologue consisting of straight lines, letting the audience fill in the obvious punch line. "Someone challenged me to think of one thing that Gracie said that made sense," I explained, "and I didn't think that would be a problem. Let's see, in the department store one day at a salesgirl said, 'Mrs. Burns, if you're looking for Mr. Brown you'll find him in ladies' lingerie.' And Gracie said . . . No, that wasn't it.

"Oh, I know. In the butcher shop one day the butcher said, 'Mrs. Burns, I have pigs' feet today . . .' No, not that time.

"I remember. We were in a restaurant and the maître 'd said, 'Mrs. Burns, walk this way . . .'

"But later, when we were ordering, the waiter explained, 'We serve the lamb chops with little panties on . . .' no, that's not it.

"I got one. Gracie was driving along and she

stopped and waited because the sign said, 'School crossing' and . . . no, that wasn't it either.''

That was the Gracie the audience knew. The most difficult part of bringing Gracie to television was adding visual humor to the silly dialogue. She was superb at that. In one episode the postman was delivering a special delivery letter to her. He held it out in his hand and said, ''You're going to have to sign here for it.''

''That's silly,'' she said. ''Why do I have to do that?''

''Postal regulations.''

''That's ridiculous . . . but give me your pen.''

And then she took his pen and did exactly as he asked—signed her name on his hand.

Sight gags were a very important part of most popular situation comedies, but Gracie wasn't a physical comedian like Lucille Ball or Joan Davis. We did 299 shows and she never threw a pie in anyone's face, took a pratfall, or wore a ridiculous costume. That wasn't Gracie. Imagine Gracie throwing a pie at someone. She would have been mortified. She would have immediately demanded that they take off their clothes so she could put them in the washing machine.

And then she would have offered to have their clothes cleaned too.

Gracie's sight gags were very subtle. In an early episode of the series, for example, I brought home a dozen roses for her. She already had two vases with flowers in them. While we were having a silly discussion about something else, she took the flowers out of the first vase and put the roses in. Then she took the flowers that had been in the first vase and put them in the second vase. Finally she took the flowers that had been in the second vase to the first vase, removed the roses, put the flowers from the second vase in the first vase, and told me to throw out the roses. "There," she said with satisfaction as she admired her flowers. "Aren't they beautiful?"

At the end of many of our shows, after the final commercial, Gracie and I would come onstage and do a few minutes from one of our old vaudeville routines. We usually had something prepared, but sometimes we'd improvise. I could feed Gracie a line from any of our vaudeville routines and she'd know the right answer. Or the wrong answer. We both loved doing these old bits. Most of the time, though, we'd do an updated version of our material. Once, for example, I told the audience, "Gracie and I would like to do something for you, but we don't have anything prepared, so . . ."

"I do," she interrupted with perfect timing.

I continued, ". . . so I'd like to thank you very much . . ."

"Mr. Paley came to my dressing room."

". . . you've been a wonderful audience and . . ."

"He had two bottles of champagne with him."

". . . we'll be back next week at the same time . . ."

"Two," she repeated, holding up two fingers in front of my face. "Two bottles of champagne!"

". . . on the same station . . ."

"Bill Paley just walked into my dressing room with two bottles of champagne and opened them up and said, 'Let's have a drink. Bottoms up.' "

I finally stopped and looked directly at her. "And?"

"And I said to him, 'Isn't that an awkward position?' "

"Say good night, Gracie."

"Good night," was all she said, and took her bow.

※

We only did the first few shows in New York, then moved to the General Service Studios in Los Angeles. For two years we did the show live, appearing every other week. Until the two coasts were finally connected by coaxial cable, we had to put a movie camera in front of a monitor and make a kinescope, kind of a primitive tape, which was flown to the other coast and shown a few days later.

In 1952 we began filming the show and went on weekly. That meant we had to shoot thirty-nine new episodes a season. It was a tremendously difficult job, much harder than anything Gracie and I had done before. As it turned out, I'd been wrong—even after giving up eating, sleeping, and breathing, I still didn't have enough time to do everything I was supposed to do. Besides standing next to Gracie, I was the executive producer of the show and worked on the script with the writers. I had so little time that I had to learn my lines while I walked along the corridors of the office or when I stopped at a traffic light driving home or to the studio.

But compared to what Gracie had to do, I had it easy. She'd often have as many as twenty-six pages of dialogue in a forty-page script. It was the same type of confusing material she'd done on radio, but in television she couldn't read from a script. She had to memorize everything, her lines as well as everybody else's lines in her scenes, and that was tough. The first few years we did the show we didn't use cue cards. Because the show was live, if someone made a mistake there was nothing we could do about

it. The worst thing that would happen is that people
would laugh at the mistake, which was not a terrible
thing for a comedy show. It was only after we'd
started doing the show on film, when we could stop
and redo a scene if someone blew a line, that we
started using cue cards to help people remember their
lines.

In fact, we were one of the first shows on TV to
use cue cards. I know they didn't use them on other
shows like "Meet the Press," the baseball game, or
test patterns. But before we started using them,
whenever Gracie was having trouble with a line,
we'd write it on an index card and paste that card
inside the sink or on the back of a cabinet door or
inside a hat, anywhere that couldn't be seen by the
camera. But even that was only partially helpful.
Gracie was such a perfectionist that she insisted on
knowing her lines cold when she walked on the set
in the morning.

Just like in the movies and on radio, her lines were
tough to remember because they didn't really make
sense, they only sounded as if they made sense. But
she had to say them exactly as they were written or
not only wouldn't they make sense, they wouldn't
be funny, either. For example, the very first show
we filmed opened with Gracie and me sitting in our
living room. Gracie was sewing and I was supposedly
looking at the script for our next show.

"George," Gracie said, "I wish you had been
under the dryer with me at the beauty shop yesterday."

"Under the dryer? What'd I miss?" Notice how
important it was that I said my line exactly as it was
written.

"Well, the operator turned off the dryer and we

got to talking about different countries. She said that in Spain the national sport is bullfighting and in England it's cricket. So I said, ''Well, I'd rather live in England because it's easier to fight a cricket.''

See how she needed my line to cue her? I could have quoted Jack Benny and it wouldn't have made any difference. That's why it was so tough for her to learn her lines.

Doing the show was a full-time job for Gracie, just what she had wanted to avoid. Every Monday, thirty-nine weeks a year for eight years, she'd spent at least four hours and sometimes many more in the wardrobe department having her clothes fitted for the show. She often wore as many as three outfits on a single half-hour show, and every one of them fitted her perfectly. Gracie picked out her own wardrobe; everything she wore had to have long sleeves long enough to cover her scarred arm. But even with that limitation she was still the best-dressed star in television comedy. One year, in fact, the California designers voted her the best-dressed woman in California. She earned it, though, Gracie was one of the very few women who wore high heels to do the dishes.

After spending most of Monday in wardrobe, she spent the entire evening studying her script.

We rehearsed all day Tuesday. Because we had a very small budget, we had to film the show in one day, and in order to do that we had to shoot the scenes out of order. We'd have the different sets we were using all properly lit and decorated and we'd simply move from one set to the next, filming whatever action took place on that set. Fortunately, with our plots and Gracie's lines, it often didn't make any difference in continuity how we shot the scenes. The important thing was that every scene had to be very carefully blocked out in rehearsal.

On Tuesday we would start rehearsing by nine A.M. We'd go through the entire script, line by line, movement by movement, so we would know exactly where to position the cameras when we were shooting. It was always late in the evening by the time we finished, and the last thing we would do was meet with the director to get his "notes" or comments. By that time everybody was exhausted and wanted to go home. We'd all be slumped in our chairs, trying to stay awake. Not Gracie. I'd look at her, and even though she had been in more scenes than anybody else, she'd be the only one sitting up straight in her chair, eyes wide open, listening attentively. The best pupil in the class. At moments like that I would just look at her with wonder. That was her upbringing: she was a tough, proud little Irish girl. How was I lucky enough to find her? And watching her, I just assumed she would live forever.

We filmed every Wednesday. That was the longest day of our week. Gracie would have to be at the studio by six A.M. to have her hair and makeup done so that she would be on the set by nine o'clock. Usually someone from our office, either Tommy Clapp or Jack Langdon, would sit next to her and go over her lines. Even when she was under the hair dryer she was working. Sometimes Charlie Lowe would join her, and he would pretend to be reading the show-business gossip columns from *Variety* and *The Hollywood Reporter*. "Oh, here's something interesting," he'd tell her. "Mamie Eisenhower's pregnant." And then he would proceed to make up some really outrageous stories. The more ridiculous they were, the more Gracie would love them. Charlie would make up stories about who was sleeping with whom, or what, or quote people we knew saying incredible things about other people we knew, the kind of items that if I repeated them here would enable a good libel lawyer to buy a new Manhattan co-op.

The only thing Charlie couldn't say was "God damn." Gracie was always trying to get him to stop using the phrase, so every time he said it, he had to pay her a dime. And she collected too, you can be gosh darn sure of that.

Starting precisely at nine o'clock, we would rehearse a scene first, then shoot it. Rehearse, then shoot. Rehearse, then shoot. Gracie never allowed rehearsals to affect her performance. Although she was careful to always hit her marks, so the camera would be able to film her, she always did her scenes the way she felt at that moment, and rarely did she feel the same way while we were filming as she had during rehearsal. That was one of the exciting parts about working with her. She was just so good she made everybody she worked with better. The rest of the cast had to react to her, and that created a kind of energy that was so important to the popularity of the show.

We'd sometimes work until midnight to get the whole show done. Nobody complained. I also produced a series called "Mr. Ed," that starred a talking horse. When we were filming that show, that horse would start stomping his foot at six o'clock. He knew when it was time to quit. Nobody in our cast did that, although I have to admit Harry von Zell would have looked awfully silly stomping his foot.

While doing the show thirty-nine weeks a year,

Gracie proved what an incredibly talented actress she was. "I never wanted to play Shakespeare," she once said, a statement she had proved by becoming my partner. Instead we played Cleveland. For Gracie, acting was just another reality—onstage she became a dizzy dame. She actually changed physically: her voice got just a little higher, her smile a little wider, and her eyes were fixed on the person she was talking to. The transformation was just as complete on that Hollywood sound stage as it had been twenty-five years earlier in a drafty vaudeville house in New Jersey.

Gracie's acting technique was simple: she did exactly what the script told her to do. Once, I remember, while we were doing the show live, she was supposed to make a false exit; she was to walk out the door and return when Bill Goodwin called her back. So she walked out the door—and Goodwin forgot his line—and she kept going, right into her dressing room. We still were on the air for another twelve minutes, but as far as Gracie was concerned Bill Goodwin hadn't called her back, so she was done. I had to run to her dressing room and bring her back to finish the show.

While we were rehearsing another scene, she was supposed to exit through a door, and Hal March decided to play a joke on her—he was going to block the doorway and see what she would do. He knew how determined she was onstage. You couldn't play any jokes on Gracie on the stage. When she got to the door and saw him blocking her way, she shoved him so hard she knocked him down. And then she made her exit.

Between scenes Gracie didn't sit around the set with the cast and crew and gossip and joke. She went to her dressing room and stayed there. She always kept a very low profile on the set; when she wasn't working we didn't even know she was there. But when it was time to start filming she'd be ready, standing on the side of the stage as if she'd been waiting there forever, prepared to do her scene.

If we'd just taken a short break, she'd usually take off her high heels and put on a pair of comfortable old shoes, then lean against a slant board—a big slab of plywood with armrests, tilted so that she could lean back and relax without wrinkling her dress. Most of the time she'd be right next to Bea Benadaret, who was also on a slant board. The two of them looked like the Dolly Sisters getting a suntan. Gracie never told me what they talked about, but Bea did, just once. She took me aside and reminded me that I was a very lucky man. Well, I knew that. "But what are you talking about?" I asked.

She'd been telling Gracie about a man she was going out with, Bea explained, and said she couldn't decide how she really felt about him. "So," Bea said, "Gracie asked me, 'Is he like George?' I asked her what she meant by that and she said, 'Oh, you know, is he smart, like George is?' "

I like that. That was what was really important to Gracie. Not, is he good looking, or is he successful, or does he have a magnificent singing voice, but is he smart, like George is. I liked that a lot.

As we finished shooting each scene, Gracie would neatly fold over those pages in her script, and when we'd completed the entire show she would put down that script and never pick it up again. The only time of the week that she was really free of the show was from the moment we finished shooting until we got into our car to be driven home. On the back seat of our limo, waiting for her, was the script for next week's show.

Thursday was supposed to be her day off. That was her day to relax. All she had to do on Thursday was take care of all those things that she'd previously had the entire week to do. Thursday was the day she was allowed to be sick, spend extra time with the kids, or see the dentist, or buy things for the house, or just do nothing. But she had to finish doing nothing very quickly, because there was always something that had to be done.

Every other Thursday we would screen two new episodes of the show for an invited audience of about two hundred people so we could add their laughter to the sound track. Doing comedy on television required exceptionally good timing—you told a joke and two weeks later the audience laughed.

Before we screened the programs Bill Goodwin, and later Harry von Zell, would bring me out to say a few words about the shows, then I'd introduce Gracie. Gracie always got a standing ovation. That must have been some great introduction I gave her. After both programs had been shown, Gracie and I would return and do a few minutes from one of our old routines. This was the only chance Gracie and I had to work in front of a breathing audience. I really looked forward to these moments, I loved being onstage in front of an audience. I don't think Gracie even minded too much. I think that's where we felt we belonged.

We did the show live the first two years and worked with an audience in the studio. But when we began filming the show, we had to eliminate the audience because we shot the scenes out of sequence. But television executives insisted that a comedy show had to have a laugh track so that the audience watching at home would know when to laugh. I told them we didn't need one on our show because the audience knew something funny had happened when I puffed on my cigar. They still insisted we use the laugh track. I guess they'd seen me smoke.

Maybe they figured the people at home were laughing at the laughter. If that was true, they could have saved everyone a lot of time and money by eliminating the show and just running the laugh track.

There were three ways to get laughs on a film track: film in front of an audience, which we couldn't do; show the completed show to an invited audience and tape their response; or use canned laughter. Canned laughter was mechanically produced. Using a little machine, we could generate any type of laughter we wanted, from outright prolonged hysterics to a mild chuckle. Technology had really changed show business. When Gracie and I started out, we told our jokes to an audience and they laughed; now all we had to do was show a film to a box.

We rarely used canned laughter on the show. We only "sweetened" the laughter, as adding laughs to the sound track is called, when a joke went flat and there was no way of eliminating it from the film. Even then we never added more than a gentle chuckle.

Friday was the day that Gracie selected the clothes she would wear on the show the following week. A lot of her dresses came out of wardrobe, but she also did a lot of shopping. That woman made such sacrifices for her career. Bea Benadaret often went with her, although Bea didn't enjoy shopping as much as

Gracie did. R. H. Macy didn't enjoy shopping as much as Gracie did.

On almost every show Gracie wore an apron. That was her tribute to her Aunt Clara. Some of the aprons she bought, but many of them were gifts from fans. I remember once Gracie and I were making an appearance somewhere and a lovely older lady came up to her and said, "Oh, I love your show so much. I never miss it. I just can't wait to see what kind of beautiful apron you're going to wear."

We spent a fortune on sets and actors and production values—and it turned out it was Gracie's aprons that were making us so popular.

We'd spend some time every weekend memorizing our scripts and working with the director on the next show. On Sunday night we'd put our scripts away and sit in our den and watch television. Sandy was married and Ronnie had taken an apartment, and we were alone. It was the only time during the week that we could relax together. Gracie loved watching TV just as she had loved listening to radio. She was a fan of other actors. On Monday the cycle started again.

Gracie used to study her script by herself in her bedroom. She'd have a tough time with it and she'd get very frustrated. Sometimes she'd get so angry she'd heave the script across the room, but she'd always pick it up again. "No matter what I do," she once said, "I'm always thinking about the script. I just can't get away from it. Even when I sit down to write a letter, I'm thinking, 'I should be working on my lines.' "

In addition to doing our show, Gracie and I occasionally appeared on other TV shows. One night we did Garry Moore's quiz show, "I've Got a Se-

cret.'' I don't remember what our secret was. I didn't
have any secrets. My secret was that Gracie did all
the work, but everybody knew that. In September
1955, they surprised me on ''This Is Your Life.''
Gracie knew all about it—she even helped them plan
it—but she told Sandy that she knew the truth: they
were really going to surprise her. The entire time
she was helping people from the show make contact
with The Pee Wee Quartet and Billy Lorraine and
other important people in my life, she remained convinced this was all an elaborate means of surprising
her. It worked, they did surprise her—they did my
life.

❧

When Gracie retired in 1958 and ''The Burns and
Allen Show'' went off the air, we were the longest-
running situation comedy in television history. The
reason was obvious. ''In order to have a successful
TV show,'' I explained to our audience in one episode, ''you need something a little bit different,
something out of this world . . .''

Just then, in the background, Gracie could be
heard lovingly telling our visiting nieces, ''Oh, children, it's cold out today, so if you're going swimming make sure you wear your sweaters.''

''. . . and,'' I continued, ''I think I've got it.''

We had a very simple program. None of our characters got involved in absurd situation, as they did
on ''I Love Lucy'' or ''I Married Joan.'' We didn't
have any fantastic characters, like Mr. Ed, the talking horse, or Cleo, a basset hound who thought out
loud on ''The People's Choice,'' or even a sexy ge-
nii. We had our son, Ronnie, going out with pretty
girls. And we had Gracie, trying to deal with the

same types of problems our viewers had to deal with on a daily basis. Ours was the humor of recognition.

For example, on radio, on television, and in real life, Gracie had difficulty handling money. Our viewers could really relate to that. We made a lot of money, enough money so that Gracie could have afforded anything Mary Benny would have wanted. But Gracie wasn't a spender; she was a very careful shopper. She often waited until the things she wanted went on sale, and always bought on a layaway plan. At home she made sure we used a bar of soap until we could see though it, and nobody in our house dared open a new tube of toothpaste until we couldn't get another drop out of the old tube with a sledgehammer.

She never really accepted the fact that we were rich. Once she went to the Hollywood Park racetrack with my brother Willy and his wife, Louise. Willy knew how careful Gracie was with money, so he told her, "Gracie, listen to me—you don't have to worry about money today. There's nothing you can't afford if you want it. If you want to bet a thousand dollars today you can do it, and even if you lose every penny you're still going to have more than enough money to take care of your family. Okay?"

"Really?" she asked.

"Really." My brother Willy was always very generous with my money.

Relieved, Gracie immediately went over to the $2 window and bet on the favorite.

Gracie was an extremely intelligent woman, but like a lot of intelligent women she just wasn't good with money. In real life as well as on the show. I remember once we got a bill from Chasen's that she didn't understand. She never asked me about these things, maybe because she knew that like a lot of intelligent men I just wasn't good with money. Instead she called Jack Langdon. "Jack," she said in a nervous voice, "I'm a little concerned about something. I've just gotten a bill from Chasen's and there's a sticker on it that says, 'This was sent to our auditor.' What does that mean? Have we done something wrong? Are they going to send us to jail?"

Jack laughed. "Of course not, Gracie."

"Then what does it mean? Are they going to dun us?"

She was really upset about it. Jack told her to relax. "It's just a little notice they put on their bills. It doesn't mean anything. Now, tell me what the bill is for—did you go to the restaurant?"

"Yes, Jack, we did. We went there. But I don't understand this bill at all, because here it says $13.50 and it has a B after it, then it says $39.85 and that has an F after it, and then it says $5.60 and it has a T after that, and I don't know what those things mean. Do you know what they mean?"

Jack thought about it for a moment, then said, "Well, how about this? Maybe the B is for beverages, the F is for food, and the T is the tax. What do you think about that?"

Gracie was silent, then started laughing delightedly. "Oh, Jack," she said happily, "you see how smart we are when we put our heads together."

Checking accounts mystified her, again in real life as well as on the show. Our banker on the show, Mr. Vanderlip, once came to the house to try to straighten out Gracie's checking account. The bank claimed her balance was $1200. She had it figured at $2,800,000. "Now," he began, showing her a check, "this check for $500 is made out to me. What's it for?"

"It's very simple," Gracie explained, but of course it wasn't. "The next time I've used up all the money I have in the bank, you won't have to notify me. Just cash that check and put it in."

Vanderlip shook his head in disbelief. "I can't wait to get back to the bank and talk to the examiners."

"Why? Is the roof leaking?"

"Now, Mrs. Burns," he continued, "this check made out to Bullock's is torn into several pieces. I guess that was an accident?" Silly man.

"Oh, no," Gracie corrected him. "I sent it to them that way."

"But why?"

"Well, I didn't know how much I owed them. This way they can keep what I owe them and send me back the change."

Now, that was dialogue from the show, but it almost could have come from real life. Gracie tried very hard to keep her bank account balanced. She didn't have to, we had a wonderful business manager named Annabelle Brown who took care of our finances, but Gracie insisted on taking care of her own checking account. I never knew why, maybe it made her feel like she was just like every other housewife trying to keep up with the bills, maybe it made her feel like she was in charge of her own life, but at the end of every month she'd sit down at her desk with her checkbook and all her receipts and stubs and slave over the figures for hours. And she would be so proud when she finally managed to get that checkbook balanced. Of course, she was always wrong, but we never told her that. She wasn't even close. She'd send her figures and receipts and stubs to Annabelle Brown, who would put them away, then call the bank and ask, "Where are we now?" A bank officer would tell her the status of the account and she would deposit whatever was necessary and Gracie would be so pleased that she had successfully kept her account in order.

When Gracie and I started working together in vaudeville we'd split our salary evenly, but after we were married we deposited everything in a single savings account. Gracie had her checking account, but I also gave her an allowance. I think it was about $250 a week. Now that was funny. Me giving Gracie an allowance. She could have written a check for as much as she needed, but she never did. Instead she tried very hard to make that $250 last the entire week. She never did that, either.

At the end of each year the stores she regularly shopped in would send me a bill for the outstanding balance on her charge accounts and I'd pay it. As far as Gracie was concerned, though, the cash she had in her pocketbook was the only real money she had, and as long as she had a few dollars she could put her hands on, she was solvent.

We did a funny bit on the TV show one night in which I tried to explain how community property worked to Gracie. I know it was funny because the laugh box gave us outright prolonged laughter.

"Community property," I said slowly, "is a law that says half of everything you've got is mine, and half of everything I've got is yours."

That confused Gracie. "Then how come I only get one-fourth of everything we make?" See how confused she was.

"I'll show you how it works. Here in my hand

I've got a dollar in change. Half of everything I've got is yours. Here's fifty cents. Half of everything you've got is mine. How much have you got there?''

"Fifty cents."

"Okay, give me a quarter. There, see how it works?''

Gracie still didn't grasp the concept; as I said, she wasn't very good with money.

"This time I'll start with the dollar," she said. "Now, half of everything I've got is yours. Here's fifty cents. And . . . and how does that second part go again?''

I had to explain it to her one more time. "And half of everything you've got is mine. How much have you got?''

"Fifty cents."

"Fine. Give me a quarter."

"Oh, now I see how it works," she said.

It worked pretty much the same way in real life too. Whatever Gracie owed, I'd call up Annabelle Brown and say, "Pay it," and it worked. In fact, because Gracie worked as hard as she did, we never had any problems with money.

Another subject we often dealt with on the TV show that reflected what was going on in the lives of our viewers was women and the automobile. In the early 1950s, families began moving out to the suburbs and women started getting their own driver's licenses and cars. Gracie was no different, again in real life as on the show. Once we did a show in which she went to the Department of Motor Vehicles to try to get her license. Doing this show was a challenge, because anybody who has ever been to the motor vehicle bureau will tell you there is nothing funny about it. On the show Gracie often went up against the bureaucracy, and our viewers always felt the bureaucracy deserved it. In this episode she took her test for a permit and Mr. Harkness of the motor vehicle bureau told her, "Mrs. Burns, I've been going over your test. Never in the sixteen years I've been here have I seen anything like it."

"Thank you," Gracie said proudly.

"When you wrote these answers you obviously had something in mind," he continued, but maybe he should have stopped right there. "For instance, this question: have you ever had a license before? You said you did. How long?"

"Oh, it was about four inches," Gracie said. "It fit right in my wallet."

"I see. Well, let's try the eye test. That doesn't require any thinking."

"All right with me, but why don't you like to think?"

"Now, Mrs. Burns, please concentrate on the chart on the back wall. Close one eye," he continued, handing her a white card, "and what do you see?"

Gracie held the white card in front of her. "I see the white card."

"No, no, no, no, what do you see with the other eye?"

"Nothing, that's the eye that's closed." Finally Harkness convinced her to try to read the eye chart. "I wish I could," she admitted, "but I can't pronounce any of those words."

When Gracie decided in real life to get her driver's licence, we got her a copy of the motor vehicle regulations and she studied the booklet for weeks, just as diligently as she studied her scripts. I suspect she was one of the few people in history who could have recited lines from the booklet. When she was ready to take the test, Jack Langdon went down to the motor vehicle bureau with her. In Hollywood celebrities were permitted to take the test in a private room so they wouldn't be bothered by people asking for autographs, but Gracie insisted on taking it in the main room just like everybody else.

The clerk corrected her test right in front of her. She got 100 percent. And she was absolutely thrilled. She was so excited, so pleased with herself. She told Jack smugly, "Just wait till I show this to Nattie, he'll just eat his heart out." Jack thought she was going to have her test framed.

Then they had to take her picture for her permit. Practically everybody in the office squeezed into a small area to watch Gracie getting her picture taken. She'd come a long way since people had laughed at her in Macy's for trying to buy a rolling pin; now they were laughing at her at the motor vehicle bureau for trying to get a driving permit.

Of course, Gracie took the whole matter very seriously. Anything that had even the slightest connection to the government she always took seriously. I guess that was a remnant from her presidential campaign.

After she got her license I had to buy her a car. On the show she was always trying to get me to buy her a new Cadillac. Once she told me, "I dreamt that you bought me a brand-new Cadillac and I bought you a necktie." Then she handed me a necktie and told me she'd kept her part of the bargain.

She asked me again on another show, but I refused, telling her, "It would be difficult if the car we had was a wreck."

Maybe that was the wrong thing to say. "It would be, huh?" she asked with a mischievous smile.

In real life I did buy her a Cadillac, a large blue Cadillac convertible. That car was really much too big for her. When she drove it she'd have to sit on cushions so she could see over the dashboard. She'd grip the steering wheel with both hands and stare straight ahead. Even when she spoke to the person in the passenger seat she wouldn't take her eyes off the road. At least that's what the people brave enough to drive with her told me.

The car didn't have power steering and sometimes she had a little trouble keeping it under control. One night she offered Jack Langdon a ride home from the office. He remembers that she drove out of the parking lot and when she stopped for a light three blocks from the studio he got out, telling her, "This is as far as I go."

When I asked him what it was like to drive with her, he said, "You can only say so many Hail Marys, then it's time to abandon ship."

She never was much of a driver. Once, on the show, she told me that a policeman had stopped her and tried to give her a ticket.

"What'd you do?" I asked.

"I was so angry that I refused to accept a gift from him," she said, "so I insisted on paying for it!"

I only remember her getting one ticket in her life. She went through a stop sign. "Didn't you tell them who you are?" I asked.

"I showed them my driver's license," she said, shrugging. Of course, her license was made out to Grace Burns. Apparently she'd gotten stopped by the only cop in California who didn't watch television.

She had one minor accident. We had a white

picket fence in front of the house, and twice, within
a brief period of time, drivers backing into our driveway to turn around knocked it down. So I put up a
little sign near the fence reminding drivers to be
careful. And right after I put up that sign, Gracie
accidently stepped on the accelerator instead of the
brake and knocked over the sign and the fence.

So we had the fence fixed again. Now, I didn't
know it at the time, but because Gracie was only
about five feet tall, the sun visor in the Cadillac
didn't cover enough of the windshield to block out
the sun for her, so she had a special long visor made
for the car and installed. But she didn't tell me about
it. A few weeks later I was driving home from the
studio and the sun was in my eyes so I flipped down
the visor—and all I could see was the visor. I drove
right into the white picket fence and knocked it over
again.

If you see the house today, you probably notice
that there is no white picket fence around the front
lawn.

On the show Gracie explained that she always
drove with the emergency brake on to prevent emer-
gencies, and we all laughed. But after Sandy had
gotten married she came to visit us one day and
parked her car in the driveway without putting on
the emergency brake. The driveway has a little slope
to it, and as we were sitting at the table we heard a
terrible crash—Sandy's car had rolled backward,
knocking down one of the posts holding up the roof
of the carport, which had fallen on the car. What
could I do? I looked at her and said, "You know,
you get more like your mother every day."

Gracie really didn't know anything about cars.
Nothing. One week she told the audience that she

wanted to have the windshield wipers put inside the car so they wouldn't rust. But in real life she once took the wrong car and never realized it. Saks had valet parking. Gracie had come out of the store and seen a blue Cadillac convertible sitting there with the keys in the ignition, so she got in and drove it home. A few hours later someone called from the store to tell us she'd taken someone else's car.

"Didn't you notice anything different about it?" I asked.

"It did seem a little different," she admitted, "but I thought it was just me."

That was the kind of thing Gracie could get away with in real life because everybody wanted to believe she really was a dizzy dame, but we couldn't have done anything like that on the show because no one would have believed it was possible.

But she really didn't understand how cars worked. Another evening she was driving down North Maple Drive with Ronnie and it was very dark out. "You know," she complained, "we should get up a petition and make them improve the street lighting in Beverly Hills." With that, Ronnie reached over and turned on the car lights. Gracie was silent for just a moment, then she said, "Ronnie, you should never argue with your mother."

In 1958 Jack Benny and I did a television commercial for which we were each to receive a brand-new Thunderbird. We decided to give them to our wives. Gracie picked out a standard model while Mary wanted a special interior in hers. Because of that, Gracie's car arrived several weeks before Mary's did, causing Mary to insist that the Ford Motor Company liked Gracie better than they liked her.

That Thunderbird convertible was the perfect car

for Gracie. She just love it. It was a small car, so it fit her well. That was her last car.

❀

Gracie worked harder than anyone else on the television show and probably enjoyed it less. She did it because that was her job, and she had been brought up with a strong work ethic. She knew that there were a lot of other people whose job depended on her doing the show. That was a tremendous amount of pressure. But she never missed a single show, not one. She worked when she had colds, she worked when her headaches were so bad she could barely get out of bed, and she worked when her heart started going bad.

Gracie first started talking about retiring while we were still doing the radio show. I didn't pay any attention. I thought Gracie wanted to quit show business the way Jack Benny was stingy—it was just part of the act. I mean, it was inconceivable to me that anyone would voluntarily quit show business. Gracie had been a star for only thirty years, how could she want to give it up so quickly?

But the television show just never had the same importance to her that it did to me. I remember the third or fourth year CBS picked up our option. This was one of the most important contracts I'd ever signed and I was very excited. I raced home to tell Gracie. I practically ran into the house and shouted, "Googie, I've got great news!"

She was busy listening to the radio. "Not now, dear," she said. "Ma Perkins is in trouble." With the contract I'd just signed I could have hired a top attorney for Ma, but instead I had to sit there quietly for fifteen minutes while Ma Perkins got out of trouble. Then I told Gracie the news. I know she was very pleased that I was so happy.

❧

I don't spend too much time thinking about the past; I'm a lot more concerned about where I'm going to be working next year. But when I think about Gracie, when I think about our life together, the thing that always surprises me is that her heart went bad. When I think of Gracie I remember a little girl with more energy than anyone else around her; a strong, vibrant, sometimes tough woman. When I think about someone with a bad heart, that wasn't Gracie at all.

She suffered her first heart attack in the early 1950s. We were going somewhere on a train. She was sleeping in the lower bunk and I was sleeping in the upper—the star always got the lower—and suddenly she said, "Nattie, I have pains in my chest."

For Gracie to admit that something was bothering her it had to be pretty bad. And because her mother had died of a bad heart, we were both pretty knowledgeable about heart problems. I jumped down from my bunk and held her in my arms, telling her, "It's going to be all right, Googie, it's nothing," and the attack passed very quickly.

When we got back to California she immediately went to see our doctor, who diagnosed it as a very mild heart attack. But Gracie seemed fine, and she certainly didn't want anyone making a fuss over her, so we didn't tell anyone. She wanted to go right back to work, probably as much to prove to herself as to everyone else that there was nothing really wrong with her. She never missed a call or a cue.

That was the beginning. Over the next several years she had several extremely minor attacks. Today it would be called angina, but at that time everything was a heart condition. If you ate too many spicy foods and got chest pains, that was a heart condition. If the network didn't pick up your option, that was a heart condition. And if you had severe chest pains caused by a bad heart, that was a heart condition. Only the last two types were really serious, though.

Gracie's heart condition didn't seem that serious. She was always able to work and shop. Each time she had one I'd hold her tightly in my arms and talk to her until the pain subsided, and it always did. Eventually Dr. Kennamer gave us some nitroglycerin pills and told us that whenever she had an attack we should put one of them under her tongue and the pains would go away. So that's what we did, and the pains always went away. I figured as long as we had a good supply of pills we had nothing to worry about.

Those pills worked so well that we began to take Gracie's heart condition for granted. We figured it was just something we would have to live with, like her migraine headaches. As my mother used to say, we should've been so lucky.

❧

I don't think I ever realized how much Gracie wanted to retire. Starting about 1954, each time CBS picked up our option I had to talk her into doing the show just one more season. One more season eventually became four years and one hundred fifty shows, but throughout our life and career together I'd had to talk her into doing so many things that she eventually enjoyed doing that I'd stopped taking her objections seriously.

When Gracie was angry, or when she really didn't want to do something, she told me. She was never shy about making her wishes known. And she was never intimidated. If we were in a restaurant and her food wasn't prepared correctly, she'd send it right back. If she didn't like a line, she wouldn't read it. Maybe the angriest I've ever seen her was the day she was late for a rehearsal because a parking lot attendant wouldn't admit her to the studio lot without a pass. Gracie was a vaudevillian—she knew that if you weren't there on time the show went on without you. Being late was about the worst crime a person could commit, and this parking lot attendant had caused her to be late. She was furious. Her face was red, her mouth was rigid, her hands were balled into fists. "Nattie," she lectured me, "you told me that CBS was a first-class network."

"Well, it is. What's the matter, Googie?"

"I want you to call Bill Paley right this minute and tell him that his parking lot attendants are inattentive." And she kept after me every day until I called him.

So I thought that when Gracie was really ready to retire she would tell me. And when she did, that would be the end of it. Unless I could talk her out of it. The only thing that would have changed that would have been a warning from one of her doctors telling her to slow down, but nobody ever said anything like that to me.

I have to admit that those last few seasons I didn't look forward to telling her our option had been picked up again. I was thrilled that it had been picked up, I just didn't want to tell her. When CBS picked us up in 1957–1958 for our eighth season, I found out how really happy Gracie was about it—she was staying with Jack and Mary in Palm Springs, and when I called with the news I decided to be forceful: I asked Jack to tell her. He refused. "You're not that good a friend," he said. Jack told me he was afraid to tell Gracie, so he called her to the phone.

"Hi, Googie," I said. "Listen, I have some bad news."

"What's the matter?" she asked anxiously.

"Don't get upset," I told her, "all the kids are fine." After that, I figured, my news would come as a relief. "CBS just picked up our option again."

I could tell she was very mad because of what she said. Nothing. She hung up on me. That was even more meaningful than anything Jack Benny didn't say. It was then I realized how serious she was about wanting to retire.

During that season I began watching her more carefully. Little things were different—maybe she had a little extra problem with a line, maybe she took a slightly longer break between takes. But things were different. Those signs might have been there for a while and I hadn't recognized them, or maybe they were just beginning to become obvious. But they were definitely there.

For example, we were filming a scene between Gracie and Ronnie on a very hot, smoggy day. Suddenly, in the middle of her line, Gracie stopped and said softly to the crew member holding the cue cards, "Excuse me. I'm sorry, but I just can't see the card."

"My fault," the man said instantly, gathering up his cards and moving closer. Everybody knew it wasn't, the cue cards were in exactly the same spot they'd been in since we'd started using them.

"Let's take a little break," I said. I thought maybe the heat was affecting her. I hoped it was the heat. It wasn't. Gracie had been working since she was five years old, she'd done thousands of performances, she'd been a star for more than three decades—and all that work, all that tension, all that traveling was beginning to take its toll.

One Sunday night a few months later we were sitting by ourselves in our den watching television. On those nights we never looked at our scripts, I didn't discuss the show, we just sat together and watched the screen. As we were sitting there I asked her, "You really want to stop?"

"I really do," she said.

It was that simple, that easy, that final. On the show I would occasionally joke that I was going to try to change Gracie's mind—for one that worked. But this wasn't the show and she wasn't going to change her mind. She just didn't have anything left to give.

I decided to make a public announcement. On February 16, 1958, we called our close friends and relatives and told them that the next morning Gracie was going to announce her retirement. Nobody believed it at first, but nobody tried to talk her out of it. They all knew that this was what she wanted; maybe they knew it better than I did.

The following morning we let our friend Louella Parsons make the announcement in her column. "At first I'm going to sleep for six months," Louella quoted Gracie. "I'm going to invite people in to dinner and visit my grandchildren. And I'm going to clean out my bureau drawers."

The telephone started ringing as soon as Louella's column hit the streets. "She had to do it," I told one reporter. "Those bureau drawers were really getting messy." Another reporter asked me exactly what the announcement meant. I told him the truth. "It means I'm out of work." Then I added, "Look, no one deserves to rest more than Gracie does. She's worked all her life."

When asked what she intended to do when we finished filming our shows for the season, Gracie had no real answer. "I haven't any hobbies," she said. "I've never had time for hobbies. It'll be nice just to be able to be free and have some time of my own. I told someone I would probably have lunch with the girls and play gin rummy all afternoon and she told me, 'Good heavens, that would be a terrible rut to get into.' And I said that it sounded like a lot of fun to me.

"Certainly one of the things I'm most looking forward to is sleeping late—as late as I like without waking up with a script under my pillow."

I never put a script under her pillow. Oh, sure, maybe I left one on the bureau or on her makeup table, but under her pillow, never.

The telephone didn't stop ringing for weeks. Reporters phoned from all over the world. A British journalist reminded Gracie, "We're two full seasons behind in showing your films, so as far as we're concerned you're working for at least two more years." Newspapers ran editorials asking her to change her mind. I couldn't count the number of letters and telegrams she received, even with my fourth-grade education. *Life* magazine asked to cover her final performance. As usual, Gracie was surprised, and overwhelmed, by all this attention. "I'd thought perhaps one of the trade papers would run a sentence about it," she said, "but that's all. People retire every day, you know. I honestly don't understand all this fuss. I'm just retiring, that's all." Even then she didn't realize how much people loved her. Maybe that was one of the reasons people loved her so much.

During that last season we finally got to do a show we'd been afraid to do for thirty-eight years—Gracie gets smart. It was a two-parter in which Gracie mistakes a British professor, who is the president of the Royal Society for Hypnotists, for a French dress designer, and is hypnotized into becoming a genius. If you don't understand how Gracie could have mistaken a proper Englishman for a French dress designer you'd better reread the earlier chapters. The professor didn't know who Gracie was until a reporter told him, "In this country she's a symbol of complete confusion." And then the professor decided to prove the power of hypnotism by making Gracie the smartest woman in the world.

In my monologue during that show I said I'd once worked with a hypnotist who'd convinced a man he was a rooster. The man's wife was terribly upset because ever time she brought home a dozen eggs he handed out cigars to his friends. Then I explained that the potential consequences of Gracie becoming a genius were too awful to think about—I'd have no act.

Gracie a genius? No one believed it was possible. But after the professor had hypnotized her she told Harry Morton, who by this season had become a successful accountant played by Larry Keating, "I think you'll find the discrepancy in your figures was in your failure to amortize the depreciation in the value of steamships over a ten-year period.''

And Harry said in response, ''Who is this?''

Imagine playing the Palace with material like that? The only good thing about that line was that Berle couldn't steal it. Steal it? He couldn't even say it. And Benny? Benny was speechless. And he still got more laughs than I did.

At the end of the first episode Gracie wanted to discuss nuclear fission, but I pointed out that people watched television to be entertained. She suggested that if they wanted to watch something frivolous they should watch ''Meet the Press.''

In the second episode Gracie went on a quiz show and I became the homemaker. That was a serious problem. I didn't look nearly as good in an apron as she did. Gracie was so brilliant I couldn't understand a thing she said. Of course, I couldn't understand the old Gracie either, but at least we made money out of it.

Finally the hypnotist took Gracie out of her trance. ''Repeat after me,'' he said. '' 'My mind is a perfect blank, ready to accept any suggestion.' ''

''My mind is a perfect blank, ready to accept any suggestion,'' she repeated.

'' 'You are now the old Gracie Allen . . .' ''

''My mind is a perfect blank . . .''

❧

We filmed our final show in June 4, 1958. It was the last time we ever worked together. I guess I really didn't believe it at the time, so I wasn't particularly upset. Our act was breaking up, not our marriage. When I stopped working with the seal, he went back to the zoo. But in the middle of the night, when I rolled over, Gracie was still lying next to me.

A few months, I figure, maybe a year. Then she'd be ready to go back to work.

Life magazine not only covered our final show, they put us on the cover. "To millions of husbands," they wrote, "she was the exasperating essence of all wives as she cut the hedge with George's electric razor and sewed shirt buttons on his shirttails so nobody would notice if he lost them. But to her profession, she was a matchless comic artist, the girl who got the most laughs for the longest-running comedy team in the U.S.

"But George has not altogether written Gracie off as a partner. 'Maybe after six months one of the kids will spill a glass of milk on her,' he says hopefully. 'Then maybe she'll retire from the kids too.'"

Our crew treated the filming of that final episode no differently than the 298 that had come before it. It was a typical Burns and Allen show—our son Ronnie was worried he was going to lose his girlfriend. We didn't even mention the fact that it was our last show together. But there was a tremendous amount of emotion on the set. Gracie finished her last scene about seven o'clock. "That's a wrap!" our director, Rod Amateau, shouted. It really was her last scene, the last time she ever appeared on a stage. But who knew? Who could have imagined? The crew gave her a standing ovation. Someone popped open a bottle of champagne and paper cups were passed around. Bea gave Gracie a big hug. Gracie took one sip of the champagne, just to be polite, and said, "Okay, that's it." Then she paused for just a second, really no more than that, took a long look around the set, and added, "And thank you very much, everyone." Then she walked off the set without looking back. And she never looked back.

Several months later Mary Benny announced her retirement.

It was impossible to believe Gracie was really finished with show business. Gracie was the most successful comedienne in history. Her career lasted more than thirty years. She had starred in practically ever form of entertainment. Who could believe a career like that could end so quietly?

I thought maybe the television industry would recognize Gracie's contribution by finally voting her the Emmy she deserved. I put an ad in the trade papers that read:

> I'm paying for this ad, so I can say what I want. I think my wife, Gracie Allen, is a great artist and deserves an Emmy. My son, Ronnie Burns, is a promising young actor and should get an award too . . . next year. Bea Benadaret deserves an award as a supporting actor. Larry Keating deserves an award as a supporting actor. Harry von Zell should have gotten an award years ago. My writers, Keith Fowler, Harvey Helm, Norman Paul, and Willy Burns, should get an award. Rod Amateau, my director/producer should get two awards. As for me, I'm pathetic. Vote for Jack Benny.

In the eight seasons we were on the air, Gracie received six nominations as Best Actress/Comedienne. Bea Benadaret was nominated as Best Supporting Actress twice, and the show received four nominations as Best Comedy Series. "I'm not interested in awards," Gracie would say every year, and every year someone else would win. But I know she felt slighted, I know it hurt her.

Gracie and I had fulfilled a lot of bookings together. I'd changed, she'd changed, even our act had changed. Instead of rewriting jokes from *College Humor* I was paying five writers. We once did a television show in which we reminisced about our life in vaudeville. I told Harry von Zell that a real vaudevillian never forgets a routine. I said that Gracie would never forget a single word from Lamb Chops, the routine that had made us famous. I offered to prove it, so when Gracie came into the living room, I asked proudly, "Gracie, do you like to love?"

"What?" she said, straightening the sofa cushions.

"Do you like to kiss?"

She was embarrassed. "George, please."

"Gracie," I explained, "I'm talking about Lamb Chops."

And then she laughed. "Oh, George," she said, "Who wants to kiss lamb chops?"

About six weeks after we'd filmed that final show, we were having dinner with Charlie Lowe and Carol Channing. "So, Gracie," Charlie asked, "have you gotten those dresser drawers straightened out yet?"

She looked him right in the eye and said firmly, "Yes, dammit!"

8

I was sixty-three years old when Gracie retired, too young to stop working and too old to start a new career. What was I going to do, stay home and cough? There's no money in coughing. I had to keep working—Saks was depending on me. One of the first lessons Gracie and I had learned in vaudeville was that the audience doesn't care how you feel, they care how they feel. If people wanted to see something that would make them feel bad, hospitals could sell tickets. As Sophie Tucker said after breaking her ankle, "What ankle?" So we didn't tell anyone that Gracie was sick. I didn't need any more sympathy; anybody who'd seen me work alone already felt sorry for me.

At first I wasn't even sure how serious Gracie was about not working again. But in addition to the thousands of letters from her fans, we'd also received some big offers to make a farewell appearance. One Las Vegas hotel offered us $50,000 to do a final show. Gracie turned it down. She wouldn't even consider it. So I knew she was at least $50,000 serious about not working again.

For the first few years of her retirement I know

Gracie was very happy. Her angina caused her to have some bad chest pains from time to time and she still suffered from the migraines, but she was well enough to go shopping and visit with friends and play cards and spend time reading and redecorate the house and keep the drawers neat. One night in a restaurant someone asked her if she missed the good old days. She laughed. "They're always talking about the good old days," she said. "Believe me, the really good days are right now. What was so good about running from train to train, living out of a suitcase, and having a quick bite if we had time? Now I have two people at home who'll get me anything I want, I have time to do whatever I want to do, and I have a little money. Maybe they were the good old days for somebody else. I'll take these days."

Well, I sort of liked running from train to train.

I think the only thing Gracie missed about being on the set was hearing the gossip. I know that I was a big disappointment to her because I never came home and told her good stories. "You never tell me anything," she once scolded me. "Don't you care?" Of course I cared, but what was I going to tell her? Mr. Ed was seen in somebody else's barn?

Fortunately, Orry-Kelly, the Oscar-winning costume designer, made up for me. She'd spend hours on the telephone listening to him. Orry knew more about what was really going on inside show business than any gossip columnist, and he told Gracie everything. They were a perfect match: Orry loved to talk and Gracie loved to listen. I'd know she was talking to him when I heard her say every few minutes, "No?" or "Really?" or "Oh, my . . ." The two of them were so close that we would all go to a party and spend the entire time together, and as soon as we got home they'd call each other and spend hours talking about the party. One morning I left the house about nine-thirty and I went to give her a little kiss and she was on the phone with Orry. I came home for lunch four hours later—and she was still on the phone with Orry.

When Gracie was talking on the phone she'd rest the receiver on her shoulder and tilt her head to the side to hold it so she could keep her hands free. Sometimes, by the time she hung up, her shoulder was numb and her neck was stiff. Angina and migraines were one thing, but this was serious. Those were her telephone muscles. Orry solved the problem by buying her a $2 rubber shoulderpiece so she could cradle the phone comfortably. Gracie thought this was the greatest invention in history. I'd bought her cars, jewelry, even fur coats, but none of them pleased her more than this rubber shoulderpiece. She was so excited when Orry gave it to her that she spent more hours on the phone with him telling him how well it worked.

Orry really was a delightful guy. He started out in New York hand-painting the dollar neckties that his roommate, Cary Grant, sold for $3. A lot of the women in Hollywood confided in him, so Gracie really knew everything that was going on. He'd tell Gracie, "I don't know why Tallulah insists on taking off her clothes every time somebody walks into the room. It just isn't pleasing. And I'm just so tired of her cocktail parties. When I went to her house the other day she was wearing shoes and pearls and her hat and that's all."

"Really," Gracie would say, happily shocked. "Oh, my . . ."

One reason Gracie and Orry got along so well is that they understood each other. That was important, because nobody else understood them. Orry told stories in real life the way Gracie did onstage. He'd constantly get people and facts confused, then he'd be amazed that we'd misunderstood him. We were out one night with Orry and Charlie Lowe and Carol Channing, and Orry was telling a story about an old vaudeville act called Savoy and Brennan. Somehow Bert Lahr's name was mentioned and Orry said, "Did you know he went to Alaska and they shot his right eye out and that's why he always wears those hats dipped over one eye?"

"He did?" Carol asked, her eyes wide open with delight.

"Yes," Orry said, "and the only reason he became a female impersonator was so he could wear the Garbo slouched hat."

Carol was amazed. We all were. "I didn't know Bert Lahr was a female impersonator," she said.

Orry looked at her like she was dizzy. "Who said anything about Bert Lahr? It was Brian Brennan." Of course Gracie had understood him.

Many people, when they retire, go fishing, or they travel; Gracie went shopping. That was her sport, her recreation. Gracie traveled to the store. If she wanted fish, she knew where to buy it. We had often talked about shopping on our radio and television shows. It was a subject our audience knew a lot about. Once, for example, on the radio, Gracie told me she'd bought ten pogo sticks for $50.

"Pogo sticks?" I said, "Why'd you buy ten of them?"

Why else? "Because that was all they had."

"But, Gracie, what do you want with them?"

"George, those sticks will come in very handy if you're attacked by a pogo."

Of course, that really wasn't Gracie at all. As far as Gracie was concerned, there was nothing funny about shopping. She took it very seriously. As she said on another show, "You know how when you go to the office you drive right past Bullock's?"

"Yeah?"

"I didn't."

That was Gracie. She would often spend most of the day in Saks. I never minded. Gracie was a shopper, not a buyer. She'd always go with somebody else, maybe Mary Benny or Flo Haley or, after her first serious heart attack in 1961, her nurse-companion, Claribel Crewell. She'd find an outfit she liked, then try to find all the right accessories that went with it. A purse, shoes, a bracelet. Eventually she'd find an accessory she loved that didn't go with the outfit, so she'd try on new outfits until she found something that went with the accessory. Then she'd try to find other accessories that went with the new outfit until she found something else she loved that didn't go with it.

But Gracie would worry about buying anything that cost more than a few dollars. Before making a final decision she'd tell me, "I saw this dress at Saks that I really liked. Do you mind if I buy it?" Mind? After what she'd done for us she could've bought the whole store. Now, if Billy Lorraine had asked me I would have minded.

When she did finally buy something, she'd always try to talk the salesgirl into giving her a discount. She was a terrible negotiator, but she loved bargaining. Sometimes the salesgirl would give her a few dollars off, and that would make Gracie's day. I'd come home at night and she'd show me her new outfit and tell me, "Look what you bought me today." And then she'd boast about how much money she'd saved by buying it.

The stores were closed at night, and Gracie loved to go out at night. Because she no longer had to get up early in the morning to report to makeup or wardrobe, she often went to the theater or dinner or friends' houses. She always seemed to have something important to do. She loved going to the theater as a patron—any theater. I know she enjoyed watching shows much more than she enjoyed being in them. Tom Clapp, a close friend who worked in the office, was a member of a small acting troupe called The Hollywood Shakespeare Festival, which performed Shakespearean plays in the park. Tom was very skinny, he had spindly legs, but for some reason he was cast to play Falstaff. Gracie had a basic knowledge of Shakespeare's plays and she knew that Falstaff was supposed to be fat.

"With those legs you're going to play Falstaff?" She laughed. "This I have to see."

I had to work, so Jack Langdon agreed to take her. She told him, "I want to read the play before I go so I'll know what it's about. What play is it?"

Jack told her it was Henry IV, part 2.

So Gracie got a copy and started reading it. About a week later Jack asked her how she was doing with it. "Not very good," she admitted. "Every time I start reading, they have these little numbers next to the words and I look down and see it's a footnote and it gives you some information. But by the time I've finished reading the footnote I've forgotten where I was in the play. So far I've read the first act five times."

She eventually got through it, though. Gracie always finished what she started.

The night of the performance Jack picked her up and they drove to the park. On the way there she started discussing the play. After she'd finished describing a certain scene, Jack said, "Uh, Gracie, I don't think that's the way this play goes."

"What do you mean?"

"I think maybe you read the wrong play." She'd read Henry IV, part 1, instead of part 2. Gracie just laughed and laughed. She knew how much in character it was that Gracie Allen had read the wrong play.

It made no difference to her. By the time they reached the theater she was already thinking about something else. They got caught in some traffic and she said to Jack, "Isn't it remarkable that all these people would know to come here at this particular time?" No wonder she understood Orry-Kelly.

After her heart attack in 1961 she couldn't go out at night as much. She just didn't have the energy. She hated that; she hated the feeling that she was missing something. But she never complained. Maybe the closest she ever came to feeling sorry for herself was late one Saturday afternoon. She was sitting on a couch, staring into space. I asked her what she was thinking about. "You know," she said wistfully, "right now in New York the orchestra is playing the overture and Carol is getting ready to go onstage." She was thinking about Carol Channing, who was starring in *Hello, Dolly!* That was all she said, but I knew what she meant—the world was going forward without her.

It was sort of surprising to me that Gracie had trouble with the footnotes, because she spent so much time reading. Until we started doing the television show she always seemed to have a book with her. In fact, almost all vaudevillians were great readers because we spent so much time on trains and in hotel rooms and in dressing rooms between shows, and there was nothing to do except read and write. Gracie even had her own bookplate, showing her as a cartoon character sitting on top of a giant hat, her face buried in a book, and stating in bold, capital letters: GRACIE ALLEN—HER BOOK. Her library in our house included books like *Aesop's Fables, Oscar Wilde: His Life and Confessions, Murray's Manual of Mythology,* dozens of detective stories, a collection of sayings entitled *Uncommon Common Sense, The Complete Mark Twain,* and probably her favorite book, a first edition of *Gone With the Wind.* Once we started doing the television show, she had absolutely no time to read, so after her retirement she'd stay up in our bedroom reading for hours and hours.

Gracie's only other hobby during her retirement was gambling. Gracie had a gambling problem—she was bad at it. She'd play cards with her friends or go to the racetrack, and when I played Las Vegas she always came with me. For Gracie, it wasn't the winning, it was the playing. And the way she played that was a very good thing.

When they were building Hollywood Park racetrack, we bought a box that she used every few weeks. Believe me, I knew more about horses than Gracie did. I knew that if you put a string in Mr. Ed's mouth and pulled it, it looked like he was talking. That's what I knew about horses. Gracie used to tell everyone she had a system for picking horses, but she never told anyone what it was. I had my own theories about her system—I suspect it worked best when the winning horse had the same name as one of our relatives. I do know that when she was having a bad day at the track she'd bet across the board, $2 on every horse in the race. That guaranteed she would be able to cash a winning ticket.

She computed her winnings at the races the same way she did in Vegas. I'd give her $50 to bet and at the end of the day I'd ask her how she did. "Great," she'd tell me, "I won ten dollars." Anyone else would have said they'd lost $40.

In Las Vegas she played blackjack and the slot machines. Blackjack is a card game in which the object is to get cards whose face value is closer to 21 than your opponents, but not more than 21. An ace can be worth either one or 11, which sometimes confused Gracie. At a casino everybody plays against the house. To begin, the dealer gives each player two cards, then asks if they want additional cards. One night Gracie's two cards totaled 15 and she couldn't decide whether to take another card or not. Finally, she had to make a decision. So she laid her cards down on the table, faceup so the dealer could see them, and said to him, "I just don't know. What would you do?"

All the other players in the game started laughing. Only Gracie Allen could get away with something like that. Actually, I don't think she was trying to get away with anything, I think she just wanted expert advice. But usually card players don't ask their opponents for help. The dealer was amazed. "Uh, Mrs. Burns," he mumbled, "I'm sorry . . . I can't . . . I don't think . . . "

The pit boss, the man who runs the game for the casino, interrupted and told the dealer, "You can advise Mrs. Burns if you'd like to—it's perfectly all right." He did, and Gracie won $3. But she was just as delighted as she would have been if it had been $3.50.

Half of everything she won went directly into her purse. This money was to be used to tip the attendants in the ladies' room, with the remainder added to her personal building fund. "This is for my castle," she used to say. But as soon as she got back to her hotel room she'd open her purse and dump her winnings onto the bed and start counting. It usually didn't take her very long. To Gracie, totaling her winnings was the best part of gambling.

❦

So, at least for the first few years of her retirement, I think Gracie was finally able to enjoy herself. The only thing in her life that made her unhappy was the condition of her sisters. And that was a real tragedy. Senility, Alzheimer's, whatever you call it, their minds were gradually slipping away. Eventually Hazel, Bessie, and Pearl each had to be put into a rest home.

It was so tough for Gracie. She loved her sisters very much and went to see them as often as she could. Most of the time they didn't recognize her. Pearl had had a stroke and couldn't speak or even feed herself. On occasion, Bessie would respond when Gracie came to see her, and she would try to get out of bed so they could dance together as they had when they were little girls, when they were The Four Colleens.

No matter how difficult it was, Gracie maintained her composure. Only once did she let her frustration out. She went to visit Bessie, and it was about ten o'clock in the morning when she arrived, but Bessie still hadn't been bathed and dressed. And Gracie started screaming. Everything she had been holding in came out in an angry torrent. "My God!" she screamed at the woman who ran the place, "I keep my sister supplied with nightgowns and bed jackets and brushes and ribbons and look at her. Look at her! I want my sister taken care of right this minute." At the end of the month, Gracie had Bessie moved to another home where she would get more attention.

I know Gracie was terrified that the same thing was going to happen to her, but she never said a word about it. And when she died, she was the Gracie I'd always loved.

After she retired I didn't get to spend as much time with her as I had in the past because I was still going to the studio every day. While we were doing the television show, I'd started producing several other programs. McCadden Productions, as Gracie and I named our company, after the street that my brother Willy lived on, produced "Mr. Ed," "The Bob Cummings Show," "The People's Choice," with Jackie Cooper, "The Marie Wilson Show," and "Panic," as well as hundreds of commercials. We had more than three hundred people working for us. Television was still so new that nobody really knew what kinds of shows the audience would watch, but I figured that people would like the same things on television that they liked in vaudeville, so we did shows with pretty girls and animals. Bob Cummings played a fashion photographer always taking pictures of beautiful models; Marie Wilson played Marie Wilson. I couldn't convince my old partner, the seal, to come out of retirement, but I had a thinking dog on "People's Choice" and Mr. Ed, the talking horse.

"Mr. Ed" wasn't my concept. Someone came to me and started telling me about an idea he had for a show. I wasn't particularly interested until he told me, ". . . and then the horse says—"

"Wait a second," I interrupted. "This horse talks?"

"Yeah. This is a talking horse."

"I'll do it."

That's how Mr. Ed was born. Well, not how Mr. Ed was born—he was born in a stable the usual way—but that's how the show began. One show I tried to develop that I was never able to sell starred a talking dog. I thought that would be terrific. I liked Mr. Ed, but what kind of intelligent conversation can you have with a horse?

Running McCadden was interesting, but I had stocked too many cigars to quit performing. I wanted to stay on television and I had an entire cast of wonderful actors looking for work, so we created "The George Burns Show." We went on the air in October 1958. I played George Burns, a television producer with an office in Beverly Hills. That had nothing to do with real life, because in real life my office was in Hollywood. Harry Morton, played by Larry Keating, was my accountant and worked in the same building I did. Blanche Morton, played by Bea Benadaret—or maybe it was the other way around—was my secretary. She spent most of her time keeping beautiful young starlets away from me so Gracie, who was at home, wouldn't have to worry. Ronnie Burns played my son—the kid was typecast—and Harry von Zell played the announcer. Our writers were our writers. The show had everything it needed to be successful except Gracie. The audience was so used to seeing this cast working with Gracie that everybody kept waiting for her to open the door and walk in. It was like sitting down to a big meal and having the soup, salad, and dessert—while the main course was home playing with her grandchildren.

The television critics reviewed Gracie's absence more than the show itself. In vaudeville they would have given me back my pictures. What could they do on television, give me back my film? Gracie was very sympathetic—she was always there for me to talk to and let out my frustrations—but the one thing she could have done to change things was the one thing I would never ask—come out of retirement. That just wasn't going to happen.

The show lasted one season. Actually, it turned out to be a very important show in television history. If it had been better it wouldn't have been canceled, and Bea Benadaret never would have created the role of Cousin Pearl on "Beverly Hillbillies" and Kate Bradley on "Petticoat Junction" and finally received the acclaim she deserved.

The failure of the show was tough for me. I'd been a failure until I'd met Gracie, and now I'd failed at the first thing I tried after she retired—if that kept up I was going to start believing there was a pattern. I still had my cigars, though, so I decided to go back onstage. I put together an act in which I did a monologue, told a few jokes, and sang a few old songs, then I convinced Bobby Darin and the DeCastro Sisters and Brascia and Typee, a great dancing act, to work with me, and signed to play Las Vegas. I figured if people didn't think my jokes were funny, they always had my songs. Actually, "The George

Burns Stage Show'' was so good it didn't even need me. But I needed me, so I headlined it.

When I walked out onstage for the first time, Gracie was sitting at a table directly in front of me. I introduced her and the audience gave her the usual standing ovation. Then I did my act. I thought it was pretty well received, even though Gracie got more applause just for showing up than I got for doing my entire act.

Afterward I asked her what she thought of the show. She didn't hesitate. ''Wasn't Bobby Darin wonderful?'' she said.

Bobby Darin was wonderful, I loved Bobby Darin, but that wasn't what I meant. ''Come on Googie,'' I said. ''You know what I mean.''

''Well, Nat,'' she said, ''I think you're reciting your monologue. You know how you always say that honesty is the most important thing onstage, and if you can fake that you can do anything? I don't think you're faking it very well. And if you don't believe what you're saying, how do you expect the audience to?''

I was still good at accepting criticism. By this time I'd had enough practice. ''So then tell me,'' I asked, ''what'd you think of the DeCastro Sisters?''

Gracie was absolutely right, of course, I was just saying my lines without any real feeling. If I wasn't selling my material, how could I expect the audience to buy it? At my next show I slowed down and thought about each story as I told it. It made a big difference. I still didn't get as big an ovation from the audience as Gracie did for showing up, but the audience responded very well.

I started playing Vegas regularly and Gracie was always there for my opening night and my first few shows. I always introduced her, the band played "Love Nest" and she always got a huge hand. That delighted me. Besides, I always figured that if I wanted a big ovation all I had to do was announce my retirement.

No matter how much time Gracie spent in Vegas, she never managed to figure out how to tip correctly. Gracie prided herself on always doing the correct thing, but since I'd always been right next to her to handle the tipping, she'd never learned what was right. In our hotel room after my show she'd tell me, "Nattie, I just can't figure out who I'm supposed to give the money to. Am I supposed to tip the man who greets us when we walk in the door or am I supposed to tip the man who shows us to our table? The man who greeted us at the door didn't seem to do very much, so I didn't give him much of a tip. The girl who brought the drinks to our table did most of the work, so I gave her most of the money. Is that right?"

I asked her how much she had tipped in all.

"Almost six dollars," she said. "Do you think that's too much?"

After watching me work over a period of time in Las Vegas, Gracie felt that there was something missing from my act. I knew what that was too. Gracie. I needed somebody to talk to onstage. What was I going to do, ask the curtain, "How's your tailor?" Obviously, nobody would try to replace Gracie Allen. Nobody could be that dumb. I needed somebody who would work well with me, but would also bring something special to the act. Gracie picked her out for me: Carol Channing.

Carol and Gracie had been friends for a long time. They were two extremely talented women who had only one thing in common: both of them had a voice like absolutely nobody else. Their voices were unique. Both of them had been asked the same silly question countless times: When did you decide to have that voice?

Carol's husband, Charlie Lowe, had represented our long-time sponsor, Carnation Evaporated Milk, ever since they'd been with the show, and the four of us had spent a lot of time together. In fact, the morning after Charlie and Carol had gotten married, Gracie was the first person to call.

"Is this Carol Lowe?" she asked when Carol answered the phone. Then they laughed their unique laughs. "Isn't that a funny name, Carol Lowe?" Gracie continued. "I mean, think of my name, Grace Burns, but Carol Lowe is really funny. But don't you just love it, don't you just love being called Carol Lowe?"

Carol was a major Broadway star, she'd created the classic role of Lorelei Lee in "Gentlemen Prefer Blondes," stopping the show when she sang, "Diamonds Are a Girl's Best Friend," and had made her nightclub debut in Las Vegas a few years earlier. She had a wonderful act and had been very successful. She didn't need to work with me and I wasn't sure she'd want to. The television critics had been very tough on "The George Burns Show" because Gracie wasn't there; the variety critics might be just as tough on the person who stood in her place onstage.

Carol and I had worked together only once in our lives. We'd done a big production number in my living room. Gracie, Willy, and I used to do a risqué version of the old song "On the Sunny Side of the Street." Gracie would stand between us, and Willy and I would sing special lyrics and Gracie would sing the title line. We were all at the house one night and Gracie said, "Nattie, please let Carol stand between you and Willy when you do your number." So we got the old, beat-up hats out of the closet and started working. We'd sing, "And where do you want to be kissed, Carol?"

And she'd sing, "On the sunny side of the street."

Well, in Gracie's living room that was risqué.

Gracie decided she would speak to Charlie about Carol and me working together. "If Carol isn't busy next season," she told him, "I would love to have her work with George. I just think they would work so well together, don't you?"

"Gracie," Charlie answered, "I know Carol would be honored." I don't think he meant she would be honored to work with me—I know that the seal wasn't too thrilled about it—I think he meant she'd be honored that Gracie thought so highly of her.

Not only did I start working with Carol, Gracie did too. Gracie had been very disappointed that she had no one to whom she could pass on all the knowledge she'd acquired, so she sort of adopted Carol. Carol was a Broadway star, but she was still pretty inexperienced about doing a double routine, so Gracie tried to teach her everything she knew about onstage appearance and working with me.

The two of them spent hours hidden away in Gracie's bedroom. "You've got to have a certain chic," Gracie told her. "I don't think you can really be funny unless you look as good as possible. Like Cary Grant looks so good and is so perfectly dressed and all of a sudden he walks into the pool. Nobody expects it. You have to look as good as you can when you walk into the pool.''

Gracie convinced Carol to get new glasses and a new hairstyle and gave her lessons in the proper way of wearing a fur coat. ''Your fur coat is part of your business,'' she said, and I hoped the IRS was listening. ''It's part of your career. There is a right way and a wrong way to sit in a fur coat. First of all, you must never sit in the same place on the coat all the time.'' At the end of that particular lesson she gave Carol a mink-covered hanger for her own fur coat, because Gracie believed fur coats should be hung on mink-covered hangers so their seams wouldn't split at the shoulders.

''Now, Nattie is absolutely fanatical about looking perfect onstage,'' she said, as though she weren't, ''so when you've got your clothes on you mustn't sit down because if you do you'll crease your dress like Tony Bennett did once and he'll get upset.'' I know she meant Tony Bennett's pants. In Vegas one night he went on-stage with creased pants and I told him it didn't look good. Brian Brennan was the man who wore the dress.

''So after you're finished dressing,'' Gracie continued, ''if you want to check your makeup, you have to get down on your knees and look in the mirror.'' And then Gracie got down on her knees to demonstrate.

''Working with Nattie is very easy,'' she told Carol another time. ''Sometimes you have to wait for him to finish puffing on his cigar, but trust him. All you have to do is stand up there next to him and have a conversation, you just have to act as if it's perfectly normal to be having a conversation in front of three thousand people.''

More than anything else, Gracie stressed the fact that Carol had to make the material her own. "Don't pay any attention to the way I did it," she'd tell her. "Don't do an imitation of me." Then Carol would read her lines and Gracie would just roar with laughter, as if she hadn't done exactly the same jokes herself. Eventually Carol did make the material her own. We used a lot of the same bits I'd done with Gracie, but in Carol's mouth they sounded new.

When Gracie was finally satisfied she'd done all she could to help her prepare to work with me, she gave Carol her personal dresser, the woman who helped her get ready to go onstage. And then she added her most precious compliment, she asked Orry to do Carol's wardrobe for the show.

The night before Carol and I were supposed to open in Lake Tahoe, Carol got a very bad sore throat. Naturally she asked Gracie what to do about it. "Oh, don't worry," Gracie said, going into action, "I've got my list." Gracie had lists for everything, and she opened the proper address book. "There's a man I know who's very good for sore throats," she said as she began searching for his phone number. "I think it's under D, for doctor." The number wasn't there. "Oh, well, then it must be under T for throat." Not there either. "Then it has to be under M for medical." It wasn't under M for medical, S for sore throat, C for cough or P for pills. She finally found it under B, for Jerry Boggio, the woman who ran our office. "Of course," Gracie explained to Carol. "You see, whenever I need the number I just call Jerry, because I know she'll have it."

Carol and I opened and closed the act together, a total of about twelve minutes. The nicest thing I can say about Carol is that she wasn't Gracie. She was Carol. She made our old material her own. I felt very strange standing there next to someone who wasn't Gracie, but I'd always wanted to work with a woman I could look up to.

Maybe that's a bad joke, but it lets me take a puff on a good cigar.

We were a hit, and I don't think anyone was happier about that than Gracie. She was so excited for me and Carol. And herself, too. It was very important to Gracie that I prove that I could be successful without her. That enabled her to really enjoy her retirement.

So Carol Channing took Gracie Allen's place onstage, and that part of my life with Gracie was really over. But offstage we were still a team. About the only things in our lives that were different were that I left the house alone in the morning and all the dresser drawers were neat.

For the first time I was like almost every other husband in America—I was supporting my wife. The change didn't affect our marriage at all. When we were sponsored by Carnation we were billed as "America's most contented couple," and that really wasn't just advertising. We were very happy with each other. We had been married for almost four decades, and our marriage just grew stronger and stronger. People ask me how to make a marriage work. I tell them the answer's easy: marry Gracie. Gracie was so easy to be married to. We loved each other, we liked each other, and we respected each other. And she listened when I sang. Gracie and I never worked at being married. We worked at not failing onstage. I don't know of many couples who spent as much time together as we did. We'd get up together in the morning, go to the theater or the studio together, come home together at night. On tour we would spend almost all day together. Believe me, when you have to spend that much time with your wife, you'd better make sure you marry Gracie.

I learned a lot about marriage in forty years, and I can give some pretty good advice. I know all about the importance of respect and trust and honesty and generosity and sharing, but for me it still comes back to one thing: marry Gracie.

❧

I made some mistakes in our marriage. I made one big mistake that I've never talked about before. I cheated on Gracie once. That's why I've never talked about it before.

Georgie Jessel used to give a lot of advice, some of it worthwhile. He used to say, for example, never forget the salami in your stomach. That was his way of saying, never forget where you come from, never think you're so important that you forget who you really are. The other thing he said that always made a lot of sense to me was that a man only gets in trouble when he thinks from his waist down.

He usually said that during his latest divorce.

It was easy to have an affair in Hollywood. It was hard not to. Even Lassie had puppies. Blanche Morton's character on "The George Burns Show" spent a lot of time keeping starlets away from the producer. Her character wasn't real, but the situation was. A lot of people in Hollywood, a lot of our friends, had affairs. One actor I knew had a rule that he would never sleep with a married woman, as it turned out that included his wife. Even I had plenty of opportunities, but I got pretty good at turning them down. I once turned down Marilyn Monroe.

I am absolutely not puffing on my cigar.

When I was still doing the radio show I'd go to the fights every Friday night with Harpo and a fine comedian named Lou Holtz. Because my office in the Hollywood Plaza was only a few blocks from Legion Hall, I used to pick up the tickets during the week, then meet Harpo and Lou there at eight o'clock. One week I got a call from an agent named Joe Cooper, who told me he was representing "the most beautiful girl you've ever seen," and he was hoping I could find a small part for her on the radio show. Of course it was easy to be a beautiful girl on the radio. If one of the characters said, "Oh, look, there's a beautiful girl," you were a beautiful girl.

I told Joe Cooper, "The only time I've got to see her is if she comes up to the office before the fights, at about seven-thirty. If she comes up here, I can talk to her for a few minutes. I'll see what I can do." About getting her a part on the show, I meant.

At seven-thirty Friday night Marilyn Monroe walked into my office and I took one look at her and knew an historic event had taken place: for the first time in history an agent had been telling the truth. She was probably about eighteen years old, and one of the most beautiful women I'd ever seen. And she was wearing a very tight sweater that accentuated her positives. She seemed like a nice kid, too. We spoke for about twenty minutes, then I told her, "I'm sorry, but I've got to leave because I've got the tickets to the fight and my friends are waiting for me."

We stood up and shook hands and she walked to the door. She put her hand on the doorknob and stopped. She pointed to her chest with her index fin-

ger and said, "These are real, you know." I guess
she was pretty surprised that I hadn't made a play
for her. But I took her word for that.

Gracie was not naive. She knew what was going
on in Hollywood. But she was very practical about
it. When Meredith Willson was our music director,
for example, his wife found out he was going around
with his secretary. "I'm going to leave him," she
told Gracie. "I'm going to divorce him."

Gracie asked, "Does Meredith still love you?"

"Oh, yes."

"Is he there for you when you need him?"

"Yes, he is."

"And you're leaving him because he's having an
affair with his secretary? Don't be so silly. If you
leave him, he'll be all alone, and he'll marry her.
Then what will you have?" That was good advice.
Meredith Willson's wife didn't follow it. He married
his secretary, but it was still good advice.

I had my affair in the early 1950s. It was with a
beautiful starlet. I don't remember her name, but she
was very pretty and very sexy. I actually don't remember what she looked like, either, but this is my
book and if I'm going to have an affair in it, it's
only going to be with someone beautiful and sexy.

Gracie and I were having a little fight at the time.
She wanted to buy a silver centerpiece that cost
$750. I didn't want to buy a silver centerpiece at any
price. We had silver centerpieces. "What do we need
another one for?" I asked Gracie. "We already have
two. You can only use one at a time." But Gracie
wanted this centerpiece.

Then I cheated with this girl. I had my one-night
affair. I don't know why I did it, maybe I had had
too much to drink, but it had nothing to do with the

centerpiece. I wasn't very good at cheating, maybe because I hadn't done it before. Somehow Gracie found out, and I found out that Gracie had found out. So she knew, and I knew she knew, but I didn't know if she knew that I knew that she knew. If that had kept up we might have had a whole new act.

I didn't know what to do about it. Gracie never said a word. That was even tougher than if we had gotten into a big fight. The longer she went without saying anything, the more guilty I felt. Finally, after a few days I couldn't take it anymore. I went out and bought her the $750 silver centerpiece and a $10,000 diamond ring and gave them to her. I never told her why I'd bought them for her and she never asked, and she never said a single word about my affair. At least she didn't say a word for seven years.

Seven years later she was out shopping with Mary Benny and they were in the silver department at Saks. Gracie found a centerpiece she really liked and she said to Mary, "You know, I wish George would cheat again, I really need a new centerpiece."

Look, I was very lucky that Gracie handled it the way she did. My mistake could have ruined both of our lives. But she was so smart, she just never mentioned it. If she had decided to make a big deal about it, we might not have had another decade together. And, in her own way, she forgave me. So today I think about Gracie every single day, and at least once a month I go to the Forest Lawn Cemetery to visit her and tell her all about my life. And the other girl, the starlet? I wouldn't even recognize her if I ran into her. That's how smart Gracie really was.

❦

Gracie got sick gradually. The changes in her health took place over such a long period of time that I really didn't notice them. Sometimes, when she had an angina attack, she wouldn't even tell me. I'd find out from somebody else. She lived only six years after she retired; it seemed like one day she was fine, the next day she was sick. Her heart was bad and there was nothing we could do about it. We had the best doctors, but this was long before they started doing bypass operations. In those days when your heart stopped, you died. Today things are much more complicated—when your heart stops they call your relatives, who argue about what to do.

The only thing that really helped Gracie was her nitroglycerin pills. Whenever she had an attack she'd put one under her tongue and within two or three minutes she'd be fine. These pills were very strong. I remember Eddie Cantor carried them around in his pocket for years and he never had a heart attack. That's how strong those pills were.

For the first few years these painful angina attacks and a shortness of breath were her only symptoms. She wouldn't even call them attacks, they were "episodes." "Oh, Nattie," she'd tell me. "I had just a little episode today." She was very sensitive about being sick, and tried very hard not to inconvenience anyone. One night we were at a party at Vincent Minnelli's house, and not too long after we got there she started getting terrible pains in her chest. We went into the kitchen and I gave her a pill, then took her right home. By the time we got home she was fine. She insisted that I go back to the party: "But, Nattie, please try to remember everything that goes on because you know you're not very good at remembering those things and Orry-Kelly will want to know everything that happens." I was sort of hoping she might add: "And no matter what they say, you just go ahead and sing," but she didn't. When I came home from the party later that night she was in bed reading, and I sat down next to her and very sweetly told her the most outrageous lies.

When she did have an attack she was always the calmest person around. There was one night when she was at a restaurant with Tom Clapp and Jack Langdon and the three of them were just chattering away when all of a sudden she got very quiet.

"Is something wrong, Gracie?" Jack asked.

"I don't want either of you to get excited," she said easily, still smiling as if nothing were wrong. "I just want you to keep talking like we're doing. Jack, would you please reach into my purse and take out my pills and give me one, please." Then she turned to Tom and told him, "Please reach around my shoulders and undo the clasp at the top of my dress and just let the zipper down a little because it's a bit tight right now. Don't let anybody see you doing it though, or they'll think we're doing something funny and throw us right out of here."

The thing Jack remembers most about that night is how incredibly calm and composed she was the entire time, and that she kept smiling.

Maybe even worse than the "episodes," which didn't occur that often, was the shortness of breath that just sapped all her energy. From the first day I met her, Gracie had always been so full of life, so energetic, and slowly that changed. She had to learn how to pace herself, which she hated. If she stayed out too late, she'd get tired; if she had to stand up too long, she'd get tired; if she had to walk even a moderate distance, she'd have to stop and rest. This was a problem because Gracie always believed she could just do a little more than she really could.

She shopped mostly at Saks because the salesgirls there protected her; if she tried to shop anywhere else she would attract attention. And attention was the one thing she didn't want. She was such a private person, and she didn't want anybody knowing how sick she really was. It wasn't just that she didn't want sympathy, but she didn't want anyone to think she was weak.

We went to a puppet show on Santa Monica Boulevard one night and by the time the show ended she was exhausted and I just wanted to get her home. But the owner of the theater insisted she go backstage to meet the young puppeteers. I kept saying no, no, no, and he kept saying how disappointed everyone would be if she didn't. Gracie was never very good at saying no. So she went backstage and for ten minutes she was great, she was animated and lively, and no one could have guessed she was sick. But it took a lot out of her. On the way out we had to go up a small flight of stairs. Gracie and I had spent decades running up and down theater stairs in practically every city in the country. We'd run for buses and trains and planes, and she'd never slowed down and never complained. But this time she walked up about four steps and had to stop to catch her breath. "Let's just wait here for a moment," she said, breathing deeply. "We'll stand here and turn around and act like we're looking over the theater, okay?"

She was a great actress and she was putting on a great act. I don't know if she ever realized how sick she was, but she must have known that she wasn't getting any better.

She suffered her first serious heart attack in 1961. We'd done a show once in which I went to the hospital to volunteer to test a miracle drug that was supposed to let me live to be more than one hundred years old. Who knew? As usual, Gracie mixed things up and thought they were operating on me, and rushed to the hospital to save me. As soon as she got there she demanded to see the general in charge. When the head nurse told her there was no general, Gracie insisted there had to be a general because this was the general hospital. After being convinced that there was no general, she agreed to speak to the private. The nurse told her that there was no private either, but Gracie was too smart for that. She'd seen his name on his office door, she claimed, and she was not going to leave the hospital until she spoke to Private Ward.

But the heart attack she suffered in 1961 was terrifyingly real. We were in the house and she had an episode. I gave her a pill, but her chest pains got worse instead of better. So I rushed her to the hospital. They gave her a shot of something and attached her to the machines and eventually the pains went away. That was the first time I ever got scared. I'd spent our life together believing Gracie was eternal. I couldn't imagine life without her.

They told me she had the same condition as President Eisenhower. Dr. Kennamer prescribed some medicine that thinned her blood and explained that as long as the medicine was effective she would be all right. He also suggested that Gracie have one drink a day to help improve her circulation. She had never been much of a drinker, but she always followed doctors' orders. So when we went out for dinner she would order her one drink—and ask the waiter to put it in the biggest glass they had in the restaurant. The doctor said one drink—but he didn't say what size.

For me, the most frustrating thing was knowing there was absolutely nothing I could do to help her. I kept asking myself, what if we hadn't done that last season of the show? What if we hadn't done the last two seasons? I'll tell you what the difference would have been—we would have done fewer shows—but it wouldn't have made any difference as far as Gracie's health was concerned.

In a situation like this it's natural to look for a reason or an answer or some way of changing things. But there was nothing anyone could do. Sometimes you just have to accept things as they are and make the best of them: if the Cherry Sisters could have sung, they wouldn't have had an act.

When Gracie came out of the hospital we hired a nurse-companion for her, a lovely woman named Claribel Crewell, who was with her all day, and we installed an electric chairlift to help Gracie get up and down the stairs in the house. One of the gossip papers reported that Gracie had terminal cancer and we had put in life-sustaining machinery. The only life-sustaining machinery we had in the house was the refrigerator.

After the heart attack the doctors prescribed some stronger medicine, causing her to lose much of her appetite. Gracie was always more of a nibbler than an eater; she was always worried about gaining a few pounds, and I don't think I ever saw her finish an entire meal. But now she started losing weight. Ronnie tried to kid her about it, telling her, "Oh, good, I need to lose some weight too. We can go on a diet together."

Gracie was as much of a fighter as she had always been and she insisted on leading as normal a life as possible. She'd sleep late in the morning and go out for lunch; she loved going to the Polo Lounge in the Beverly Hills Hotel, and then going downtown with Claribel to get her hair done or her nails done or to do some serious window-shopping. Sometimes she'd play cards with her friends. If she had the energy she would walk around the neighborhood for exercise with Claribel or one of the girls. The kids would come by from time to time, which is exactly the way kids are supposed to come by. One afternoon Gracie called me at the office, and she was all excited because Ronnie had stopped by for lunch with Richard Chamberlain, who was then starring in one of her favorite shows, "Dr. Kildare." Gracie didn't watch a lot of TV, but she liked the doctor and lawyer shows. Show business had come a long way since Hammerstein's—now the most popular form of entertainment was watching shows about disease and murder.

I'd spend my days at the office, or I'd be on tour, but we would speak several times every day. What would we talk about? Nuclear physics? We talked about the same things that every husband and wife who have been a famous comedy two-act for forty years talked about: the kids, who was sleeping with whom, when I was coming home, and what Jackie Kennedy was wearing.

We settled into a comfortable period. As long as Gracie didn't expend too much energy, she was fine. She could go out, go to parties, shopping; she just had to be careful. I thought that maybe she wasn't going to get any worse. And if her condition had stayed like that we would have been fine, and we could have been happy together for a long, long time. But gradually she did get worse. The new medicine thinned her blood, and every once in a while she'd have a brief fainting spell. Outside Saks one afternoon, for example, she passed out as she was getting into her Thunderbird, and Claribel couldn't get the doors open so she could drive Gracie for help. Claribel didn't know whether to call a doctor or a mechanic. Another time she fainted in Las Vegas just before I was supposed to go on. The doctors told us that these fainting spells didn't mean she was getting worse, and that we shouldn't worry about them. When the woman I loved passed out and fell on the floor no matter what the doctors said, I worried a lot. Sometimes, at night, I'd lie awake in bed, just listening to her breathe.

I know one of the things that bothered her terribly at first was having to wear a wig. Gracie had always been so proud of her beautiful hair. She loved sitting at her dressing table in one of her brightly colored silk kimonos, brushing her hair. She probably had fifty different hairbrushes, and each one of them had some special purpose. But she needed the wig. Until the day she died Gracie would not set foot outside the house if she didn't think she looked perfect—and until she took off just one thing. A lady just didn't go out of the house any other way. But the medicine also caused her hair to get thinner, and it took her a lot of time and energy to set it and style it, so she went to Max Factor's with Claribel and both of them bought wigs. Gracie bought seven of them, each one exactly the same color and length as her real hair. Those wigs made it much easier for her to get ready and go out.

Actually, wigs, or toupées, had a long history in

our marriage. One of us besides Gracie had been wearing a toupée since that person was twenty-seven or twenty-eight years old, and the other person had never said a word about it. I would have had my toupée made to look exactly like my hair had looked too, but who could remember what it had looked like? At night I'd put my toupée on a dummy head, and Gracie would put one of her wigs on a dummy head, and the two heads would be right next to each other on the bureau. I got a strange feeling when I looked at them; I felt like I was sitting behind ourselves in the theater.

Maybe Gracie's body was sick, but not her spirit. She refused to let anyone see her depressed or unhappy. If she wasn't feeling well, she would stay in her room by herself. Maybe this sounds sad, but it wasn't really. Gracie wouldn't let it be. She still had many more good days than bad days, and on those days she was alert and active and happy. She was Gracie. For example, it was during this time that they instituted zip codes. Our zip code is 90210. I know that's our zip code because I wrote it down. But Gracie memorized our zip code instantly. I asked her how she did it. "Oh Nattie, it's so easy," she explained. "I looked at it and said, ninety. Well, ninety is a nice old age to get to be. Then twenty-one. Twenty-one is when you get to be an adult. And zero is either before or after. It's nothing. So I thought, old age, young adulthood, nothing, ninety, twenty-one, zero, and I never had any trouble remembering it."

That's the Gracie I remember. The zip code I still don't remember.

In early 1964 she started to get worse. She started spending more time in her room. It was tougher for her to come downstairs. I did my best to make her feel better, but there wasn't very much I could do. One day when I knew she was having a particularly rough time with the pains, I did something that was very unusual for me, I went shopping for her. I bought her an expensive mink coat. When the saleslady asked me how tall Gracie was, I turned to my right, because she'd been standing right there for most of our life together, and imagined myself looking down at her onstage. I held out my hand a few inches lower than my head. "She's this tall," I said.

I brought the coat home that night. She was in bed and I walked in carrying a big box. This might have been the first time in forty years that she didn't have to show me what I'd bought for her. "Look what I bought for you, Googie," I said. She opened the box and started crying. "What are you crying about?" I asked, "I paid for it." Then I started crying. Finally she got out of bed and put on the coat. And she looked lovely. For the next few days she couldn't stop talking about it. She called all of our friends and told them, "I can't be dying. You know Nat— if I was dying he never would have bought me this coat."

She started to fail that July. Her birthday was July 26, just a few days after Sandy's, and Sandy had planned a party to celebrate both their birthdays. She'd bought a new dining set for the party and was anxious for her mother to see it. On the day of the party Gracie started to get ready, then had to stop. It was just too much for her. She had an attack and we gave her a pill and put her back to bed.

About two weeks later I was opening in Las Vegas

with Connie Stevens. Connie and I were doing a new
television show called "Wendy and Me." Connie
was Wendy, I was me. Who else was going to play
Me? If anybody else had played Me, they would
have had to change the name of the show to "Wendy
and Him." Connie and I were also working together
in Vegas. The whole family came down for the
opening. Sandy and Ronnie and Willy and Willy's
wife, Louise, and Claribel and the Bennys and Jack
Langdon. Gracie played hostess. For a moment I
could have closed my eyes and it would have been
ten years earlier. Gracie was running around making
sure everybody knew where they were supposed to
be seated and that the food was right and that there
was enough champagne, and I could see that she was
loving every minute of it. But a few minutes later I
looked around and she wasn't there anymore. The
strain had been too much for her and she'd had an
episode. Claribel had given her her medicine and
taken her upstairs for the night.

The following morning several people came by
the room to see how she was feeling. She was better;
she was sitting up in bed and anxious to hear all
about the show. Then everybody said goodbye and
went back to Los Angeles. For some of them it really was goodbye—that was the last time they saw
her.

❧

Gracie fought to the very end. I remember, in early
August she went shopping with Claribel and bought
a lovely pearl ring. On time, naturally. The ring was
for her right hand, because she never took off the
$20 wedding band I'd given her in Cleveland thirty-

eight years earlier. That pearl ring was the last thing she bought.

In mid-August she was feeling better, so she got dressed up and we put on our hair and went to a wedding reception for Edie Adams and Marty Mills. It was a nice party and we both had a nice time. Maybe that's the best way to remember Gracie, in a swirl of happy, laughing people.

One day in August she woke up in the morning and was feeling very well, so she called Ronnie on the set of "Wendy and Me" and told him she had decided to come down there for lunch. That was very unusual; it was the first time in six years, since the day she retired, that she expressed any interest in going on a set.

It was a special day. A lot of the people on the crew had worked on "The Burns and Allen Show" with us, and from the way they reacted you would have thought the Queen was coming. Well, maybe she was. They made up a special director's chair with "Gracie Allen" written on the back for her.

When she walked on the set everything stopped. She looked so lovely, so full of life. People just started applauding. We stopped shooting and went across the street to a small restaurant for lunch. For a minute, for a second, Gracie was back where she belonged, in the middle of show business. But it only lasted a minute, then she was gone.

We were home alone the next night. The Democratic Convention was on and they were showing a special tribute to the late President John Kennedy. Gracie was crying as she watched it. When the convention went off the air for the night I turned off the television set and went downstairs to work on my script. A few minutes later I heard the set on again.

"Com'on, Googie," I shouted upstairs, "turn it off and go to sleep."

"I'm watching an old Spencer Tracy picture," she said loudly. "It's almost over."

A short time later I heard her calling for me. She was having trouble breathing. "I'll be all right," she said. "I'll be okay—just give me a pill." I gave her a pill and held her in my arms, but the pill didn't seem to be working. She started breathing more heavily and she was sweating. I gave her another pill, but the pains got worse. I called Dr. Kennamer and he rushed right over. I don't remember how long it took him to get there; I don't remember too much about the whole night.

As soon as he arrived, he listened to her heart, then said, "I think we should call an ambulance, George."

While we were waiting for the ambulance to arrive, I called the kids. I called Willy. I wanted them to be there.

The ambulance came about ten o'clock. I was holding her hand and I kept telling her, "It's all right, Googie, you'll be all right."

When the ambulance attendants picked her up to put her on the stretcher, she apologized to them, saying, "I'm sorry boys, I'm all wet."

Dr. Kennamer told me to sit in the front seat of the ambulance. In the back the attendants gave her oxygen. The driver put on the red lights and the siren and we raced to Cedars of Lebanon Hospital. I didn't say anything. Maybe I did, who remembers? I do remember thinking, Gracie was right, Beverly Hills does look different from so high up.

When we got to the hospital they rushed her upstairs. I waited in the hallway. Ronnie and Sandy arrived. Willy and Louise arrived. We weren't there very long, ten minutes, an hour, not very long. Dr. Kennamer came through the door and I knew. He didn't have to say anything. "I'm sorry, George," he said. "Gracie's gone. We couldn't save her."

Gone? How could she be gone when I had all those pills left? He asked me if I wanted to see her. Of course I did. I wanted to talk to her for just a few more minutes. I wanted to stand next to her onstage and hear the laughter of the audience. I wanted to see her smile and hear that birdlike voice and that unmistakable cackling laugh. I wanted her to look up at me with her trusting eyes. I wanted to fight my way through the ring around the piano and sing for her one last time. And I wanted to ask her just once more, "Gracie, how's your brother?"

So I went into the room. She was lying there and she looked so peaceful. I didn't know what to do. For the first time in forty years I was alone. So I did the only thing there was to do: I leaned over and I kissed her on her lips and whispered, "I love you, Googie."

Then I gave her back her pictures and walked out of the room.

There's an epidemic with 27 million victims. And no visible symptoms.

It's an epidemic of people who can't read.

Believe it or not, 27 million Americans are functionally illiterate, about one adult in five.

The solution to this problem is you... when you join the fight against illiteracy. So call the Coalition for Literacy at toll-free **1-800-228-8813** and volunteer.

Volunteer Against Illiteracy. The only degree you need is a degree of caring.